Guide to Biometrics for Large-Scale Systems

Julian Ashbourn

Guide to Biometrics for Large-Scale Systems

Technological, Operational, and User-Related Factors

 Springer

Julian Ashbourn
Verus Mundus
Hertfordshire
United Kingdom
biometrics@1to1.org

ISBN 978-1-4471-5886-8   ISBN 978-0-85729-467-8 (eBook)
DOI 10.1007/978-0-85729-467-8
Springer London Dordrecht Heidelberg New York

British Library Cataloguing in Publication Data
A catalogue record for this book is available from the British Library

Printed on acid-free paper

Springer is part of Springer Science+Business Media (www.springer.com)

Endorsement

Julian Ashbourn has been at the forefront of the biometrics industry since its inception, not as a creator or seller of biometric systems but as an implementer and user of the technology. This book picks up where his previous book, *Practical Biometrics: From Aspiration to Implementation*, left off, providing an authoritative understanding of both the technical and human factors involved in implementation of this important technology.

– William Saito,
Founder & CEO, Intecur, K.K., Tokyo, Japan

Preface

It seems almost bizarre to consider that contemporary biometric technology, which many still see as very advanced, even within the context of fast-moving Information Technology, has been with us for over 20 years. At first glance, it may seem to the casual observer that little has changed within that window of time. After all, we are still speaking of fingerprint readers, facial recognition, iris recognition and the other popular biometric techniques, and even their physical implementation does not seem to have changed all that much. However, behind the scenes, there have been many changes, some of them significant. Furthermore, these changes have not been restricted to the technology itself, but include changes of attitude, changes in the way the technology is deployed and changes in the context of our understanding of primary applications.

One aspect that has not perhaps changed as much as it might have done is the continuing focus upon the front end technology. Many technology suppliers, systems integrators, consultants and users still seem rather preoccupied with the front end devices and their theoretical performance. Attend any conference on the subject and you will surely encounter discussions upon matching algorithms, the physical design of biometric reader devices and theoretical performance. This is understandable, as it is mostly the device manufacturers who have driven the technology forwards, and theirs is a language of matching algorithms, equal error rates, degrees of freedom and other such parameters which serve to define the relative performance of one device in comparison with another. Consequently, systems integrators, consultants and even implementing organisations have largely adopted both the language and the focus upon biometric devices when considering applications for the technology.

It may be argued, with some justification perhaps, that the approach outlined above has served us well enough up until now. However, the world is changing fast, in terms of technology, business models, politics and even culture. It is time to consider biometric technology in a broader light. To integrate the concept more seamlessly into mainstream Information Technology while also striving to understand cultural attitudes and the societal impact of identity management as we progress into the twenty-first century. Make no mistake. This idea represents a step change in our thinking and many currently held tenets may come under a less than comfortable scrutiny in the process.

This book itself consequently represents something of a milestone in the development of biometric technology. It will be interesting to revisit it in another 20 years and align it with developments undertaken within that window of time. No doubt we shall have retained much of the technical terminology, but it is likely that we shall be looking at a different implementation model, and perhaps a different understanding of the concept of biometric identity verification. In the chapters which follow, we shall embark upon a voyage of exploration and clarification, striving to develop a new and robust understanding of biometric technology and its application, to serve us in coming decades.

Julian Ashbourn

Contents

Introduction

Abstract Within this chapter we shall travel through a logical progression, starting with discussion around the natural forms of identity verification practised by animals and humans. The techniques involved are actually quite complex and often involve multi-modal methodologies, sometimes distributed spatially and temporally within the identification process. Such identity verification processes are embedded into everyday activities and transactions, almost subconsciously, and involve impressive feats of memory and information processing, intertwined with elements of learned and inherited experience.

Moving the focus to human activities, the idea of biometrics as a relatively new concept is flawed as there exist clear evidence that ancient civilisations utilised similar concepts, albeit in a non-automated manner. In this respect, the Sumerians, Egyptians, Chinese, and others have effectively used biometrics for identity verification purposes. The modernisation of such techniques may be considered the culmination of an interesting thread of fascination with anatomical measurement and human character, which blossomed in the nineteenth century via the work of several pioneering individuals including Franz Joseph Gall, whose interest in whether character was reflected in physical appearance and how the brain might be segmented via function sowed the seeds for what he termed as Cranioscopy but what became more broadly recognised as Phrenology. Cesare Lombrosco moved the thinking forward into the realms of criminology and Adolphe Quetelet brought statistical thinking and methodologies into the fray, establishing, among other things, the Body Mass Index, still effectively used today. Alphonse Bertillon gathered together various measurements to more formally establish criminal anthropometry as a police procedure for the identification of criminals. His system, which he named Bertillonage, was becoming widely used prior to the advent of fingerprinting, which followed naturally from the work of several individuals including Jan Evangelista Purkyne, Juan Vucetich, and Francis Galton. It was Juan Vucetich who really pioneered the use of fingerprints from a policing perspective in Argentina, although the Galton–Henry system, as introduced to Scotland Yard, eventually became pre-eminent.

The chapter then moves into modern times with the advent of electronics and the automation thus facilitated. Such developments paved the way for automated identity verification via biometrics, although this was to take some time before being considered a reliable methodology. It is interesting to note the dichotomy between this modern, automated approach and the capabilities of the biological brain and the natural identity

J. Ashbourn, *Guide to Biometrics for Large-Scale Systems: Technological, Operational, and User-Related Factors*, DOI 10.1007/978-0-85729-467-8_1,
© Springer-Verlag London Limited 2011

verification that this allows in animals. This chapter effectively sets the scene for our deliberations into biometrics and identity management from the broader contemporary systems perspective.

Introduction

Before we enter into the detail of contemporary biometric technology, its application, and associated implementation issues, it would be useful to establish some fundamentals around the process of identity verification and how such ideas have developed over time. Actually, identity verification is a perfectly natural process, practised by animals and humans in everyday activities and, in this context, it is illuminating to understand the distinction between these natural processes and their modern, computer-aided equivalents. It is also interesting to understand how the concept of identity verification has been used in ancient times and, similarly, the explosion of interest in the nineteenth century which, in many ways, paved the way for later ideas as we applied electronics and information technology to synergistic issues. Indeed, much of the thinking of these early pioneers prevails, in one form or another, to current times. However, the modern approach to technology, coupled with the logistical challenges of managing an ever-growing population, introduces a new raft of issues to contend with, some of which are not as well understood as they might be. This introductory chapter consequently places biometrics and identity management into context and establishes a pattern of thinking which will serve us well as we progress through subsequent chapters and explore some of these issues.

Identity Verification in Animals and Humans

It is interesting to contemplate the manner in which different species within the animal world utilise techniques of identity verification. There exists a view which suggests that this is primarily focused upon kin recognition, in order to protect and perpetuate the gene pool; however, a closer study reveals a more complex capability which, in some instances, is simply astounding.

The methods employed by animals for identity verification vary. In some cases, one method appears dominant. For example, the extraordinary ability of penguins to locate their offspring, initially by voice recognition, from within a population sometimes numbering hundreds of thousands. Similarly frogs have been shown to identify neighbours by voice recognition and discriminate between known neighbours and strangers by the same method. Wolves undoubtedly recognise the voices of kin and strangers as, no doubt, do many other species. Bats, for example, are able to locate individuals within large populations within dark caves, primarily by aural clues. Others use visual clues. The ability of birds to recognise individuals is commonly understood and, interestingly, this applies across species and is clearly not limited to kin recognition. Hawks have an incredible aptitude for processing visual information, often at high speed, as has been understood since ancient times. It is logical perhaps that the Ancient Egyptians identified the deity

Horus with the all-seeing hawk. In recent times, cattle have also been found to readily identify each other and discriminate between kin and strangers by sight alone. Such powers of identity verification are not restricted to mammals and birds. Insects similarly seem to have well-developed abilities to recognise kin and discriminate between kin and strangers. Bees are legendary in this respect, but wasps, ants, and many others also practise identity verification routinely. Recent research indicates that even at amoeba level, there is a positive discrimination between kin and strangers, with some surprising responses when the two come together.

While we tend to align a particular sense, such as sight, smell, or hearing, to our understanding of how animals practise identity verification, the likelihood is that, in many cases, multiple senses are being employed in order to arrive at a conclusion as to the identity of another individual within observable range. Furthermore, these sensory perceptions are feeding into an intelligent processing engine which has the ability to reference memory and quickly reach conclusions as to the identity of a given individual. They are indeed employing multi-modal biometric techniques in a sophisticated manner, selecting a range of sensory clues in order to reach a conclusion. These may include visual parameters such as outline, colour, pattern, and relative contrast; dynamic visual parameters such as movement, relative speed, and what we might refer to as 'body language'; aural parameters such as timbre, pitch, emphasis, and precise sound sequences; and scent, in a variety of ways, including individual and gender recognition. Individual cues may be employed in different situations. For example, a wolf may recognise an individual voice at a distance and corroborate this information by visual cues and scent at shorter distances, synthesising this information into a conclusion and responding accordingly. There are countless examples of animals using sophisticated techniques in order to verify the identity of kin, strangers, and even individuals within other species, including of course humans. Indeed, one could fill an entire book with interesting examples and hypotheses as to the processing mechanisms being employed.

Humans use exactly the same techniques to discriminate between kin and strangers and to recognise individuals within a population. When we recognise a relative or friend at a distance, we may employ several identity verification techniques. For example, overall appearance and colouring, outline, body language, and so on. As we get closer, we can corroborate this evidence with recognition of specific anatomical features as well as sound and even scent. It is understood, for example, that human mothers recognise the scent of newly born babies and may easily discriminate between them based upon scent alone. No doubt the babies similarly recognise the scent of the mother, although, in both cases, this information would ordinarily be corroborated by other factors such as visual and aural clues. Just as with animals, humans are routinely employing multi-modal biometric techniques for the purposes of identity verification, even if somewhat subconsciously.

Identity verification is an integral part of animal existence and everyday life, from the smallest of insects to larger mammals, birds, other species, and of course humans. Mostly, we practise these identity verification techniques without consciously choosing specific parameters to measure against our memory and understanding. Consequently, we tend to automatically deploy a range of measures and techniques in order to reach a conclusion as to the identity of the creature within our sphere of recognition. There are many factors which feed into this multi-modal identity verification functionality, some of which may be quite complex. For example, the distinction between learned and inherited experience is particularly interesting, and there is little doubt that many animals instinctively distinguish between friend and foe, even without the benefit of direct experience. Distinguishing features such as colour, patterns of marking, and anatomical construction seem to be pre-programmed in various species in order to raise awareness of potential danger. This very capability may even be exploited, as with certain species of butterfly who adopt colours and patterns which they know to be abhorrent to predators. These mechanisms can become very complex within the broader evolutionary cycle. Such realities place into context the remarkable processing capabilities of the biological brain and how, in comparison, the artificial brains of computers may appear relatively crude. While it is true that computer processing speeds and the consequent ability to process huge amounts of information are becoming very impressive indeed, there are still differences in the application of logic between the computer and the biological brain which we have, so far, failed to grasp or replicate. This is an interesting point to ponder as we continue our journey through the pages of this book.

The Use of Biometrics by Ancient Civilisations

There is a tendency to imagine that the very concept of biometric identity verification is a uniquely modern phenomenon. Actually, nothing could be further from the truth and there exists clear evidence that even ancient civilisations practised the technique routinely. For example, it is understood that the Sumerians considered a hand print a good identifier, and would occasionally imprint the outline of a hand into an important clay tablet as a statement as to the identity of the individual, or individuals, associated with the attendant transaction. Given that the Sumerians were pioneers in written language, and that the use of clay tablets with indented marks was an integral part of this visual expression of thought, it is an entirely logical approach to capturing the identity of relevant individuals. The practice aligns well with the concept of the written signature on later documents created with coloured dyes and inks upon parchment and papers.

It was perhaps the ancient Egyptians who brought the concept of biometric identity verification into the mainstream. The Egyptians were of course masters of organisation and, to a degree, documentation, at least as was necessary to enact everyday transactions and to maintain a duty of care towards them. Functions such as the definition and collection of taxes, the acquisition and distribution of foods, the administration around procurement of materials associated with public works, and a wide range of everyday commercial transactions, all benefited from the accurate identity verification of those individuals involved. They were various ways of accommodating this requirement, from discreet anatomical measurements to a more general notification of individual features, and these would be recorded and aligned with details of specific transactions. For example, one such record reads: Nechutes, son of Asos, aged 40, of middle size, sallow complexion, cheerful countenance, long face with straight nose and a scar upon the middle of his forehead. There is, in fact, a considerable amount of verifiable information captured within that simple description. If required, such information could be, and often was, accompanied by an anatomical measurement such as the distance measured between the individuals outstretched thumb and the tip of the elbow. Thus, the ancient Egyptians had an effective method of personal identity verification which was also extremely flexible, drawing upon multiple parameters as required in relation to the importance of the transaction. In some respects, this approach was more sophisticated than contemporary methods. But then, the ancient Egyptians were an extraordinary people.

It is perhaps less clear whether the ancient Greeks or Romans practised what we would recognise formally as biometric identity verification today as, by that time, passwords and tokens were becoming popular as a means of identifying individuals. However, there is little doubt that they would have used such techniques informally. Similarly, when one considers the Mesolithic and Neolithic tribes meandering across Europe and elsewhere before those times, as well as the Nordic peoples, no doubt they would have practised the natural methods of identifying kin and discriminating among non-kin, as described previously in this chapter. They were indeed distinguishing the individual from within the broader population, or, in other words the particular from the universal, within a real-time context. The more sophisticated civilisations utilised elements of those natural methods in a way that could be documented for subsequent verification, even by a third party without prior knowledge of the original transaction or event. This development represents an important step towards contemporary thinking around a formalised identity verification methodology. As such, we have much to learn from the natural world and from early human civilisations with regard to identity verification. It was, relatively speaking, a good deal later before we expanded significantly upon these ideas, via the application of science and scientific thinking.

Early Pioneers in Anatomical Measurement

It is appropriate, in order to inform our thinking around contemporary biometric techniques, to consider the development of thinking around the use of anatomical measurement for identity verification and other purposes. Much progress was made in the nineteenth century in this respect, with several strands of thought existing in parallel for a time, before polarising into a near-universal methodology.

Franz Joseph Gall (1758–1828)

Franz Joseph Gall was born in the little town of Teifunbrunn in Baden, Germany, to a prosperous family who thought that he might go into priesthood. Instead, he decided to study medicine, firstly at Strasbourg under J Hermann, and later in Vienna, where he qualified and began practising as a physician in 1785. While proficient as a medical practitioner in the accepted sense, Gall was always fascinated by the idea that character and aptitude might be centred in specific locations within the brain and reflected in external physical appearance. This thinking originated with the conjecture that those with exceptional memory tended to have protruding eyes.

Gall developed his theories into the discipline of cranioscopy, whereby it was posited that personality and the development of mental, and even moral faculties, could be determined by the precise shape of the skull. This technique was later renamed as phrenology by Gall and his followers. Unfortunately for Gall, the idea, while arousing initial curiosity, was ultimately not well accepted, especially by the church and even within the realms of contemporary science. Consequently he was much criticised and, in 1802, the idea was officially indicted by the government of the time as being dangerous to religion. In 1805 Gall left Vienna and toured Germany, giving a series of lectures, before finally settling in Paris where, while practising again as a physician, he continued to develop the concept of phrenology. His studies lead him to the conclusion that the brain was divided into 27 distinct areas, each corresponding to a particular human faculty, although 19 of these were thought to be shared with animals. In such a manner, individual aptitude for mental acuity, the arts, courage, arrogance, memory, and other factors were all catered for and represented by cranial physiology. Within this architecture, there was even an area defined for religion.

Gall and his concept of phrenology may not have been universally well received among scientists and priests, but he nevertheless attained a certain celebrity, arising no doubt from enduring curiosity regarding his ideas. Unfortunately, this curiosity soon developed into the high-jacking of these same ideas by opportunist quacks who set themselves up as phrenologists, lending fuel to the fire of Gall's opponents. He visited Britain briefly before retiring to France, where he died in August 1828. It is interesting that curiosity around the concept of phrenology endures to this day. More important perhaps is that Gall actually made genuine contributions to neurological science and was in fact intuitively correct in his theories of brain functionality being localised, even though phrenology was ultimately headed in the wrong direction. The concept of identifying individual characteristics by anatomical measurement, and therefore, by inference, was a powerful one, as we shall see.

Cesare Lombrosco (1836–1909)

Cesare Lombrosco was, by all accounts, a fascinating character whose interests spanned psychiatry, forensic medicine, criminology, and evolution among other things. Born in Verona, Italy, to a wealthy family, he studied linguistics, literature, and archaeology at universities in Padua, Vienna, and Paris, eventually becoming, of all things, an army surgeon in 1859. He went on to become the director of an insane asylum in Pesaro in 1871, before becoming a professor of forensic medicine and hygiene at Turin in 1878, then a professor of psychiatry, and, finally, a professor of criminal anthropology in 1906.

Lombrosco took the concept of phrenology several stages further and into the realms of criminology, whereby he suggested that criminal tendencies were expressed in physical features and anomalies. These ideas were mixed with theories of atavism wherein he claimed that criminal tendencies were a throwback to the primitive characteristics of a subhuman type of man, or 'savage'. It was postulated that such traits found physical expression in primitive features reminiscent of apes and lower primates, including sloping foreheads, extended arms, heavy jaws, asymmetry of the face, and so on. Indeed, Lombrosco suggested that even specific criminal activities such as thieving, rape, and murder could be aligned with physical characteristics. It is interesting that, in stark contrast with Gall, Lombrosco and his work were taken very seriously by the establishment. His ideas were reinforced by many years of detailed post-mortem measurements and, of course, he had a ready stream of interesting examples upon which to work.

In time, Lombrosco expanded his thinking into areas of the mind as he attempted to align physical and mental characteristics within the sphere of criminology. Factors such as a lack of morality, an absence of remorse, vanity, impulsiveness, vindictiveness, and cruelty began to fascinate him, as did the distinction between predisposing factors and precipitating factors such as lack of opportunity, poverty, and general environment. He was indeed laying the foundations for criminal anthropology, a doctrine which is very much to the fore in modern times. Lombrosco's contribution to science was ultimately significant and he enjoyed the acceptance of the scientific community, along with position and distinction. It is curious, in a way, that much of this stemmed from the identification of human characteristics with anatomical measurement, a concept which has little support today. However, it continued the stream of thought initiated by Gall and provided momentum towards a more specific methodology for identifying individuals.

Adolphe Quetelet (1796–1874)

Adolphe Quetelet was born in Ghent in Belgium and studied there at the Lycée, where he also started to teach mathematics at the tender age of 19. Indeed, Quetelet was fascinated by mathematics and statistics throughout his life and applied statistical reasoning to many social situations. After receiving a doctorate in mathematics from the university of Ghent in 1819, he became interested in astronomy and eventually founded the Royal Observatory of Belgium, persuading a consortium of government and private investors to establish an observatory in Brussels. In fact, throughout his lifetime he established several institutions and journals and contributed significantly to various statistical societies.

Quetelet brought statistical thinking and detailed measurement to social factors such as criminology and the prevalence of behavioural traits among human populations. He borrowed from astronomy concepts of the laws of error and probability and applied these to what we would now call sociology, determining what he referred to as the 'average man'. Included in his work was a good deal of precise anatomic measurement of various human types, predicting the discipline of anthropometry. However, it was the categorisation and determination of behavioural characteristics according to statistical evidence and the laws of probability which particularly interested him, and he saw this as a new science which he called social mechanics. Criminology was a key component of this science and Quetelet studied the relationship between criminal behaviour and other social factors via statistical analysis. This was perhaps Quetelet's great strength: taking ideas which had previously been discussed and hypothesised over in an intuitive fashion, and tying them to sound statistical thinking, producing reliable and repeatable results accordingly. The concept of aligning behaviour with measurable anatomical traits had not entirely gone away, but now the two areas were crystallising into separate disciplines: the study of social phenomena and straightforward anatomical measurement. From the latter perspective, Quetelet defined a simple formula for estimating whether a given individual was under- or overweight in relation to their height, based upon his average man concept. This formula – weight in kilograms/height in metres^2 – would become universally recognised as the Body Mass Index (Quetelet Index), and is still used today in order to gauge obesity in individuals over the age of 20.

Quetelet published many papers and several books, bringing new perspectives to the study of criminology and social behaviour, as well as methods of anatomical measurement based upon sound reasoning. His considerations of statistics, averages, and probabilities are highly pertinent to our contemporary view of biometric identity verification.

Alphonse Bertillon (1853–1914)

Continuing the statistical theme, Alphonse Bertillon was born in Paris to a father who was a statistician and he had an older brother who was also a statistician. Alphonse himself, while clearly obsessive about order, did not immediately distinguish himself. In fact, he was expelled from the Imperial Lycée in Versailles and drifted along, taking jobs here and there until, in 1875, he was conscripted into the French army. The army similarly failed to inspire him and he left without any particular distinction or the acquisition of any particular skills. His father managed to get him a basic clerical job at the Prefecture in Paris where he started his police career as a lowly copyist. However, as often happens with individuals who are naturally inventive and bright, Bertillon soon started to devise and implement his own ideas for the identification of criminals against prior records. His main theme was one of precise measurement of anatomical features, coupled with an orderly and logical record-keeping system. In this, as with everything, he was somewhat obsessed with detail and strove for a very high precision in his measurements. To Bertillon is usually attributed the establishment of anthropometry, at least with respect to official use of the technique, although others undoubtedly had similar ideas. Much of his early work was conducted in his spare time, often utilising the infamous La Santé prison in Paris for gathering precise measurements of various anatomical features of the inmates, no doubt to their initial amusement.

In 1882, Bertillon was ready to show his system of anthropometry, which was later renamed to Bertillonage in recognition of its inventor. It involved precise measurements of various features including the head, body, and various distinguishing marks such as scars and tattoos. Note the similarity, in principle, with the methods employed by the ancient Egyptians. Bertillon's methods were moulded into a precise formula which would be used consistently for each individual, yielding results which would reliably verify their identity. In 1884, he was able to identify 241 multiple offenders using his Bertillonage system, which was quickly adopted in France and then in Britain and America. The precise and consistent measurements, coupled to an ingenious record-keeping system, allowed police departments to quickly reduce the list of possible identities against which to verify a given individual. With the aid of photographs, a final comparison and positive identity verification could often be made. This was a significant step forward for police departments who had previously lacked any particularly scientific methodology for the identification of criminals.

The Bertillonage system, while undoubtedly popular, was not infallible and mistakes could be made, especially regarding the initial measurements which, undertaken by a broad cross section of police officers, tended to be inconsistent. Furthermore, the measuring apparatus was itself often inconsistent if not carefully maintained. Not everyone was as precise or as obsessed with detail as Bertillon himself. Consequently, it became obvious that the system was slightly flawed, especially as some of the measurements taken were subject to natural change, with ageing for example. Nevertheless, Bertillon continued with his experiments, especially with photography, wherein he standardised what we would now call the 'mugshot' and worked on various ideas for using photography at the scene of the crime.

As an individual, Bertillon was thought to have become increasingly eccentric and, in later years, was responsible for some particularly strange testimonies on all sorts of questionable evidence. By then, however, he had become something of a celebrity and was well received at various international expositions and other such events. Bertillon's contribution was significant in several respects, not least by bringing order and a scientific approach to identity verification within the field of criminology.

Jan Evangelista Purkyne (1787–1868)

Jan Evangelista Purkyne was a truly remarkable individual and a groundbreaking scientist, as well as something of a Czech nationalist. It may not have turned out that way, as Purkyne was born into a humble and poor family in the little town of Libochovice near Prague, who would not have been able to afford him a proper education. However, he had a talent for singing and was effectively adopted into the monastery at Moravia, where he also received a classical education, after which he subsequently entered into properly as a teacher in 1804. He was fascinated and absorbed by the library at the monastery and quickly acquired a taste for scientific learning. His thirst for knowledge quickly overtook the facilities at the monastery, however, and in 1807 he decided to leave and embark upon a momentous 300 km walk to Prague, where he started studying philosophy at the Prague University, while also acting as a tutor. Philosophy merged into medicine and, in 1819, he graduated in medicine with a groundbreaking thesis on human vision. Thus was born a notable career in human physiology.

Purkyne moved to Poland and became established at the university at Wroclaw in 1822, where he was to remain for 27 years. Throughout that time, he developed a dynamic and demonstrative approach to teaching which was unusual for the time and no doubt much appreciated by his students. He also developed many ideas and made important discoveries via his research into the human body, and in 1842 established the world's first proper physiological laboratory. His research was broad and encompassed cardiology, studies into the brain, human vision, speech, and many other areas. While studying sweat glands, he realised that human fingerprints appeared to be unique and could thus be used for identification purposes.

Purkyne eventually returned to Prague where he was to be instrumental in the Czech national revival, championing the use of the Czech language and continuing his teachings at the University of Prague, where he also established the Ziva scientific journal, an important vehicle for Czech science. His discovery of the relative uniqueness of human fingerprints was to prove hugely significant in the field of criminology.

Juan Vucetich (1858–1925)

Juan Vucetich was born in what we now call Croatia but moved to Argentina as a young man, where he landed a job at the La Plata Police Office of Identification and Statistics. Argentina had a particular focus in this area and had embraced the methods established by Bertillon, following a report by Dr. Augusto Drago, which led to the establishment of anthropometry within the Buenos Aires Police Department. Vucetich meanwhile had been reading about the research of Francis Galton and became convinced that fingerprints represented a better and more reliable method of identification than the complex mechanisms of anthropometry. He further developed a method of fingerprint collection and classification which he continually refined, effectively inventing the process of dactyloscopy: the taking of fingerprints using ink.

Vucetich pioneered the use of fingerprints in a practical sense and, in 1892, made the first positive criminal identification using fingerprints in the notorious case of Francisca Rojas, who had murdered her two sons. He continued to develop the system which started to become adopted by police forces in many other countries. Vucetich himself travelled widely and produced many papers on the subject, including his seminal Comparative Dactyloscopy of 1904 which became a universally accepted reference.

While Vucetich had initially included Bertillon's anthropometry techniques in his thinking (indeed he was now leading the Office of Anthropometric Identification), he quickly dropped these ideas and focused uniquely upon fingerprints as a superior method. The Argentine government made good use of his expertise and its deployment included the use of a fingerprint on the standard internal identification document. Considering that this was around the turn of the twentieth century, the idea of having an effective biometric on an identity document was indeed far-sighted.

In terms of biometric identity verification in the form of fingerprints, the world owes a great deal to Juan Vucetich, who effectively moved us on from the inconsistencies of anthropometry to a far more reliable and more workable system of fingerprinting. He was a good scientist with a steady methodical approach, who employed high standards of documentation, which he readily shared. While he rightly achieved international recognition, it is fitting that he is remembered at La Plata where both the museum and local police academy bear his name.

Francis Galton (1822–1911)

Francis Galton was an exceptional individual with interests in many areas, most of which he made a significant contribution to within his lifetime. Born in Birmingham to a prosperous family of bankers and gun manufacturers, he was a half cousin of Charles Darwin, sharing the common grandparent Erasmus Darwin. He was consequently well placed but, even so, demonstrated remarkable capabilities from an early age, reading at the age of 2 and absorbing a certain amount of Greek and Latin before the age that most would have started primary school. Indeed, when he did go to school, he was somewhat surprised that the other children were not familiar with some of the concepts and philosophies which were everyday fare for him. Similarly, at secondary school in Birmingham he was frustrated by what he saw as a narrow scope of studies. He went on to study medicine and then switched to mathematics, which he studied at Trinity College, Cambridge, although ill health prevented him from going as far as he might have in this field.

In 1844, his father died, leaving Galton financially independent and secure. He decided to travel, initially through eastern Europe to Constantinople and then to Egypt, where he followed the Nile down to Khartoum and then on to Damascus and further afield. Fired with an enthusiasm for travel, he joined The Royal Geographical Society in 1850 and embarked upon an expedition into South West Africa, for which he was subsequently awarded the Royal Geographical Society's gold medal as well as a silver medal from the French Geographical Society.

Galton gave his attention to several areas including meteorology, biology, psychology, and criminology. In each area he made significant contributions, often fuelled by his penchant for observation and measurement. When half cousin Charles Darwin published his revolutionary work, *On the Origin of Species*, Galton was hugely impressed and immediately turned his attention to exploring variation in human populations and the implications thereof. His research embraced many aspects of human variation, from anatomical measurement to mental faculties, but he was particularly interested in understanding inheritance and the probability of aptitudes and capabilities being passed on genetically. He undertook a good deal of work in this area, publishing his conclusions in seminal works such as *Hereditary Genius* and *English Men of Science: Their Nature and Nurture*. He was the first to use this term 'nature and nurture' and distinguish between the two with regard to mental faculties. He also invented the term 'eugenics' in 1883 and, in doing so, effectively founded a new branch of science.

Given his interest in human variation and inheritance, coupled with a keen sense of precision and measurement, it is logical that he would, sooner or later, stumble upon fingerprints and the idea that they are unique among individuals. As mentioned previously, Juan Vucetich was hugely impressed and inspired by Galton's work in this area. Galton had amassed a large collection of around 8,000 sets of fingerprints and had studied the variations in minutiae, applying statistical tests to show that they were indeed unique. Indeed, his study of minutiae formed a basis for meaningful comparisons between fingerprints. He went on to develop a sound classification system and was an early advocate of fingerprints as a means of identification, producing a number of papers on the subject between 1888 and 1909. In fact, early work on fingerprints had been conducted in India from around 1860, particularly by Sir William Herschel and it was another from this area, Sir Edward Henry, who, like Juan Vucetich, saw the potential of Galton's work for law enforcement, and this eventually led to the Galton–Henry system of fingerprint classification which was published in 1900 and adopted by Scotland Yard in 1901 for purposes of criminal identification. Henry of course went on to become Chief Commissioner of the London Metropolitan Police.

Francis Galton's contribution to the understanding and classification of fingerprints cannot be overestimated. Yet his interest in fingerprints was as of a small pebble on a large beach of scientific endeavour. His contribution to science overall was simply immense. He received many accolades for his pioneering work and was eventually knighted in 1909, at the tender age of 89.

1

Modern Times

The nineteenth and early twentieth centuries saw tremendous advances in applying scientific principles to the concept of identity verification. Ideas and methodologies introduced at that time have endured, in one form or another, until the present. The great wars intervened of course and it wasn't really until after the Second World War when rapid advances in electronics provided the foundation for another revolution in identity verification and management. The key factor in this respect was the promise of automation: automation in the search and comparison of records and, ultimately, automation with respect to real-time identity verification checks. We use the term 'biometrics' in a rather loose fashion to encompass various distinct disciplines within this automated, electronic identity verification world. However, there are various complexities to understand in this context, many of which will be explored elsewhere in this book.

In this chapter, we have explored various factors from natural processes in animal and human identity verification, through to the more formalised approach taken in ancient times and the later appliance of scientific principles to common ideas. In this there exists a logical progression from something we do naturally as individuals to something that may be done in a formal manner with respect to collections of individuals within a societal and legal framework. The latter concept has naturally been subject to continual development and remains so today. Even so, we are a long way from replicating electronically or mechanically the natural identity verification processes practised by the most humble creatures on this earth. Indeed, the relative performance of some of our automated processes appears decidedly crude in comparison. Nevertheless, in some areas we have been able to develop capabilities which are not mirrored in the natural world, mostly because the natural world has no need for them. This is a significant point, as we are departing, in some respects, from the natural way of things. Furthermore, in so doing, we are introducing a new raft of societal issues associated with our modern view of identity verification and identity management, which has progressed way beyond the simple requirements of criminology. Such issues are further confused with the universality of computers and computer networks, which, themselves, introduce significant new challenges to this area. This book will similarly explore many of these challenges and attempt to illuminate somewhat the darker corners of the automated, identity verification world that we have created in modern times.

It is perhaps time for another revolution. Not necessarily one of evolving technology. Nor of providing additional functionality or new methodologies. But more a revolution of attitude and understanding. Revolutionary ideas around what identity verification really means to the modern world and its collective population. Revolutionary ideas around both individual and public sector responsibilities. Revolutionary ideas around the use of technology in society. However, before we can architect such a revolution, we must first understand the current position, its strengths, and its weaknesses, from both a technological and operational perspective. We must further understand the logical future extrapolation of this position in accordance with synergistic developments in information technology. Within the chapters of this book will be found a foundation for such an understanding.

Review Questions

1. Identify and discuss the various ways in which animals may undertake identity verification within the natural world, and compare such techniques with those naturally practised by humans.
2. Explore the use of identity verification using biometric techniques within ancient civilisations.
3. What is the significance of criminal anthropometry in relation to identity verification as practised in contemporary times?
4. What was the primary contribution of Jan Evangelista Purkyne's work to current methods of criminal identity verification?
5. Consider and discuss the impact of computers and computer networks upon the practice of identity verification.

Biometrics Revisited

2

Abstract There are many popular assumptions around biometrics and what a biometric identity check really means. Some of these assumptions properly belong in the world of mythology. This chapter clarifies exactly what a biometric identity verification check actually means and how it works technically, covering factors such as matching thresholds and degrees of likeness. Similarly, there exists a degree of misunderstanding around the finer points of individual biometric techniques and their principles of operation. The primary biometric techniques are therefore clarified and placed into perspective. Applications are also discussed with respect to biometric functionality and associated aspirations. This chapter consequently provides an overview of biometric technology, explaining how the technology has evolved, how it works and what it may and may not provide, exploding a few myths along the way. It explores how identity verification has developed as a separate function from early access control systems and looks at some of the currently popular biometric techniques, exploring their strengths and weaknesses accordingly. This chapter provides a solid foundation for those which follow, ensuring that the reader has an adequate working understanding of the technology upon which to develop further thinking.

Biometrics Defined

The word *biometric* means literally a measurement of life. Many years ago, the author offered another definition as follows: *A physiological or behavioural trait which may be measured, stored and thus utilised in subsequent comparison with a live sample for automated identity verification purposes.* This definition aligns well with the way we think about biometrics today and seems to have been universally adopted. It follows that there are potentially many biometrics although, in practice, just a few have endured as popular techniques for automated identity verification purposes.

Before we go any further, it is appropriate to clarify what a biometric identity verification check actually means and to address a few myths in this context. There is a fundamental distinction to make here between a one-to-one check, wherein we are comparing one stored biometric with one live sample, and a one-to-many check, wherein we are comparing one live sample with many stored biometrics. In the former case, we are seeking

J. Ashbourn, *Guide to Biometrics for Large-Scale Systems: Technological, Operational,*
and User-Related Factors, DOI 10.1007/978-0-85729-467-8_2,

2

to corroborate a claimed identity by comparing the live sample with a stored biometric, claimed to represent the individual concerned. In the latter case, we are seeking to identify the individual by comparing the live sample with a population of biometrics, in order to find a match.

When we undertake a biometric identity verification check, we are essentially comparing two sets of computationally derived, digital information in order to ascertain how closely they match each other (we do this many times in a one-to-many check). Of course, they will never match each other absolutely, due to natural variances in the way the live sample is presented, environmental conditions and a host of other factors. Consequently, we place a condition upon this match, effectively agreeing that a match has occurred if a certain threshold of likeness has been reached. In simple words, you may think of this in terms of a percentage. Any matching transaction result which falls beneath this threshold will consequently be seen as a non-match, and the transaction will fail. Therefore, a match is always a relative match according to the predefined parameters, which, if satisfied, we consider to represent a match. In the majority of systems, this set of parameters, or match threshold, may be adjusted. Therefore, at a specific point of presence, a system may be tuned according to local conditions. Figure 2.1 illustrates this. We shall revisit this idea later in the book. Suffice it to say that there are no absolutes with respect to biometric identity verification; it is always a question of degrees of likeness when comparing a stored biometric with a live sample. Even when comparing sets of stored biometrics, the same principles apply.

When we refer to a stored template, we should understand that this template could take a variety of forms. It may quite literally be an image of the biometric trait as captured by an optical device, or it may be a digital representation of the trait derived according to

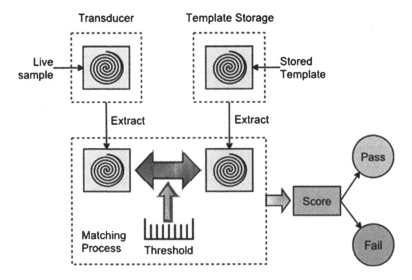

Fig. 2.1 A simplified view of the biometric matching process

vector or feature information. In either case, it is likely that a certain amount of processing will have taken place, both with respect to feature extraction and removal of unwanted noise. Such processing will be undertaken both at the time of template creation and at every subsequent matching transaction. It is possible therefore that the processing itself may, under different conditions, introduce a small amount of errors. Whether these errors are significant or not may depend both on the biometric technique employed and the precise configuration of the biometric transducer and matching algorithm. We shall consider other types of errors elsewhere in the book.

Assumptions

Let us explore a few of the assumptions often made around biometrics and individual identity verification.

- A biometric match proves that I am who I say I am.
  Absolutely not the case; a biometric match proves nothing of the kind. It simply provides a level of confidence as to the likeness of two sets of information. Other information aligned with the stored biometric record may or may not be correct and may or may not have been edited or tampered with.
- A failed biometric transaction proves that I am an impostor.
  Incorrect. It simply shows that two sets of information have failed to match according to a predefined likeness threshold.
- A biometric check is infallible.
  Not at all; there are many factors which may conspire to give a false result, either a false positive or a false negative.
- Biometrics cannot be spoofed.
  Certainly some biometrics and associated devices are more resistant to others in this respect, but most have been successfully spoofed at one time or another.
- A biometric will protect my privacy.
  Absolutely not. Indeed, the opposite is often the case. In any event, such an assumption cannot be made out of context; it all depends upon the application and associated infrastructure.
- All biometrics are stable over time.
  Not necessarily the case. Some are certainly subject to change and others are more resilient. This factor, and the implications for live matching transactions, is often not well understood.

One could continue with a long list of assumptions and half-truths which are often claimed or promoted with respect to biometric identity verification. However, I believe that we have made the point that biometrics are not infallible and that we should beware of attaching too much importance to a biometric identity verification transaction in isolation. As part of an intelligent brace of measures and checks, defined in relation to the perceived risk at hand, a biometric check may provide an increased level of confidence as to the identity of a given individual, providing the information aligned with the stored biometric is indeed correct in itself. If the associated information has been falsified, then the biometric check simply serves to augment the fraud. This is an important point which needs to be properly understood.

Biometric Methodologies

Now that we have placed the value of a biometric check within a proper perspective, we might usefully consider some of the currently popular biometric methodologies and their associated development. Back in the 1980s when there was a lot of activity and research into what we would perceive today as contemporary biometrics, the focus was predominantly upon physical access control; in other words, gaining entry through a physical portal such as an internal door or external gate. In fact, many early systems were described simply as door entry systems. The electronic control was often centred around a keypad and personal identification number, although, often, even this was shared among all users. Keypads were slowly joined by card or token readers, which could be used either in conjunction with the keypad or in isolation. Cards became more sophisticated, the humble magnetic stripe card being joined by infrared cards, Wiegand cards and a variety of other tokens including short-range transponder cards for 'hands-free' operation. Developments in card technology were mirrored by increasingly sophisticated control mechanisms which could cater for hundreds of entry points and provide additional functions around alarm monitoring and building management.

The access control market consequently blossomed and many sophisticated systems became available. However, the concept was not without shortcomings. As systems became larger, card and token management became more of an issue. Furthermore, the instances of individuals passing tokens between them increased, throwing doubts upon the accuracy of transactional records. We may know that a particular token had been used at a given point of presence on a particular day, but we could not be absolutely sure that the individual using the token was the same individual to whom it had been assigned. If the system was additionally being used for time and attendance purposes, this was an unfortunate reality. In very high security access control scenarios, the limitations of tokens were particularly pertinent. If, however, we could incorporate a biometric check, either with or without a token, then we could surely have an increased confidence as to the true identity of the individual concerned. This was the driver behind most of the early, pioneering biometric systems. Indeed, many of them were physically implemented within an access control like architecture; one can recall early implementations of hand geometry, voice verification, fingerprint scanning and retinal scanning, which were effectively access control systems that happened to use a biometric rather than a token. Slowly, the biometric functionality divorced itself from the control functionality, although there are still examples where the two are usefully combined. Let us consider some of the popular biometric techniques.

Hand Geometry

Hand geometry was one of the early pioneering biometric techniques that originally measured the position and length of the fingers when placed upon a platter surface. The original device was rather large and cumbersome, but this was soon refined into the ID3D hand geometry device (from Recognition Systems Inc., the primary advocate of hand geometry), which was much neater and, as the name suggests, introduced a three-dimensional factor via the use of mirrors. There were many strong points associated with this device, including relative ease of use and an unusually small template of around 9 bytes, facilitating its storage upon portable media as well as having low system resource usage if stored centrally or, as was possible, within the device itself. The ID3D was also well considered from a systems perspective, facilitating simple RS485 networks to be created with nothing more than the readers themselves and effectively providing distributed template storage. Current versions of the original hand geometry reader continue to provide good functionality, ease of use and a quite reasonable performance. They remain particularly well suited to certain types of applications and are often used in the context of physical access control, time and attendance monitoring, benefit provision and similar applications.

Voice Verification

Voice verification was another early pioneer and there were a few different systems available for a while, some of them quite well considered from the systems perspective. Typically, voice verification systems analysed the individual dynamics inherent within the annunciation of a given pass-phrase, creating a template accordingly which could be used for subsequent matching with the live sample. While the theory is logical enough and, no doubt, some of the matching algorithms well developed, voice verification as a technique is disadvantaged in several ways. Firstly, if using commercially available transducers such as telephone handsets, the quality of mass-produced low-cost transducers is not only relatively poor in terms of frequency response and dynamic bandwidth, but notoriously variable from sample to sample. Secondly, we have the inconsistencies and noise within the communications channel (e.g. telephone lines, routers and exchanges) to consider. Thirdly, variable point-of-presence environments will have equally variable ambient noise levels and acoustic properties such as reflectivity, absorption, preponderance towards standing waves and so on. Lastly, the consistency with which users interact with the transducer device often leaves much to be desired, especially with non-habituated users. Such issues, when summed, can create enormous challenges for voice verification systems. Nevertheless, they may be well suited to certain, closed-loop applications where voice is the biometric of choice.

Signature Verification

Signature verification as a technique was also among the pioneers and there were several competing systems at one stage. It seemed like an obvious application of biometrics as there were so many familiar processes that used a signature as a means of identity verification.

Furthermore, signature verification biometrics, in theory at least, provided a further depth of analysis as one could measure the dynamics inherent in writing the signature as well as the precise geometry of the signature. In isolated tests, signature verification could give a reasonable account of itself. However, in live situations, using commercially available graphics tablets and existing systems components, things were often not so easy. Furthermore, it is interesting, when considered in proportional terms, how relatively inconsistent some users are in signing their name, both dynamically and graphically. While a human observer might, even subconsciously, make allowances for such inconsistencies while still correctly recognising a signature, a signature verification matching algorithm has a harder time, especially when attempting to function within tight tolerance levels. Consequently, signature verification has yet to fulfil its promise as a viable mainstream biometric technique, although there may be applications where it could prove to be useful.

Keystroke Dynamics

Keystroke dynamics is another early technique in which a great deal of time and effort was invested, including by some major information technology companies. The idea of recognising an individual by their particular keystroke dynamics was clearly an attractive one from an information technology and networks perspective. While it did seem possible to determine an individual dynamic signature under carefully controlled conditions, real users under real operational conditions were not perhaps as consistent in the way they used a keyboard as one would have liked in order to implement this technology. Furthermore, using standard keyboards, there wasn't really a wealth of individualistic information with which to work. After much research and some interesting demonstrations, the idea of keystroke dynamics as a viable behavioural biometric seemed to fade, especially when other techniques were seen to be making good progress.

Fingerprint Recognition

Fingerprint recognition is probably the biometric technique which most people are aware of. It was always going to be an obvious choice of biometric for those in law enforcement, where matching fingerprints has been fundamental to the identification of criminals since the turn of the last century. This reality in itself initially introduced something of a stigma, due to the strong alignment with criminology in most minds. There is a dichotomy here between automated fingerprint identification systems (AFIS) as used by law enforcement agencies to search large databases, often off-line, in order to identify criminals, and discreet fingerprint biometric systems, which typically function in real time in order to verify an individual identity, within a range of scenarios. The two functions are increasingly interlinked in areas such as border control, and this raises some interesting questions.

The technology itself, however, has progressed quickly into workable systems which are considerably easier to use and more reliable than some of the original implementations. Fingerprint readers may use either an optical or capacitive sensor, each of which has their own advantages depending upon the application. Optical sensors may offer high resolution and be easily able to capture a full grey-scale image of the fingerprint. Capacitive sensors tend to be smaller, easily integrated and less sensitive to the build-up of grime on the surface of the sensor. The fingerprint matching process may be based upon identifying minutiae according to a spatial vector, or may be based upon image matching by pixel contrast or grey level. Some systems may store both minutiae information and a full image of the fingerprint. In practice, fingerprint recognition has become well adopted as a biometric methodology across a broad variety of applications. Many of these applications are in the public sector, for applications such as border control, national identity documentation, benefit entitlement and so on. Many more are in the private sector for applications such as network access, mobile device security, voluntary transportation payment systems and other applications. Fingerprint sensors have become almost a commodity item and are often supplied on an original equipment manufacturer (OEM) basis for incorporation into laptop PCs and a variety of other devices, as well as being provided in a range of distinct forms as commercial off-the-shelf (COTS) products for integration into other bespoke systems. The performance of fingerprint recognition can be robust, depending upon the number of fingerprints utilised and the dependence upon human and environmental factors.

Retinal Scanning

Retinal scanning was a pioneering biometric technique, developed initially for access control purposes within military environments. Its performance could be very good under certain conditions. However, its usability was typically rather troublesome, at least with respect to early implementations, although it improved a little in later iterations. This is primarily because usage originally involved peering into a binocular device and aligning one's vision upon a target – something that many people initially struggled with, especially those with impaired vision. In addition, many users did not very much like the idea of physical contact with the binocular interface. Consequently, while usage within a controlled military environment may have been acceptable (largely because such users had no choice in the matter) the technique found little favour within the broader community. The retinal scanning technique involved scanning the vein patterns on the retina with a low-powered beam shone into the eye: an intrusive function which was not typically considered an attractive proposition by potential users. Furthermore, early versions of retinal scanners were prohibitively expensive for anyone outside of the military. Later versions became much less expensive and were rather better considered in terms of connectivity, systems integration and the user interface. However, by then, other biometric techniques had found a wider acceptance and had effectively marginalized retinal scanning as an operationally viable technique.

Iris Recognition

Iris recognition has become a popular biometric technique and is generally recognised as being perhaps the most accurate technique in terms of matching individual iris patterns. Consequently, it is a useful technique both for one-to-one matching for the purposes of

2

individual identity verification, and one-to-many matching for the purposes of identifying a particular iris from within a large database. In addition, the relative operational performance of iris recognition can be very good. In early implementations, failure to acquire an image of suitable quality under real operational conditions could be an issue, as could acquiring high-quality reference templates. However, the technique quickly evolved and such issues are rarely troublesome today. Iris recognition readers tend to be rather more expensive than those for certain other techniques, largely because of their relative complexity. Furthermore, installation and commissioning may be a little more demanding, especially with regard to environmental placement and the accommodation of a broad range of individuals of differing physical size. Such deployment issues may be overcome, however, and may be considered insignificant for applications where the accuracy and performance of iris recognition is required.

In simple terms, the technique typically involves locating the iris within a human face, separating it from the pupil and sclera, dividing the visible iris into segments and analysing each segment accordingly. From this analysis, a relatively sophisticated iris code may be derived and matched against a previously stored reference. The amount of detail represented within the iris code allows for a high degree of confidence when undertaking matches, even when searching very large databases. This is facilitated by the amount of available information that may be derived from a typical iris, and the relative uniqueness of the iris within the human population. Indeed, even the left and right irises of the same individual tend to be distinct and irises are considered to remain stable throughout life, being fixed shortly after birth. Iris recognition has grown in popularity in recent years and is a technique which will no doubt continue to be widely used.

Face Recognition

Face recognition has been available as a biometric technique for a long time, although it is probably fair to say that early implementations left something to be desired in terms of accuracy and reliability of matching. However, the technique has many potential applications and continued development ensured that it quickly matured into a viable operational technique. Typically, the technique involves metrics of, and between, distinct features within the face, relying less on factors of a transitory nature such as hair style or the use of cosmetics. Nevertheless, the human face is subject to change over time and this reality will remain a challenge for face recognition systems, as will variance of expression, illness and other natural factors. In addition, environmental and human factors will almost always play a part in the efficacy of a face recognition system within a given deployment scenario. Consequently, face recognition may not quite match the accuracy provided by certain other techniques. However, it lends itself readily to applications where the face is already used within an identity verification context. Similarly, the ability to match against a stored image, perhaps from a different source, will appear attractive in some public sector applications. Face recognition has occasionally been used in conjunction with another biometric in order to increase confidence in the identity verification process. Face and fingerprint is a popular combination in this context. While not offering superlative levels of accuracy or operational performance, face recognition nevertheless remains a popular technique, and one which will no doubt benefit from further development.

Gait Recognition

The potential attractiveness of gait recognition lies in the ability to recognise an individual at a distance. However, there are serious challenges to be overcome in this respect. The idea that an individual typically walks with a unique gait is an interesting one and, under laboratory conditions, the concept of gait recognition can be demonstrated. However, real life is full of dynamic variances which render the implementation of such a system particularly difficult. In addition to the complexities of matching, there are factors such as the opportunity to even capture the moving image of an individual in isolation and in sufficient detail to be able to undertake such a match. Creating a reliable template is also something which presents real challenges. Gait recognition represents an interesting example of biometric research driven by a perceived requirement: in this case, to identify an individual at a distance beyond which contact and near-field biometrics can function. While perhaps an attractive idea for military and very high security applications, it is doubtful that gait recognition will become a mainstream biometric technique.

Vein Scanning

It has long been considered that the pattern of veins within the human anatomy may be unique to individuals. Consequently, there have been various implementations of vein scanning over the years, from hand scanning, to wrist scanning and, more recently, finger scanning. Most of these techniques have been shown to work and could certainly form the basis of a viable biometric identity verification system. The problem that they face is not one of technical capability or efficiency, but rather one of market realities. The preponderance of fingerprint, face and iris systems, readily available at a broad range of costs, makes it difficult for a distinct technique to gain market share without a clear and compelling advantage. Even early techniques such as hand geometry have an installed base which is unlikely to be impacted by a newer technique of comparable performance. Consequently, for any new biometric technique to become established in the marketplace, it must break new ground and offer clear advantages that cannot be realised by contemporary methods. The various implementations of vein scanning, while undoubtedly interesting, may struggle a little in this context. However, time may prove an interesting leveller in this context and distinct applications for vein scanning may appear.

Other Techniques

There are various other biometric identity verification techniques which have surfaced from time to time, including ear lobe recognition and scent recognition. Almost any anatomical feature or behavioural trait might be deemed a candidate for an operable biometric. However, we have to place such ideas in context and align them with the perceived requirement. If this requirement is to have a method by which we might verify an individual identity with a reasonable degree of confidence, then the existing biometric methodologies provide us with the means to do this in a variety of ways, thus facilitating a broad range of applications. Perhaps, in time, other techniques will be developed which might supplant some of the existing methodologies. For now, we might usefully turn our attention towards a better use of existing techniques within contemporary applications, and the provision of a better understanding of the future alignment with societal expectations. Such matters will be discussed within these pages.

Which Biometric Is Best?

A question that is asked perhaps more than any other in this field is which biometric technique is the best? The answer of course is that there is no *best* biometric in absolute terms, it all depends upon the precise nature of the application and the reasons for its implementation. In order to get a feel for this, it is pertinent perhaps to consider a few obvious application areas.

Physical Access Control

The original application for automated biometric identity verification, physical access control, remains a viable application for this technology. Several techniques have been used in this context, such as fingerprints, hand geometry, face recognition, retinal scanning and iris recognition. Important factors to consider include relative durability of biometric sensor devices, overall ease of use and desirability of a low false negative rate, whereby few individuals will find themselves blocked in error. Another factor has often been the integration with tokens such as conventional access control cards. In this respect, both hand geometry and fingerprints have been used quite successfully. Integration with existing systems, such as access control or building management systems for example, may be important in some cases. This will necessitate the use of a commonly used interface as well as a workable storage of biometric reference templates, either centrally, distributed among the devices themselves, or, ideally from both a performance and management point of view.

If a simple access control system is required within a new build scenario, then there are a variety of biometric-only systems, often based upon fingerprint technology, which may be easily deployed and commissioned and which will function quite well in an internal office environment, for example. Hand geometry can also work well in such scenarios. For high security access control applications, iris recognition would be a good choice, providing the sensing devices suit the environment. For example, under military or custodial scenarios, devices would ordinarily be required to be ruggedised and tamper-proof. External applications present their own challenges, particularly in harsh environments. Interestingly, voice verification has sometimes been used in such applications, via ruggedised and weatherproof handsets. The choice of a biometric for physical access control must take all such factors into account. Of course, available budget and the implications for ongoing maintenance will also factor strongly in many such situations.

Time and Attendance Monitoring

Time and attendance monitoring is a relatively specialised application area with a long history of using tokens, from punch cards to access control cards. It is also, these days, strongly driven by software, integration with payroll systems and flexible reporting functionality. Consequently, it is often the case, when implementing biometrics, of integrating biometric sensors with an existing system. Fingerprint readers have been used quite successfully in this context and there are also various dedicated fingerprint systems available. Another biometric technique which has found much favour for this application is hand geometry. Indeed the flexibility and connectivity offered by the leading hand geometry device lends itself well to such applications, as does the relative usability of the technique. Iris recognition would no doubt also work well, although the cost and operational methodology may not appear so attractive in certain environments. Time and attendance is one application area where contact-based techniques tend to be well accepted.

Logical Access Control

Logical access control, across computer networks and even within specific computer applications, is an area traditionally managed by a combination of user name and password. However, for higher security when a second factor is required, a biometric can work very well. Interestingly, this is an application area which has failed to grow in line with expectations, in spite of a plethora of low-cost fingerprint devices as well as various software-based techniques such as face recognition which can interact with existing transducers such as the webcams incorporated in many laptops. Perhaps part of the reason for this lack of adoption is the dichotomy between single device access and network access. For single devices, the user name and password methodology has become somewhat ingrained and is generally held to offer sufficient security. For network access, the necessity for integrating seamlessly with directory services may have deterred many from adopting a biometric. In addition, the question of support for a large user base in the event of persistent false negatives, for example, is no doubt one of concern for many organisations as this would be seen as a potential increase in support costs, especially if users need to be re-enrolled with their biometric. Nevertheless, it is possible that we shall see growth in the use of biometrics for logical access control. Factors such as business-to-business connectivity and the increasing reliance upon IT for many organisations in both the public and private sectors, coupled with increasing concerns around data security, may reawaken interest in this area. There was a time when it looked like capacitive fingerprint readers would soon grace the lines of almost every laptop computer, although relatively few models are thus equipped at present. More ubiquitous is the presence of an imaging device, both on laptops and monitors. Assuming an adequate resolution from such devices, perhaps a form of iris recognition might eventually find its way into this area at a low enough cost to make it viable. That would certainly be an interesting development. In the meantime, there are various fingerprint readers that may be easily integrated for those wishing to explore this area.

On-line Transactions

An extension of logical access control across public networks such as the Internet provides many business opportunities. It also has implications for security as many organisations have found to their cost. Applications such as on-line shopping and, importantly, on-line banking are increasingly becoming the norm, as are on-line interactions with public agencies. Encryption can go some way to protecting sensitive data, but access into external networks and onto external servers is always a worry, particularly access at administrator level. If a miscreant obtains the necessary identity credentials, he or she can wreak havoc in many ways, from simply stealing data to bringing down servers or even entire network segments. Furthermore, when such credentials are simply in the form of user names and passwords, their discovery may be relatively easy for a skilled miscreant. In theory, a biometric might serve to increase security within such a scenario, including that around non-repudiation. However, there are many factors to consider, especially around where the biometric is stored and at which point identity verification takes place. In this respect, it may be pertinent to consider access control within the hosting application quite separately from that of the remote client. Usability also has a part to play, as many customer users might struggle to understand and work with biometric identity verification. However, administrator access within the hosting network might well be an area worthy of investigation, although there are many issues to address. Indeed, the choice of a biometric technique may appear almost trivial compared to the challenges of designing an architecture which represents a genuine increase in security via the use of a biometric, while remaining workable and supportable. Once such challenges have been overcome, the biometric techniques of choice will no doubt be similar to those for internal network access control.

Portable Device Access

The rise in the use of portable devices has been pronounced in recent years. Furthermore, the functionality has become somewhat blurred, with devices which started out as mobile phones becoming, in effect, miniature personal computers, cameras, web browsers, data storage devices and general on-line communications devices. Mobile computers themselves have adopted a wide range of wireless connectivity functionality and may themselves operate as mobile communications devices. Even the form factors have moved closer together with the advent of the netbook PC and increasingly compact notebook PCs, all featuring cameras and often preloaded with a range of social networking software. One result of this mobile technology revolution is that such devices may hold a good deal of personal information. Indeed, modern netbook and notebook PCs have more data storage capacity than would be found on some servers not so many years ago. As such devices may easily be mislaid or even stolen, security becomes increasingly important, especially for devices issued to corporate users. It will be interesting to see how biometric technology will be used in this context. Already, one can easily incorporate face recognition into devices with an integral camera. Fingerprint sensors are small enough to be included, even in the smallest PC form factors, and they are to be found occasionally on notebook and laptop PCs. Whether such options become popular and commonplace will no doubt depend upon the suppliers and what they perceive as their primary market. However, there is certainly scope for intelligent implementations in this sphere, perhaps for corporate remote workers, for example.

National Identity Documentation

National identity documentation, in the form of identity cards and passports, is an obvious area for the adoption of a biometric, especially with the adoption of chip-cards and chips in passports. This opportunity has not escaped the attention of government agencies and there are now many implementations around the world. Fingerprints and iris recognition are popular methodologies, particularly fingerprints as these can very easily be referenced against other databases, including criminal databases if required. There is an interesting paradox here as the concept of a national identity document historically has been to affirm the right of an individual to cross a border according to their country of residence and whatever international agreements are in place. Consequently, the primary use of a biometric should be to confirm that the individual presenting the document is the same individual to whom it was originally issued. This concept has become somewhat blurred as the national identity document and the biometric it contains is being used increasingly for law enforcement purposes. Perhaps this is symptomatic of the times we live in. In any event, embedding a biometric into such a document is easy enough. The controls around registration and the processes by which such a document will subsequently be used will require careful consideration, as will the physical and technical reality at the point of checking. As a consequence of the almost universal use of fingerprints for law enforcement purposes, it is likely that fingerprints will predominate on national identity documents, although iris recognition and face recognition have been allowed for within the relevant document standards.

Border Control

Border control is an interesting area. On the one hand, some authorities may be satisfied with a simple biometric check of the user against the biometric reference embedded in the national identity document. Others, such as the USA for example, may require the collection of biometric data quite separately and will check these data against criminal databases, as well as storing it for future usage. Furthermore, they may require a much more extensive collection of biometric data, such as all ten fingerprints. Biometric data may also be used for VISA applications, enabling the checking against criminal databases before a VISA is granted, and also ensuring that the VISA user is the same individual who provided a biometric at the time of application: a useful application of biometric identity verification within the auspices of border control. Given the close association with law enforcement, it is perhaps not surprising that fingerprints predominate as a biometric technique in this area, although there are exceptions, with iris recognition in particular proving popular in this area due to its inherent accuracy. For border control purposes, it is often not essential to align the biometric with a national identity document, and various interesting schemes are in operation with or without an associated token.

Benefit Claims

Being an obvious application for biometric identity verification, it is surprising that the technique has not been used more often to control benefit fraud, especially in countries where this is a major issue and a major cost for government. It is a simple matter to issue claimants with a token containing a biometric and then check this biometric for each claim. With thorough background checks undertaken at the time of registration, such a system would no doubt provide impressive efficiencies and cost savings, as indeed has happened in areas where the concept has been introduced. Fingerprints would be an obvious biometric technique due to the relatively low cost of implementation and comparative ease of use. However, other techniques could be adopted if, for example, a non-contact methodology was preferred. As with any public sector implementation, it is the attendant technical architecture and operational process which will require careful consideration if such systems are to realise their potential benefits. The concept could be utilised across a wide range of state benefits and associated scenarios.

Industrial Processes

The use of biometrics with respect to industrial processes, such as when sophisticated machinery needs to be operated by certified trained operators, or in relation to very high security installations, may be an area where biometrics can prove extremely useful. In such applications, a non-contact, accurate methodology such as iris recognition might work well. Alternatively, under certain environments, a robust technology such as hand geometry might also be suitable. It is an area with many possibilities for creative thinking around the use of biometric identity verification. Furthermore, when aligned with safety, it would represent a valuable use of biometric technology. It will be interesting to see how things progress in this context, and one might expect to see an increasing use of biometric identity verification in this area over time.

Other Applications

There are countless potential applications for biometric technology: anywhere, in fact, where a strong confidence is required as to the true identity of an individual either performing a specific function or claiming a particular benefit. Clearly, there are areas where it would simply not make any sense at all to add the complexity of biometric identity verification to an existing process. It should be remembered that it is not simply the biometric matching process which needs to be designed, but the whole end-to-end process including registration, support, ongoing maintenance, data management and so on. There are also areas where the adoption of biometric identity verification might make considerable sense. That is for implementing agencies and individuals to decide. This section has perhaps served to illustrate that there is no single *best* biometric technique. It is a question of the application, the operational environment, the user profile and what we are trying to achieve. Furthermore, it is easy to become preoccupied by the characteristics and theoretical performance of different biometric techniques when the focus should really be upon clarity of purpose, sound technical architectures and properly considered operational processes.

Considerations Around DNA

Whenever biometrics are discussed, the thread often meanders its way, sooner or later, to DNA and the possibilities of using DNA as a mainstream identity verification method. There are many reasons why this is currently not really viable, not the least of which is the time and specialised facilities required for DNA analysis. However, it is appropriate that we consider DNA within these pages and provide a simplistic overview accordingly.

DNA stands for deoxyribonucleic acid and is the fundamental fabric of genes which, joined in a long string, make up the human genome. It is made up of nucleotide base pairs, each consisting of a purine and pyrimidine, and there are around 3.2 billion base pairs in the human genome. There are around 30,000 functional genes, that is, those that encode proteins, within mammalian genomes, including the human genome. Proteins are encoded by a transition process from DNA to mRNA (messenger ribonucleic acid), a specific sequence of which encodes a particular protein according to the genetic code.

As illustrated in Fig. 2.2, the encoded protein will depend upon the precise sequence transcribed from DNA into mRNA, a sequence which could be taken from anywhere within the genome. Furthermore, even this same sequence may be transcribed slightly differently as introns are discarded and molecules attached to the exon sequence, resulting in different protein coding. Considering the size of the genome and the degree of inherent randomisation, these processes may become highly complex. Indeed, while there remains much we do not, as yet, properly understand with regard to molecular genetics, it is clear that this DNA sequence is far from being fixed. We understand, for example, the process of exon shuffling, which can create new genes. Similarly, via a process of transposition, entire sections of

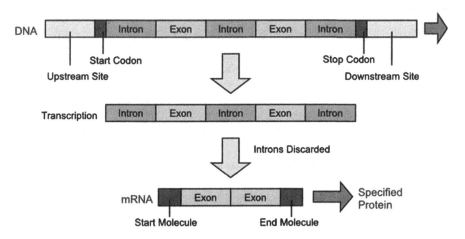

Fig. 2.2 A simple view of the DNA transcription process

2

DNA may be randomly copied and re-inserted at different points along the genome. Indeed, it is currently supposed that around 45% of the human genome consists of repeated sequences and that there exist around 4.3 million repetitive elements which we call microsatellites. This, of course, is all part of the process of mutation, which is a natural component of evolution. Genes mutate from one form, or allele, to another in order to create phenotypic effects. It is this very flexibility which allows for species to adapt. It is estimated that human babies have around 300 mutations which neither parent shares.

This very brief, high-level overview of DNA and its part in the evolutionary process reminds us that the genome is not some fixed, static entity, but a complex dynamic mechanism which can, and does, change. DNA can be damaged by chemical and physical events and altered by random mutations, all of which will result in sequence changes of one sort or another within the genome. DNA and genome analysis is thus a highly complicated affair and it is clear that we are still developing our understanding in this area. Consider, for example, the randomisation that triggers certain genetic sequences which ultimately prove to be harmful in humans (and other animals), often expressed as specific diseases which appear as if out of nowhere, often with no consistency as to age, gender, or ethnicity. This is simply the complex genetic mutational mechanism at work, and it starts with DNA.

Currently, there is a dichotomy of opinions emerging as to just how unique DNA may or may not be. Furthermore, the DNA analysis process is highly complex, exacting in its execution and subject to changing methodologies as our knowledge in this area develops. The common view of DNA as the ultimate personal identifier is consequently challenged as we increasingly understand the complexities involved. Those who dream of a commercially available, real-time DNA identity verification system might do better to employ their little grey cells, for the time being at least, to perfecting the comparatively simplistic mechanisms of biometrics. Mutation among said grey cells may of course overtake them in this quest.

Review Questions

1. Discuss the automated biometric matching process and the purpose of a variable matching threshold.
2. Review and discuss the relative strengths and weaknesses of individual biometric techniques.
3. Distinguish between retinal scanning and iris recognition as biometric methodologies and discuss relative usability.
4. Review and discuss the potential for biometric identity verification for the purposes of network access control.
5. Discuss the practical relevance of DNA as a potential automated identity verification method.

Biometric Systems Defined

3

Abstract In this chapter we shall focus upon the definition of a system and consider how identity verification has developed from simple physical access control systems to more sophisticated bespoke systems and, finally, identity verification as a service. Biometric identity verification has mirrored this general trend. An important part of this transition is echoed in networks which have developed from closed-loop wired networks using traditional protocols such as RS485 and RS422, through more sophisticated computer networks based upon Ethernet or token ring, and finally to the IP-based networks which may span continents. We also discuss applications and the impact, especially, of border control and law enforcement applications in bringing biometric technology to a much broader potential market. The fundamentals of the biometric registration process are explained in the context of systems administration and the additional factors which biometric technology introduces in this respect. We discuss system architectures and infrastructures and introduce the concept of application modelling via the Biometric and Token Technology Application Modelling Language (BANTAM). This chapter takes the concept of automated biometric identity verification and applies it to systems and applications.

Introduction

The concept of a system is an interesting one, usually defined as a complex whole, or a set of connected parts, often with a common structure or function. With respect to biometrics, the term is often used erroneously, but we understand the intent to describe a system which happens to incorporate biometric functionality of one sort or another. In practical terms, a biometric system might be anything from a standalone biometric device to an international system of connected databases and operational points of presence. In this context, it is appropriate to consider the recent history of biometric identity verification and understand the systemisation of biometrics into larger technical and operational environments.

J. Ashbourn, *Guide to Biometrics for Large-Scale Systems: Technological, Operational, and User-Related Factors*, DOI 10.1007/978-0-85729-467-8_3,
© Springer-Verlag London Limited 2011

3

Early Days

The roots of biometric systems as commonly understood lay in the concept of physical access control. Access control systems had themselves grown from simple door entry systems, often comprising little more than a keypad, a simple logic system which could store a specific code and compare this with an input, a relay output and a power supply. An advance on this basic precept was made with the introduction of plastic cards: firstly low-cost magnetic stripe cards, developing into more sophisticated cards, such as infra red, Wiegand and other formats, designed to offer higher security both in their physical form and in the associated management. For example, more sophisticated cards incorporated a site code as well as a range of card numbers, aligning a batch of cards with a particular physical or organisational entity. However, the fundamental operating principles of a token being used to gain physical access to a facility remained. It is useful to embed this fundamental principle into our thinking, for all later developments are, more or less, a variation upon this theme, as illustrated in Fig. 3.1.

In time, the simple standalone door entry system progressed into multiple devices connected together via a physical network, often based upon RS485 or RS422 communication protocols, enabling multiple entry points to be controlled using the same batch of tokens. Centralised logic was often provided via a dedicated control interface, often with little more than a small LED readout for programming purposes: remember that this was before the widespread adoption of personal computers.

When the personal computer started to appear in earnest, it was logical to use this as the central host, often communicating via a simple RS232 to RS485 converter, and configure a rudimentary control programme which allowed for tokens to be grouped, time zones to be configured and set, and individuals to be easily aligned with tokens. At this juncture, we might truly claim to have a *system*, especially when local control boxes were configured to include multiple relay outputs and voltage free digital inputs, facilitating a degree of building management functionality. However, it was an access control system, not a biometric system.

When workable biometric devices appeared, we saw a similar progression from simple standalone devices, often emulating simple door entry systems, to simple networked

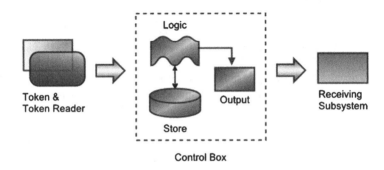

Fig. 3.1 Principles of using a token as a control mechanism

systems, often emulating access control systems, and, eventually, the interfacing of biometric readers to existing access control systems. Consequently, for some time, when people discussed biometric systems, what they really meant was access control systems with biometric devices attached. The exception to this rule was in the form of early automated fingerprint identity systems (AFIS) such as those used by law enforcement, whereby fingerprints were checked against fingerprint databases in an automated manner.

This logical progression from door entry systems to sophisticated access control and building management systems is an important factor within the adoption of biometric technology into the mainstream. Having exhausted the practical opportunities within the access control market, biometrics effectively became, for a while, a technology looking for an application. This application was to materialise in the form of border control and national identity documentation. Here was an application of global proportions which focused upon biometric technology in its own right, not as a sophisticated access control system. Thus, a new and significant wave of energy was released around creating some workable standards for biometric devices and their interfaces, looking at the possibility of incorporating biometrics into national identity cards and passports, and deploying biometric readers at border control points. In this context, several memorable pilot implementations were undertaken, using techniques including hand geometry, fingerprints, facial recognition and iris recognition. Interestingly, these early implementations often still featured relatively isolated architectures, not too far removed from that depicted in Fig. 3.1, and there was little thought around broader integration.

Rudimentary Integration

We have discussed the rudimentary integration of biometric devices into sophisticated access control and building management systems. This was usually facilitated by simply taking a binary pass/fail output and injecting it into the token reader input of the associated control box, simulating a card number and adding a unique location identifier. Indeed, many went as far as emulating a standard Wiegand format output in order that the biometric reader could simply replace an existing token reader. Certain implementations reversed the process by accepting a token and token reader input into a self-contained network of biometric readers. Actually, this was a logical approach, as it enabled token plus biometric two-factor authentication, thus providing a higher level of security to that commonly offered by token-only or token-plus-PIN systems. The principles remained closely aligned with the fundamental principles discussed earlier: that of controlling access to a physical location via the use of tokens. One complication in adopting this approach was that it necessarily entailed an additional layer of administration as now system administrators had to manage individual enrolment into the biometric database (whether hosted on the physical token media or centralised) and consider the complexities of matching thresholds, false negatives and false positives. Depending upon the overall purpose and associated level of risk inherent in the host application, this may have been considered a bridge too far for many operators.

Slowly, other ideas emerged which focused more closely upon biometrics and the possible benefits of adoption for specific purposes. One such example is in relation to ATM or cash dispenser machines. While such usage has not gained wide acceptance to date, there have been one or two specific implementations. Similarly the use of a biometric in relation to an entitlement card and the provision of an associated service have often been explored. Such ideas and applications are significant in that they start to consider the integration of biometrics into a process rather than simply an existing security system. This allows us to think, more properly, of biometrics as a sub-system or service which may be utilised within a broader process.

System Components

While adopting this 'biometrics as a service' perspective, it is helpful perhaps to consider the necessary biometric system components and how these might be aligned with, or integrated into, other systems. In this context, there are some fundamental components, or what some might prefer to consider as building blocks, with which we can effectively build a biometrics system or, alternatively, provide biometric functionality within a broader system. We shall discuss this more fully within a forthcoming chapter, but it may be useful to set a pattern for our thinking here.

Figure 3.2 illustrates the high-level system components which, together, provide biometric identity verification functionality for use by other processes or systems. These components may be distributed according to a number of different models, with more or less functionality present at the reader and host positions. The first block is concerned with capturing the biometric and undertaking whatever pre-processing is required before passing the relevant information to the host processing position. For example, this could be a fingerprint reading device, a camera assembly for iris or face recognition or some other biometric capture device. The communications channel is important, both from a reliability and security perspective. It is important that communications between devices and the host be maintained at all times and, equally importantly, such communications must be secure. If a third party or public network forms part of this channel, then security will be especially important. At the host position, the primary processing and biometric matching will be undertaken according to a pre-configured set of parameters, usually including a match threshold. The matching algorithm will undertake

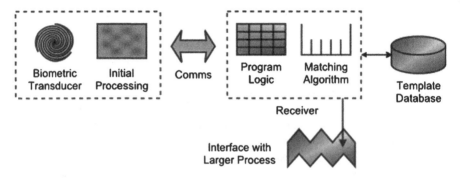

Fig. 3.2 Biometric system components

the match and produce either a relative score, indicating degrees of likeness, or a binary match, or fail according to the set threshold. The reference template will be obtained from a database, which may be centralised or distributed. The reference biometric may even be loaded from a portable token such as an identity card. Finally, when all processing is complete, the output will be fed to the master system, which will integrate this result within its own processes.

Thinking in terms of logical components enables us to design workable architectures with which to build our biometric system. However, the identity verification function, as described, is only a part of the total system. We must equally consider the enrolment process whereby individuals are registered into the system and reference biometrics created. There are both technical and operational factors to attend to in this context. Technically, we must understand what constitutes a robust biometric reference template, which will remain usable under real operational conditions. It is possible to put some metrics around this, depending upon the precise technique employed and we must identify a minimally accept-able level and strive to remain above it when creating reference biometric templates. In most implementations, by far the bigger challenge is the alignment of a biometric with a personal profile. This involves robust procedures for verifying information supplied by the individual at the time of enrolment. If these procedures are in any way lacking, then the biometric and all subsequent transactions become meaningless. Indeed, it is possible for implementing agencies to unwittingly create a brace of fraudulent identities due to the lack of a robust registration process. This of course is only relevant in systems where the bio-metric is positively aligned with an individual profile and used for verifying the identity of a named individual accordingly. It is also possible to create anonymous biometric systems whereby the stored reference biometric is not aligned with any specific user profile, and is instead used simply to verify that an individual with appropriate entitlements has been authenticated within the system.

In any event, the administration and maintenance of the biometric database is of primary importance within any biometric system. The technical capability, no matter how proficient, is meaningless if not aligned with a robust understanding and administration of the user base. This process must necessarily include the re-enrolment of templates when insurmountable errors are encountered with a given reference, the deletion of reference templates when users are no longer in the system, the maintenance of user records and the monitoring of overall database performance. Typically, such an administration will require specialist skills and this is a factor which should be taken into consideration at system design time. We might usefully consider these additional requirements as non-technical systems components. When thus considered, we may easily design an operational archi-tecture to sit atop the technical architecture. This operational architecture may be designed, using our non-technical components, in both a logical and spatial manner.

Peripheral Architectures

Having developed a workable design for the technical and operational aspects of our biometric system, we must also consider precisely why, where, when and how this system touches third-party systems or processes. Typically, there will be almost as much effort required in this area as in designing the biometric element. For example, it would be typical for the biometric functionality to support a major service provision, such as often happens with public sector applications. The provision of this service will no doubt depend on another primary system which will undertake and track the service provision, storing all such transactions within a related database. The primary system, at the point of identity verification, will effectively call the biometric sub-system and accept the result of the biometric match into its own workflow process in order to complete or perhaps reject the transaction. While this sounds straightforward enough, there may be several interfaces involved, all of which need to be configured, tested and maintained. There must also be a messaging sub-system and workflow with which to manage exceptions. Furthermore, if there is a failure somewhere in the broader workflow, this needs to be clearly identified in relation to the biometric functionality, ensuring that the cause of the failure, and the notification and remediation thereof are properly aligned.

Similarly, the biometric template database itself may be abstracted out to another layer, not necessarily on the same platform as the host application, and may be used by several applications. There may be performance implications which need to be understood with such a model. As we move more towards service-orientated architectures, these connections and interconnections become more critical. Thinking in terms of logical components and interfaces helps us to design suitable models within these architectures, in order to meet the operational realities of a broad range of applications.

Communications are very much a part of this and we must decide where our building block components sit and how they communicate with other system components. We must consider network components as part of this picture and understand precisely how our data traverse firewalls and routers and what this means from a network device configuration perspective.

Our biometric system architecture has now grown quite considerably and has likely touched many other components and interfaces along the way. At each of these points of contact we must consider security, performance, reliability and sustainability and ensure that all is properly documented, including all aspects of configuration. Our definition of a biometric system may assume different complexions according to the host application and its operational requirements. A biometric system in isolation achieves nothing. It is when we incorporate biometric functionality into broader processes and applications that the technology is effectively systemised. Consequently, we must be absolutely clear as to our overall objectives and operational requirements in order to design an effective biometric system. The BANTAM Biometric and Token Technology Application Modelling language is a freely available toolset which may prove of significant value when designing such systems, especially when consistency and repeatability are paramount (Fig. 3.3).

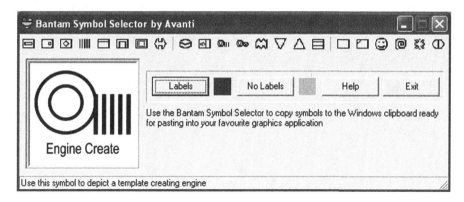

Fig. 3.3 The BANTAM symbol selector

There are many freely available tools which promote best practice with respect to defining, designing and implementing systems. The BANTAM Program Manager, for example, provides for a document repository, reports generator, project manager, personnel and supplier databases, a training management section and more, within a simple, small footprint package. There are also readily available office programs with integral drawing packages, databases and presentation packages which may be used to good effect. Indeed, there is no shortage of available tools, but we must additionally develop a rigour around policy and approach.

Review Questions

1. Define what is meant by a system.
2. Discuss the fundamental principles of access control systems.
3. Distinguish between standalone, distributed and centralised systems.
4. Discuss early and contemporary network communications protocols.
5. Define what is meant by an AFIS system.

Identity Management

Abstract The phrase 'identity management' (which, incidentally, the author first coined more than 15 years ago in the context of biometrics) may mean different things to different people in different situations. Clarifying exactly what we want it to mean within the context of a given application is important if we are to realise our identity management objectives for that application. We must also consider the mechanisms by which we aim to create, store and subsequently verify an identity, as well as the attendant roles and responsibilities around the associated processes. When we add a biometric into the equation, these mechanisms become more complex and require a more sophisticated form of management. Consequently, identity management is an area where precise definition and clarity of purpose are paramount. Furthermore, we must consider identity and identity management from the individual user's perspective, ensuring that our processes are transparent, ethical and easily understood by all concerned. This is especially important when records need to be verified or updated. This chapter presents us with an opportunity to consider the concept of identity management, as it aligns with our own situation.

What Is an Identity?

Before we can effectively manage identity, we must first define it. This presents an interesting conundrum as there are potentially many definitions. We might, for example, simply define identity as that which renders an entity definable and recognisable. Associated natural factors might include gender, appearance, personality and of course biometrics. Non-natural factors, implemented for control purposes, include recognisable tags which we associate with an identity such as national insurance number, passport number, customer number, address and so on. From a systems perspective, we might also include digital certificates and other forms of electronic token.

Identity is however very personal, no matter how impersonal we make it for commercial or national purposes. An identity from the individual's perspective is bound to self-image, self-esteem and perceived individuality within a given social environment. There is also a very strong cultural element, often bound to some sort of group identity, whether religious, professional, artistic or some other parameter. This is important for many individuals as it

J. Ashbourn, *Guide to Biometrics for Large-Scale Systems: Technological, Operational, and User-Related Factors*, DOI 10.1007/978-0-85729-467-8_4,
© Springer-Verlag London Limited 2011

provides them with a sense of belonging and, as predominantly social animals, humans often crave this sense of belonging. Indeed, the lack of a sense of belonging often leads to problems for both individuals and societies.

When an individual is referenced within a large database of individuals, they are simply a record, located by whatever key is used, whether national insurance number or some other unique identifier. The management of that record within a given transaction is a relatively impersonal affair, at least to the managers of that application or service. However, to the individual, it is a uniquely personal affair, which will undoubtedly have implications for their day-to-day activities, lifestyle and, perhaps, how they believe they are perceived externally. In fact, their external perception may be quite different from how they believe they are perceived, often as a result of the correlation of information beyond their personal control. Furthermore, this external perception may be subtly different between public and commercial agencies: a factor we shall return to later.

We consequently have something of a dichotomy of defined identity: the digital identity which exists for the majority of humans and is largely created by others, and the intensely personal identity of the individual, as understood by that individual. The two do not necessarily align perfectly. The interesting thing about biometrics is that, in some ways, they straddle this divide. They are primarily used for systems-related management or control purposes, and yet they are also uniquely personal. It is not surprising therefore that biometrics are typically perceived as being very personal from the individual's perspective. We should bear this in mind when designing and implementing systems which incorporate some form of biometric identity verification.

An identity is therefore something much more than simply a number against a database record or, indeed, whatever data that record contains. It is something of the very essence of an individual, unique to that individual and subject to subtle changes over time. It is not something that can be shoe-horned into a convenient categorisation for management purposes. It is something which should be treated with respect and understood within the broader context.

The Concept of Identity Management Within Systems

From a systems perspective, the concept of identity management is primarily one of aligning an identity reference with a transaction. That transaction may result in the provision or denial of a service, based upon correlation with other information. Alternatively, it may be a transaction undertaken by the individual concerned, either within a contained network or across networks. In any event, the transaction is aligned with an identity, or perhaps several identities, if several individuals or organisations are involved. Of course, organisations also have identities, as do physical entities or objects associated with a given transaction. However, we are concerned here with individual identities.

Consequently, the system must know which user is accessing a service or being aligned with a specific transaction. This is typically achieved by the user providing their identity credentials which are verified accordingly. When the identity is established, the identity claimant's entitlement to the service being provided is also checked, before the service is granted. It all sounds simple enough in principle. The challenge, particularly with respect to large-scale systems, is the verification of both identity credentials and entitlement. This will generally require access to one or more databases, probably over a network. If the throughput, in terms of numbers of transactions, is high, then performance can become an issue. In the realms of mainstream IT where user names and passwords prevail, user credentials are typically stored in an LDAP (Lightweight Data Access Protocol) directory which is optimised for high performance read-only access. When biometrics enter the equation, further complications arise depending on the precise nature of the application. For example, in an AFIS application which is typically matching one or more static (i.e. stored) fingerprints against large numbers of other stored fingerprints, database size and associated throughput performance will typically be of primary concern. Some of these databases number records in many tens of millions. For closed-loop systems where a live biometric is matched against a smaller, specific database, the system performance will typically represent less of a bottleneck as the acquisition of the live template will take a few seconds in any event. For a one-to-one biometric match where, for example, the reference biometric is loaded from a token such as a card or passport, systems performance becomes academic. A given system may of course be a composite of all of these models and thus have its own specific issues.

In all cases, however, the concept is similar. Identity credentials, whether biometric or otherwise, must be provided and verified. The system understands nothing about identities in the true sense; it is simply comparing two sets of data and passing the result to the next point in the workflow. This is an important point to remember. Computer systems are not intelligent; they simply perform tasks which we have been predefined and coded into them. With absolute identity credentials such as passwords or keys, the task is a simple direct match with a binary match or non-match result. With variable credentials such as a biometric, we must tell the system what does or does not constitute a match. The degree to which two biometrics are similar may be expressed, in simple terms, as a percentage. If we decide that a 90% likeness constitutes a match and anything below 90% a non-match, then we must instruct the system accordingly. The matching process will result in a 'score' of likeness which the system will compare against its instructions. There is rather more processing involved than with a simple binary password match, and this will need to be accommodated somewhere within the system. The concept of identity management from a systems perspective remains straightforward. A user (or system component) is identified according to the verification of provided credentials. If the credentials are verified, entitlement is then checked accordingly. The storage and transmission of these credentials is typically undertaken according to the established best practice within the IT sphere. The addition of a biometric introduces a little more complexity due to the non-exact matching process as well as additional data management issues.

Identity Credentials

The simple user name and short password has prevailed in IT circles for many years, perhaps partly because it is an understood and fairly intuitive mechanism and partly because the associated data storage and management issues are slight and have been well catered for.

4

Complexities arose of course when different applications took a slightly different approach to the management of identity credentials, often implementing a bespoke internal database and associated mechanism. However, over time this has been resolved into a more universal approach whereby the credential database is typically externalised and applications share a common method of access and verification via the use of directories. Thus, from a systems perspective, the management of simple identity credentials had become almost standardised. From a users' perspective, the situation was often less clear, especially if they had to remember multiple passwords for different applications. Complications arose in the form of keys and key management, a key being essentially a very large digital string which may be uniquely associated with an individual, a systems component or a software process. A digital 'certificate' may contain a key together with other information about the entity associated with this credential. A detailed explanation of digital certificates and keys is outside the scope of this book; suffice it to say that they represent a sophisticated type of identity credential. While simple enough in concept, the implementation of a key management system is usually fraught with difficulties within a large organisation. This is interesting, as the potential benefits of a full public key infrastructure (PKI) have long been agreed, and yet usage of the technology has not blossomed as originally envisaged, partly because of these complexities of implementation. Simpler methods, using symmetrical keys or simple hash values, have perhaps enjoyed a greater usage in real operational terms. Nevertheless, the usage of digital certificates and keys will increase, especially as we embrace virtualised environments and cloud computing.

A more personal identity credential is of course a biometric. For individual identity verification, as opposed to that of a system component, a biometric provides a sophisticated identity credential without introducing the operational complexities of digital certificates, keys and their associated management issues. There are important questions as to what exactly is stored as the reference, typically a choice between a raw image of the biometric and a mathematically derived template. Decisions also need to made as to where this is stored and how it is accessed. However, in all cases, these identity credentials are relatively meaningless until they are aligned with an entity such as a human being, a systems component or a specific transaction.

The Alignment of Credentials with User Profiles

The alignment of a biometric with a specific user profile represents both the strongest and potentially weakest aspects of biometric identity verification. From a positive perspective, when properly aligned with a user profile which is henceforth tamper-proof, then certainly a biometric provides a useful supplement to the methods by which an identity may be verified: A supplement because a biometric is not foolproof and consequently should never be relied upon in isolation as proof of positive identification.

The potentially negative aspect concerns the alignment of the biometric with a user profile, typically consisting of information such as name, date of birth, place of birth and changeable items such as domiciled address, hair colour, occupation and so on. It is in the gathering of this profile information where problems arise. This is especially the case when important documents such as national identity cards are being issued which either contain, or are otherwise referenced to, a stored biometric. If the information constituting the user profile is not scrupulously checked and verified, then it is an easy matter for government agencies to inadvertently create fraudulent identity profiles, corroborated with a biometric. Once created, the biometric will of course match and the fraudulent profile will be assumed to be correct. It is a source of wonder that countries who have a significant passport and associated benefit fraud issue, such as the UK, employ foreign nationals in the issuing offices and, even when serious systematic fraud by these foreigners is discovered, they continue to employ them in such positions. One wonders how many fraudulent identities have been created in this way. The problem is that once created, such fraudulent identities are unlikely to be discovered. This is an extremely attractive proposition for those engaged in organised crime who, with care, can create several such identities in different countries, all authorised by government agencies and all corroborated with a biometric. As the choice of biometric for national identity documents is not quite universal, this multiple identity fraud may be entirely realistic if carefully orchestrated. If the criminal concerned is already registered within a criminal database, including his fingerprints, then there is a risk that at least a fingerprint biometric might one day be matched and dual identities discovered, but professional criminals will understand under what circumstances such an eventuality might arise and will be on their guard accordingly.

Notwithstanding the issues from a criminal perspective, there are also potential issues for legitimate users with respect to the alignment of data with biometrics. This is not a weakness of biometric technology, but rather a weakness in our ability to manage data records properly within large-scale systems and, particularly, between large-scale systems. This returns to the dichotomy between an individual's true identity and their digital identity or, to be precise, their multiple digital identities or profiles. Multiple because, in contemporary times, almost every adult human in developed economies will have digital identities or user profiles held by several government agencies, often in multiple countries, plus profiles held by utility providers, commercial organisations, financial organisations and others. These multiple profiles should of course be identical. However, this is often not the case as simple data entry mistakes may be made, records may be confused with those of individuals with similar names, information may be appended to records by administrators who have no knowledge of the individual in question and so on. The situation is accentuated by the reality that, in spite of various in-place data protection laws, such information is routinely shared, without the knowledge of the individual, between agencies in both the public and private sectors. The reality is that a given individual will likely have many digital identities residing in several countries, administered by a range of third parties, most of whom the individual has never had any contact with. The information contained within these identities will certainly differ in detail, especially after a number of years, and may, due to mistakes, differ significantly. The problem arises when aligning a biometric against one of these profiles, which, somewhat bizarrely, is assumed to be correct, because the biometric matches. Conversely, if the biometric does not match, then the individual is assumed not to be the same individual for whom the profile exists. This is where the situation becomes problematic. Let us assume for a moment that the biometric is always going to match. We now have the situation whereby the data associated with the biometric by the agency concerned will be assumed to be correct. If, in fact, it is incorrect, perhaps because it has been either inadvertently or deliberately tampered with, the individual concerned may find it extraordinarily difficult to prove that the information held is wrong. The assumption will always be that the biometric matches the particular record and, therefore, the record is correct.

In some respects, we have completely misunderstood the potential for using biometrics within such situations. The burden of this understanding must lie partly with law enforcement agencies that have effectively hijacked the use of biometrics, at least from a national and international perspective, for their own purposes, effectively turning applications which are concerned with user's rights into supporting applications for law enforcement. They have effectively criminalized the innocent on a massive scale, assuming everyone to be guilty until proved innocent. The problem with this approach arises when the parameters of this proof cannot be relied upon. Ultimately, such an approach will prove wanting in the control of real, serious crime, whose proponents understand how to avoid such traps.

National data sources and criminology have been used to make the point around the relative vulnerability of data records and how much trust may or should be associated with them, particularly when a biometric match is assumed to corroborate such records. The same principle holds within a distinct system such as that managed by an organisation. The biometric credential is only meaningful in relation to the user profile to which it is aligned. The user profile is, in turn, only meaningful if accurate and properly maintained.

It is possible of course to have an anonymous biometric (or non-biometric credential-based) implementation whereby those enrolled into the system have previously been ascertained as eligible for access to whatever functions and benefits are available from the system and there is no particular requirement to associate individuals with particular transactions. In such cases, if the biometric (or other credential) matches, then the function and associated benefits are made available. While applications of this nature undoubtedly exist, they tend to be the exception. Ordinarily, linking the individual to the transaction is a primary objective of any system which encompasses user credentials and profiles. A biometric is simply another credential which may be utilised in such a manner. The alignment of credentials with user profiles is thus critically important. Furthermore, the management of these profiles over time and the precise administrative rights that are in place for such management are equally important factors, and become more so as data are shared and computer environments migrate towards virtualisation and the use of third-party infrastructures.

Data Management

Data management is a subject which might easily and usefully fill a book in its own right. There exist many data management methodologies and ideas around associated best practice. Unfortunately, these seem to be rarely adhered to, almost regardless of existing policies within the organisational structure. The plethora of stories around data mismanagement by government agencies and public utilities seem to be without end. It is easy to dismiss such occurrences simply as human error, which undoubtedly plays a major part in such matters. However, if such errors continue to occur, then perhaps this points to some fundamental weaknesses within the systems which contain the data and how these systems are administered.

Data do not exist in isolation of course; they must be entered and maintained as appropriate. This requires the establishment of suitable roles and permissions among those charged with administering the system as well as those who may subsequently have access to the data. These fundamental requirements are typically easily compromised if strict policies are not in place and enforced. Such polices must specify precisely who may enter the original data and under what conditions, as well as who may append to or otherwise modify the data and under what conditions. The original data should be rigorously verified before entry and, if changes are subsequently made, these should also be subject to rigorous verification and reasons given for the change. The necessary roles for these tasks must, in themselves, be rigorously maintained with individual administrators and system users similarly verified and associated with every transaction. It goes without saying that strict access control should be in place for every such task and individual transaction, with every associated transaction logged accordingly in order that a full audit trail be constructed. It also goes without saying that sensitive data, including personal information, should be strongly encrypted. All of this is particularly relevant to user profile records and one would imagine that, by now, this is all well understood and generally implemented. And yet, disasters of data loss and data mismanagement continue to occur on a worryingly wide scale.

While it remains outside of the scope of this book to explore the detail of data management, there is an important point to understand with respect to the implementation of biometrics, and that is: if we are struggling with managing data in the conventional sense, adding a biometric into the mix is not necessarily going to help in this particular context. Furthermore, if we mismanage biometric data in relation to user profiles and associated transactions, then things could become potentially confusing. We must therefore ensure that the fundamentals are well understood and are securely in place before adding biometric technology. This is particularly important with regard to the biometric enrolment process, which should be undertaken under very strict control of both administration and data management. This includes aspects of data collection, transmission and storage, all of which should be undertaken within a secure technical architecture and against equally secure and enforced processes.

When it comes to subsequent systems usage, then data integrity and security remain paramount. Part of this is dependent upon systems architecture and automated systems process, and part is concerned with systems operators and users. Generally, there should be no need for human operators to access sensitive user profiles other than in exceptional conditions. Identity verification and eligibility may be ascertained via automated systems processes and, if these are properly established and maintained, human intervention should be minimalised.

The sharing of personal information databases for both political and commercial purposes is typically where errors creep in. Even if the original host system was properly designed and operated, there is no guarantee that third-party systems have been equally well considered or are subject to the same rigours of administration. Given that associated systems are often outsourced to third-party contractors and, equally often, off-shore contractors, it is impossible for any hosting agency engaged in such outsourcing to guarantee the security of such data. This reality, in itself, makes a mockery of almost every data protection act in the developed world.

4

If we are to improve matters in this respect, we must start to think differently about the importance of personal information, how it is used and how it is managed. Government agencies in particular should be wary of outsourcing the associated systems to third parties. The advent of available third-party infrastructures, such as that promoted under the generalisation of cloud computing, should also be viewed with caution as regards the usage of sensitive or personal data. The oft-quoted theory that the externalisation of such technical infrastructure enhances security is unfounded and flawed. Given our record in managing sensitive data to date, such developments should be very carefully considered. Now, when we append to this reality biometrics and the associated user profiles, we can see that we must be particularly careful. All of the rigour associated with good systems design and good data management must be applied wherever the data exist and are used. Often, these data cross geographic borders and are used by a variety of agencies and commercial entities. It is time for us to think about how we might create assurances that data are managed to an equivalent rigour wherever they are used and whoever the users are. The payment card industry is attempting such an assurance via the PCI Compliance Initiative, which requires a certain integrity of systems design and operation. We need something similar for the usage of personal information by organisations in both the public and private sectors.

In short, good data management principles are important generally. They are especially important when we are dealing with personal information and user profiles. Similarly for systems which incorporate biometric identity verification, robust data management is critically important. One cannot overstate this importance. Its acknowledgement should be the cornerstone of all systems design.

Role-Based Identity Management

The concept of role-based identity management (or role-based access control) is particularly important with respect to systems and data administration, whereby we must assure that sensitive data may only be accessed by those with legitimate reasons to do so. Within a typical organisation, configuring a role-based identity management environment simplifies associated access control and audit logging by effectively linking access control privileges to operational policy and process. This is achieved by precise role definition, articulating precisely what a given role may or may not do with regard to systems access, down to whatever granular level is required. Users may then be simply grouped by role. This approach also supports segregation of duties, which is a key factor within many regulatory requirements.

In a role-based system, a hierarchy of roles may be defined, wherein certain roles may include the privileges defined in other roles at a lower level. It is thus a simple matter to define a role which is a superset of two or more other roles. A user may then be assigned to a role, effectively defining what that user may and may not do within the system and its operational functionality. This may include the control of access to specific files and records and the level of that access with respect to read-only or read-and-write privileges. Many organisations implement a role-based access control model of one sort or another, and many applications anticipate such a model. However, within a very large enterprise with a heterogeneous technical environment, role-based access control as described may become a little complex to administer. In such cases, purpose-built provisioning systems may offer an alternative approach, although the fundamental requirements remain similar: the ability to control access to resources and data based upon role definitions and operational processes. Such factors are important with regard to the administration of large databases, such as those containing user profiles upon a national scale. They are also important of course for any application, or series of applications, dealing with sensitive data.

The primary consideration here is that, whatever means of systems access is deployed, users will still need to authenticate themselves to the system, using whatever credentials have been decided upon, including a biometric where applicable. Now we are starting to see a layered approach as to how biometrics might be implemented within real-world systems. Wherever the biometric identity verification transaction touches another part of the infrastructure, we must understand precisely what this interface is, how it works and its level of relative security. For example, if a binary fail to match/match message is being input to another layer of infrastructure, can this message be spoofed? What of the communications path, and its security, between the biometric device and this point in the infrastructure? However sophisticated the biometric matching algorithm, the input of the identity verification result into the next layer of infrastructure is critical if we are to realise the potential benefits of a biometric identity verification transaction. Figure 4.1 illustrates in simple terms how a biometric might interface with a host application.

There are many ways in which the biometric matching result might find its way into the appropriate section of a host application, depending upon where exactly the biometric matching takes place, how the result is output, where within the system workflow this result is utilised, what the interfaces are and so on. The perceived value of implementing biometric identity verification must be aligned with the relative security and robustness of the total host systems infrastructure and how the biometric result is used within it. We have used role-based access control as an illustration of typical systems processes to which biometric functionality might be appended. It serves to illustrate that biometric functionality in isolation is of little practical value. It is the integration of biometric functionality into the workflow of other applications which typically provides value. These other applications might be national border control systems, local government systems, banking

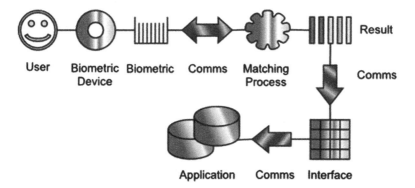

Fig. 4.1 We must consider the biometric interface into the application

4

systems, academic systems or something else. As such systems rely upon user profiles and identity verification transactions, they are effectively engaging in identity management. Now we have moved identity management from a concept to a component of systems functionality. It follows that we cannot consider the biometric element of identity management in isolation, but must understand it within a context of functional workflow and must include all other aspects of this functional workflow in our deliberations.

Review Questions

1. Define and discuss identity management in relation to different operational scenarios.
2. Define and discuss identity from both the human and systems perspective.
3. List the popular forms of identity credential and how they are typically implemented.
4. Discuss the vulnerabilities associated with maintained user profiles.
5. Discuss the importance of data management within a systems user context.

True Systems Integration

5

Abstract There are many factors to understand with respect to systems integration, and true systems integration is much more than simply connecting a biometric device to a computer system. This section starts with a discussion around systems definition in order to set the scene for the rest of the chapter. From an understanding of systems definition, we move on to the subject of systems components and, in particular, the concept of biometrics as a systems component. We acknowledge that all systems are subject to evolutionary change, as are individual systems components. The possibility of change must therefore be allowed for in systems design and systems architecture.

The registration process is a vital part of any system which features biometric identity verification. Consequently, this must be allowed for in the design of the overall system and its administration. It must similarly be reflected in the operational processes and procedures associated with the broader system. The registration process is thus discussed and feeds into a broader discussion around the operational process. Factors such as administration, including exception handling, messaging, data management and maintenance of a directory system are relevant in this context. With respect to operational data, we discuss the storage of biometric credentials on portable media and portable devices, as well as remote databases, and consider factors such as performance and administration.

The biometric matching process is explained in some detail, including discussion around the associated systems infrastructure, communications and the location of the matching process. Systems and data security form an important part of any system and the biometric element renders this area of even greater importance. It is discussed in broad terms including the importance of system component configuration, the distinction between data in transit and data at rest, and even with respect to secure application development. This discussion naturally leads to thoughts around systems scalability, operational performance and systems architecture, including network configuration and security. Supporting factors such as audit logging and centralised log management are relevant, as are applications and systems testing procedures. This chapter thus provides a framework within which many aspects of systems integration may be considered.

J. Ashbourn, *Guide to Biometrics for Large-Scale Systems: Technological, Operational,* **49**
and User-Related Factors, DOI 10.1007/978-0-85729-467-8_5,
© Springer-Verlag London Limited 2011

Systems Definition

There are many ways in which one might define a system. Typically, such a definition is often given as an identifiable entity composed of multiple discreet parts which, together, constitute an operational whole. However, this is rather a simplistic definition. In fact, systems can be quite complex and exist, in one form or another, everywhere. The whole world, indeed the universe, is composed of systems. People speak of closed-loop systems wherein there exists no external influence or connection. In reality, these are few. The majority of systems tend to have permeable boundaries which allow, or even depend upon, external communication and influence. Furthermore, systems boundaries are more theoretical than actual. Systems touch and interact with other systems. There are systems within systems and different types of systems with dependencies across and between systems. A computer is a system, so is a tree, a motor car, a mountain and a city. Cities interact within a country. Countries interact within a continent. Continents interact within global systems, and so on. We might additionally think of a system as having a defined functional goal or output. In reality, the complex web of systems will have many functions and many outputs, although we might select specific outputs from sub-systems as considered necessary for particular functions.

In the natural world, we are just beginning to understand the complex interactions and dependencies between natural systems. The large and obvious entities such as the geosphere, biosphere and atmosphere are relatively easy to comprehend. When we move down to the level of individual organisms, or indeed cells, the situation becomes rather more complex. Each of these organisms is composed of one or more systems which interact with other systems. The complete organism then interacts within its local environment. That environment is influenced by external events and other environments until, ultimately, everything is connected and interconnected in ways which continually evolve to affect both the whole and its components of constitution. Let us consider a vascular plant, for example. We might posit that it is composed of roots, stems, leaves and flowers, each of which has a definite function to perform and each of which is a component of the whole. However, the root system must interact with the soil and its various organisms in order to derive nutrients. The stems must exist and interact within a specific environment, either aquatic or atmospheric and have the necessary properties which allow for this. The leaves must interact in order to photosynthesise and harness energy from the sun. The flowers must interact both with the environment and other organisms in order to pollinate and reproduce. The plant and its constituent components may be considered as a complete system, but it is itself part of a larger system. The plant system has an overall goal of survival and reproduction and the larger system has its own goals of survival and continual evolution. Furthermore, within this veritable web of systems, various components and properties are often shared, both for the common good and, occasionally, for the selfish requirements of a particular sub-system. It follows that an understanding of these components, their properties and behaviours are also shared among and between systems, as are the rules by which they function (Fig. 5.1).

So it is with respect to what we might describe as biometric systems. It may be possible to define a particular biometric acquisition and matching system in terms of its local

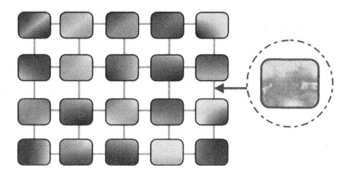

Fig. 5.1 A complex system as part of a web of complex systems

components and functionality; however, such a definition is meaningless until it is applied to the larger functional application. In turn, this larger application is itself meaningless until it is placed in the context of the broader requirement within the larger social or business-oriented system and this, in turn, relates to a broader global system of governance. The individual components such as capture devices, networks, processing, transactions, analyses, policies and so on may indeed be discussed and configured as discreet entities. However, if they are done so in isolation, they will never prove an efficient part of the broader system and network of systems. Our efforts within the realm of man-made IT pale into insignificance compared with the wondrous works of nature in this context. However, we may take a lead from nature in acknowledging the complexity and interactions which exist within true systems. This will lead us to a better understanding of true systems integration and the design requirements thereof. To date, we have adopted a rather simplistic and fragmented approach to systems design which often owes more to supplier politics than to intelligent design. It is perhaps time for a change in this respect, even if it entails a more radical approach to our deliberations. These might usefully start with an appreciation of the global systems perspective, including societal aspirations, policies and governance, before even thinking about the technical infrastructure. We must also consider interactions, dependencies and the management of change. In addition, just as nature incorporates protective elements within systems, we must consider overall security and the ability of our systems to evolve and adapt.

In conclusion, our definition of a system has, to date, often been far too constricted to allow for intelligent design. The result has been more akin to a Frankenstein's monster of bolted together parts, than a beautiful holistic creation following natural principles. Furthermore, when multiple Frankenstein's monsters come together, as indeed they must, it is perhaps little wonder that things go awry and mistakes are made. Such mistakes may be obvious and correctable or may go unnoticed. They will however have an effect, usually upon one of the constituent parts of the system, such as an individual human, or transaction, or perhaps a cascading effect throughout multiple components which still might go unnoticed for a considerable time, thus weakening the overall efficiency of the broader systems. In the natural world, this would tend to be noticed and compensated for. Our administration is somewhat lacking in comparison. Consequently, we must use our very best efforts to ensure that our systems design is as robust as possible from the outset.

5

Pertinent Systems Components

From a biometrics perspective, it is perhaps pertinent to understand the various components which, together, constitute at least the biometrics system functionality and its interfaces into the broader web of systems. In this respect, we might usefully make a distinction between those components necessary for the registration process and those required for subsequent operational transactions. We might also consider defined processes as system components, as these will surely interact with the technical infrastructure and are equally subject to dependencies and interactions with other systems.

The Registration Process

In order to realise biometric identity verification within a transactional environment, we must first register the biometric credentials and align them with a specific user profile. This is a critical part of the overall systems landscape as, if errors are made at this point, they will tend to perpetuate throughout all the other systems and sub-systems which constitute the whole. Let us be in no doubt that these other systems are likely to be many and complex and, if errors are introduced at this stage, their discovery and remediation will become increasingly unlikely as information proliferates within the web of systems. In simple terms, we might define the applicable components as follows:

- The individual user: the most vital component of all. Without users, everything else becomes somewhat academic.
- The physical registration facility and its operation. This is important as a suitable environment must be established within which users and staff are comfortable and repeatable registration transactions may be undertaken.
- The defined registration process. A critical element, especially with respect to the checking of identity credentials before an individual is registered against a profile with their biometric. This is an obvious area for fraudulent exploitation as forged credentials can result in fraudulent identity profiles being created and substantiated with a biometric, lending the fraudulent identity an air of authenticity, as it has been created under official supervision.
- The registration facility trained staff. Although the tasks involved may not be over-complex, the registration facility staff must nevertheless have a robust understanding of the registration process in context. They must also be trained to spot fraudulent attempts at registration and understand how to deal with these accordingly. Lastly, they must have a sufficient technical understanding to enable good-quality registrations and to be able to spot when this is not the case. It goes without saying that these individuals should be trained in general administration and that they should understand the seriousness of their position and the attendant responsibilities. Consequently, such staff must be properly trained and qualified as professionals. Anything less will ultimately prove to be a false economy if errors are introduced into the system and, as has already happened, fraudulent scams are established.

- The biometric capture devices and associated technology. These devices must be regularly checked and calibrated, ensuring that they perform to a consistent operational standard, thus producing repeatable, high-quality biometric reference templates. They must also be kept clean, especially when contact methodologies such as fingerprints are utilised. The operational consistency of these devices is critically important as poor-quality reference templates will affect subsequent transactional performance within the broader system.
- The reference database. Whatever database is used for storing these reference templates, it must also be subject to rigorous procedures of administration and maintenance, ensuring its operational efficacy and security. This includes all related infrastructural components, including host platforms, networks and the database software itself. In particular, a good understanding must exist of dataflows and administrative rights throughout the broader system.
- The portable token. If a portable token is used, such as an identity card or passport, its production must be carefully orchestrated and aligned with the registered biometric template. Such a token, once created, should be tamper-proof and logged against a unique reference within the database. The supply of blank or unused tokens should be subject to the strictest security procedures, with each token being properly accounted for.

The Operational Process

The operational process employs some of the same components, but used in a slightly different manner. This is typical within real systems where distinctions as to types of usage, or context, must be understood and catered for, both within process and technical infrastructure. Related components include:

- The individual user: again, without users there is effectively no system. The user, in operational terms, additionally plays an important part with regard to realised performance, a subject we shall revisit within these pages.
- The physical transaction point of presence, including important elements such as signage, local instruction, flow and exception handling.
- The defined transactional process and its articulation to users, which might include written information, personal guidance from an administrator or overall process facilitator, depending upon the application. This process must cater for every eventuality of usage, including attempts at fraud, technical errors, equipment malfunction and other exceptions.
- The process facilitator, responsible for the overall process in an attended transaction. With respect to an unattended transaction, such a person may be called upon for exception handling via a clearly articulated process at the point of presence.
- The biometric capture device. This device, as well as being generally maintained in good order, must also be configured for the precise environment in which it is operating. Furthermore, it must be configured according to a desired performance criterion. This factor will be elucidated elsewhere in this volume.

- The biometric matching process. This may be undertaken within the device itself via an explicit algorithm, or may be undertaken remotely, in proximity to a database, depending upon the nature of the transaction and the biometric methodology deployed. For example, if the reference template has been provided from a portable token for a simple one-to-one match, then this process may be easily accommodated within, or in proximity to, the biometric device. If, however, the supplied live biometric is to be matched in a one-to-many fashion against a database of reference templates, then the match may be undertaken within, or in proximity to, the database in question.
- The communication channels. Depending upon the systems topography and associated infrastructure, there will be requirements for communicating the biometric, the match result and other pertinent information, within the broader system and, possibly, externally to other systems. These communications channels must be configured to be both highly available and secure as well as offering acceptable performance.
- The reference and transactional databases. If a reference database is used to search against, using the supplied biometric, then this must be configured for high availability and high performance, as well as being made secure. In any event, a transactional database will undoubtedly be used to log the transaction and possibly align it with specific stored information, derived from other data sources. This database has simpler performance requirements, but must nevertheless be rendered secure and highly available. Furthermore, for all in-scope databases, great care must be taken as to administrative and legitimate user access rights, general security and the availability of a tamper-proof audit trail.
- The overall systems infrastructure, including links and feeds to and from other systems, for example when passing the biometric matching result or referencing other information. This entire infrastructure should be understood in great detail and engineered to be robust and resilient. Data in storage and in transit should ideally be encrypted and network components configured to allow only legitimate traffic from identified sources. This systems infrastructure may be considered the backbone of the operational system and be nurtured accordingly.
- Operational policies. Having implemented a workable system, we must understand how to interpret the information provided by it, including when exceptions occur. This requirement is generally satisfied by a series of defined policies which are articulated in various forms to all the individuals involved in the operation of the system. Such policies, which also govern systems maintenance and evolution, may similarly be regarded as system components. Components which require careful configuration and maintenance, just as with physical or technical components.

As we may appreciate from the discussion above, there are many pertinent components which together constitute our operational system. Some of these components will reside within our immediate sphere of influence; others may require liaison with other, specific departments. In any event, they must be addressed, understood and documented within any intelligent system. Indeed, a map or directory of systems components should be created wherein any component may be quickly referenced and all of its parameters exposed. Without this level of detail, our system will be, at best, rather chaotic. It follows then, that someone must be the custodian of this systems component directory and take full responsibility for its well-being and ongoing management. For a system operating within the public sector, this is particularly important, due to the responsibility of dealing with personal information, which, if compromised, may have serious consequences.

Understanding pertinent systems components, how they function and interact with other components and how they might best be configured and orchestrated within the broader system, is a crucial factor within overall systems design. At a different level, understanding how entire systems function and interact is equally important. In both cases, this understanding may only be acquired if a focus is brought to bear at the lowest possible level of technical and operational functionality. This focus may then be extrapolated throughout the higher levels, ensuring operational stability as each component is tested within its operational context. Thinking in terms of logical components facilitates such an understanding and assists its documentation in a manner that may be easily understood at all levels.

Biometric Credential Storage

There are several options for storing biometric credentials, either on portable media, portable devices or remote databases. Portable storage media allow for an individual biometric reference template to be read and compared with a live sample on a one-to-one basis at the point of presence, often within the biometric device itself, without requiring a connection to a remote database. If a one-to-many look-up is required, then a remote database must be used for comparing the live sample with many possible matches. The credentials concerned will typically consist of the biometric reference template, a unique identifier and possibly other user information, depending upon the precise nature of the application, its purpose and its technical architecture. Some of the storage options are discussed below.

Portable Media

Depending upon the application and the biometric methodology chosen, it may be possible to utilise very low-cost tokens, such as magnetic stripe cards for example, on a limited use basis. Some implementations of fingerprint technology and hand geometry can create templates small enough to be stored on such a token. This approach may be interesting for applications such as temporary travel cards, on-campus entitlement and similar applications. Concerns may arise as to the security of the biometric credentials, especially with respect to lost or stolen cards. Consequently, associated processes, operating procedures and policies must be clear and properly communicated.

A more appropriate portable token is available in the form of the smart card, or chip card as it is more properly described. A chip card may be rendered more secure in terms of how the credentials are stored upon the chip and how access to this chip is provided. The contents may be encrypted and digital keys required in order to access certain areas of the chip. Furthermore, due to the additional capacity of the chip, other pertinent information may be stored if required. Chip cards are relatively robust and, due to a wide adoption of the technology, their cost is no longer prohibitive.

Portable media in the form of cards have additional advantages in that they may be customised, branded and used as visual identity cards if required. Furthermore, they may be used

5

for applications which do not necessarily require a biometric check, thus rendering them a multi-function device. Existing documents such as passports or medical cards may be redesigned to incorporate a chip and thus provide a mechanism for biometric identity verification. This has of course been achieved and standards created around access to the chip within such public documents. In theory, any portable document or token to which a chip may be embedded could contain biometric credentials and act as a provider for such credentials within the context of a biometric identity verification transaction. Indeed, it is quite possible to encode a biometric into printed information such as OCR code, although reading this information may be quite cumbersome compared to the ease with which a chip may be read.

It is possible of course to use any form of portable media which allows for sufficient storage capacity for the chosen biometric. In principle, USB media devices, flash cards and other formats might easily be used for such a purpose, especially as many computers and other devices already feature the required connectivity. Security of the biometric credentials and their access will need to be properly addressed and there may of course be practical issues such as token cost, the ease with which such tokens may be mislaid or lost and so on. Nevertheless, applications may exist where such an approach might prove useful.

Portable Devices

In addition to portable media expressly designed for storage, portable devices such as mobile phones also have a capability to store and transmit information to a host application. It is therefore quite possible to store biometric credentials on such a device and, theoretically, load these credentials from the device into the biometric identity verification application for matching purposes. However, one must consider the data security implications of such an approach. Both security of the stored credentials and how they are accessed and the inherent security issues associated with wireless technology. No doubt all such issues may be overcome, although the cost and complexity of doing so may prove prohibitive within the context of a typical application. Furthermore, complications from a user perspective may prove troublesome in practice and, of course, there are cost implications associated with the mobile device and its operation.

However, another possibility in this respect is the voluntary storage of a biometric upon a mobile device, which the user may or may not choose to employ with respect to certain public sector applications such as government agency entitlement, banking and so on. The individual may then manage the biometric credentials and be in direct control of their usage. However, in order to make such an idea workable, the necessary technical infrastructure would need to be widely deployed and standardised in a manner which made the idea attractive to users. Currently, we are far from this position, but future developments may move in this direction.

Remote Databases

Many applications within the public sector employ remote databases in order to check the supplied live biometric sample against a number of others within a one-to-many scenario. As such, these applications are often referred to as biometric identification systems as opposed to identity verification systems. However, it may be argued that such a description is flawed as identification depends upon more than matching a biometric within a certain tolerance or threshold. In any event, in order to undertake a one-to-many search, a database of reference templates must be provided. In reality, such databases may contain millions or tens of millions of records and will need to be engineered accordingly. In particular, performance in relation to searching through large numbers of records for a possible match (or even several possible matches with respect to AFIS systems) will be an issue. There are various tactics which may be employed such as database partitioning or narrowing the search by filtering on other information and so on. In any event, such databases will require a finite time to search through a given number of records for a possible match. With certain biometric technologies, this may be undertaken in real time or close to real time depending upon the size of the database and other architectural factors. In other cases, the search may be undertaken off-line and the results fed back into a host application for subsequent resolution.

From a corporate perspective, such a database will typically be much smaller and may be more easily utilised within a real-time scenario. Much will depend upon tuning and how the database is accessed. It may be that existing corporate directories based upon LDAP could be used for such credential storage and retrieval on a one-to-one match basis. If a one-to-many search is required, no doubt that could be facilitated depending upon the number of users and the chosen database technology.

In all cases, an important factor will be the interaction between the biometric acquisition and matching functionality and the database technology. This must be securely implemented and must include exception handling as appropriate to both the technical environment and operational process. Consequently, the biometric functionality, user interface and database operation must all be closely integrated. In addition, the logging of transactions and the provision of a secure audit trail will need to be similarly integrated.

It follows that, if biometric credentials are to be stored and accessed from within a remote database, then several factors must be addressed, both from an operational perspective and of course with respect to the population of such a database and the subsequent administration and maintenance of it. It is likely that this approach will be used predominantly with regard to public sector applications, for which additional responsibilities around data security and privacy must be taken into account.

As discussed, the storage of biometric credentials may be undertaken in various manners according to the requirements of the application. It is a factor which requires careful consideration and equally careful design and implementation.

Biometric Matching Process

The biometric matching process, in simple terms, may be considered as a mathematical algorithm which compares two sets of information and outputs a score of relative likeness. A binary decision as to whether the two sets match may be made according to whether the likeness score is above or below a predefined threshold. This threshold is typically adjustable in order to fine-tune the system towards a probability of either false positives or false negatives.

5

The information sets involved are often numerical or alpha-numerical codes generated from the biometric. In order for these codes to be created, features from the captured biometric need to be defined and recognised. If we take fingerprints as an example, there are various ways of achieving this. One popular method is to plot minutiae points, deriving a set of coordinates which may be encoded and matched against those of the stored reference. Another is to analyse the image of the fingerprint via a greyscale value plotted against a grid, and either match this directly with that of the stored image or derive a code from it and match the codes. Yet another might be a more sophisticated textural analysis approach utilising Gabor filters and custom algorithms in order to derive a suitable code. With other biometric techniques, there are similarly various methods by which a comparable value for the biometric in question might be derived (Fig. 5.2).

The point within a given workflow that this matching process is undertaken may be subject to variation according to the application at hand. The majority of off-the-shelf biometric capture devices have the capability to perform the match within the device itself, thus outputting a simple binary result of match or non-match, which may be integrated into the next step of the workflow. Another approach is to take the raw data from the biometric capture device and perform the feature extraction and matching process externally within the broader workflow. Alternatively, one might take a feature generated code from the capture device and match this against stored codes from reference biometrics. Much depends upon the nature of stored reference biometric data and the application in question. For AFIS systems for example, the matching capabilities within the system would typically be utilised, taking raw fingerprint data from the capture devices. For other applications, it may be prudent to undertake feature extraction and matching within the device, or otherwise at the point of presence, thus realising a degree of distributed processing. If undertaken within a distributed processing model, attention must be given to the precise configuration of the devices and, in particular, the setting of the matching threshold. Elsewhere in these pages we shall discuss equivalence of performance across nodes which focuses upon this very point.

Architectural decisions as to where and how the biometric matching process should be undertaken will depend upon several factors including: whether the system is performing a one-to-one or one-to-many match; if a one-to-many match, how many reference biometrics

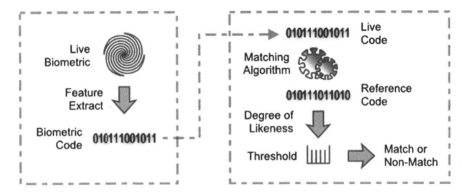

Fig. 5.2 The biometric matching process in concept

within the database; database performance; deplored infrastructure of the host application; required systems performance; linked applications and so on. There may also be situations whereby the use of more than one matching algorithm is pertinent, or where the matching algorithm may be regularly varied in an off-line scenario. Such situations would favour a matching process externalised from the capture devices. When integrating biometric functionality into the broader host application, such factors should be carefully considered, especially from the scalability and sustainability perspective. Technology providers will of course have their own views in this context, with the more experienced typically offering a degree of flexibility as to systems infrastructure and associated possibilities for where and how biometric matching is undertaken and how the result may be communicated. A good approach would be to produce a functional design using an appropriate modelling language such as BANTAM, and use this as a discussion document during the systems design process. There are many associated factors to consider and various possibilities around infrastructure topology. These should be properly understood and the overall systems design optimised in alignment with both the physical reality and operational aspirations.

Systems and Data Security

There are many ways of looking at systems security with respect to systems incorporating biometric functionality. It may help to consider systems security initially in a generic manner and then apply the same principles to the biometric components, functions and sub-systems within the broader system. We might usefully compartmentalise our deliberations as follows.

Infrastructure Security

Within infrastructure security we include the physical security of the primary data centre, security of individual devices such as servers, firewalls, routers and other components, and the security of supporting software such as operating systems, middleware and communications.

Physical security is easy to overlook when thinking in terms of applications, but if the physical environment is not secure, then everything else we might do is unnecessarily compromised. Physical security is not just a question of securing the data centre against forced access, important though that is in itself, but includes the necessary operational processes around everyday maintenance and support: for example, understanding precisely who should have access to what equipment and under what circumstances. This would usually entail some sort of physical access control as well as a detailed log of activity. We may extend this to areas of physical data destruction when tapes or hard drives are replaced within the data centre. We must also consider the operational security of individual infrastructure components. For example, which ports are open on our servers and firewalls, and why? What communications protocols are being used and how secure are they? How are our operating systems configured and to what level of security? Are they regularly maintained with security patches and updates? How is this orchestrated and who manages the process? Similarly with middleware such as web servers and databases. How precisely are these configured, to what specification and why? Similarly, we must understand who legitimately requires administrator rights to these various services and components, and for what specific purpose. How is this managed and maintained on a day-to-day basis? Our network components such as firewalls and routers also need to be configured in a secure manner, with administrator access similarly defined and controlled.

In short, the infrastructure for our system must serve a specific purpose in supporting our application and its software securely while not admitting any other activity or allowing any other connectivity. In order to achieve this goal, we must ensure that the entire infrastructure is precisely defined, managed and properly documented to the degree that we understand how every single physical and logical component is configured, why it is configured that way and who is responsible for maintaining it. Within a typical large-scale system, this is not a trivial undertaking and will doubtless require a good deal of effort. However, anything less will be a compromise and will therefore carry an element of risk. Defining whether such risks are acceptable might depend somewhat upon the nature of the application. Nevertheless, risks are risks and they should be avoided if at all possible.

Data Security

Having developed and implemented a secure and operationally stable infrastructure, we must consider how our data interact with this infrastructure, and how securely such interaction occurs. This includes data in transit, data at rest and data while being processed.

Data in transit may be handled by a variety of devices within, and possibly external to, the primary network. At any of these points the data are conceivably at risk. It may be copied, for example, and sent to destinations of which you are unaware. It may be deliberately corrupted, rendering it unusable within the system. It may be subtly altered to create a false reality within the system. It may simply be 'sniffed' and analysed by a third party wishing to extract salient details such as personal information. It may be unintentionally fragmented within the various communications processes, leading to unexpected data errors. There are two primary areas of concern: the integrity of the data and the reliability of its transmission. For the former, we will probably wish to encrypt the data, and for the latter, we shall probably wish to employ a guaranteed delivery mechanism which monitors every packet and compares that sent with that received. If we are transmitting sensitive or personal data between systems components and across networks, then we need to take positive measures to secure the data. If we are transmitting across third party networks, then we must take extra care to ensure the data are secure and transmitted reliably. There is little margin for error in this respect as our systems will be severely compromised if we cannot rely absolutely on the integrity of our transmitted data.

Data at rest present specific challenges. It is a relatively easy matter to encrypt data at rest with strong encryption methodologies, which, in themselves, are unlikely to be compromised. However, the primary weakness lies not in the robustness of the encryption algorithm, but in how it is implemented and orchestrated within the system. For example, at what point are the data encrypted and at what point are they decrypted? How precisely is this decryption undertaken and how are the necessary keys stored and maintained? Who has access to these data from a systems administration perspective? Are systems adminis- trators blocked from accessing certain fields within database tables? How is such access control defined and maintained? When the encrypted data are legitimately required by the application, how are they delivered to the application and how are they removed from the application? Are steps taken to flush the data from memory, or do they reside in the mem- ory in an unencrypted form until they are overwritten by something else? If this is the case, then the data may be rendered vulnerable for a period of time. There are many factors to consider with respect to the secure storage and retrieval of data.

When the data are being processed, they may also be at risk, depending upon the precise manner in which information is passed between functions, open to editing or perhaps auto- mated processing of some description. To understand this in detail, and therefore to be able to ascertain the degree of potential risk, we must delve into the lower-level processes and associated code. In this context, secure application development processes and procedures become pertinent. We must understand very precisely how our application and associated systems components are handling the data at every turn. The current trend towards service- oriented architectures introduces some additional complication in this respect as services being used may have been authored by different teams in a more or less secure manner. If the internal functionality of a given service is obscured, then we are at a disadvantage in understanding its precise handling of the data. When multiple services are employed, with the associated complex interconnectivity, then the issue increases in proportion. This is an area which deserves our explicit attention. There is, of course, also a human element in that data are often processed by human operators. Consequently, the proper training and secu- rity screening of these operators is important and should be given a high priority. They may be assisted in their task by robust error-checking within the software code, ensuring that errors appertaining to range or simple mistyping are highlighted. However, software cannot detect malicious editing or deliberately falsified transactions. Our human operators should therefore be selected and nurtured with the same attention to detail that we lavish upon our hardware and software. If this is not the case, they may quickly become the weakest link in our operation.

Biometric Sub-system Security

Many of the items discussed above apply to the biometric sub-system. Indeed, this sub- system also comprises hardware, software, communications, configuration and various human interfaces. As such, it has all the vulnerabilities of the broader system, albeit in a more contained environment, at least until the point of delivering the biometric match result into the next component of systems workflow.

Typically, the biometric sub-system will comprise biometric capture devices, commu- nications channels, processing functions and data search and retrieval routines. It is tempting to believe that, within the biometric device itself, data are at least secure. However, the device is connected to other systems and networks and so, depending upon precisely what is happening within it, this may not be the case. It may be possible for data to be corrupted within, or in close proximity to, the device before it enters the broader system. For example, let us imagine that a particular device undertakes a one-to-one biometric match internally via the input of a reference from a portable token and a live biometric sample, and then outputs a simple binary result via a communications channel which is not robustly secured. It may be possible for this result to be intercepted and reversed prior to further processing within the host system – unlikely, perhaps, but certainly not impossible. We must therefore consider the internal workings of the device and, in particular, its immediate communication methodology very carefully. If the device is transmitting either raw biometric data or a derived code into the host system for matching against a database, then we must understand every stage that these data pass through, their relative security and reliability of transmission. In short, we must be confident that it is received by the host system, exactly in the form that it left the biometric device, with no opportunity for manipulation, intentional or otherwise, presenting itself along the route. Such a signal should ideally be encrypted and only decrypted at the point of processing. Wherever the biometric matching process takes place, we must also ensure that the resulting data are properly secured and cannot be tampered with. This is particularly pertinent with regard to the likeness score and binary match result as it is injected into the subsequent workflow. In conclusion, we must pay attention to data security both throughout the biometric sub-system and at every juncture within the broader host system, or, as is often the case, collection of host systems and their various interdependencies.

Scalability

To many minds, scalability is simply the ability of a system to grow and expand over time. In natural systems, this is orchestrated beautifully via an organic architecture designed at the outset to accommodate such organic growth. With computer systems, things are often a little different. The reality sometimes becomes a hotchpotch of infrastructure bolted together in anything but an organic manner in order to accommodate a degree of growth never anticipated in the original systems design.

It is important therefore to consider such things at the outset and, as a rough rule of thumb, double our original estimates, before designing a suitable systems architecture which will accommodate growth in a planned, systematic fashion without altering the overall design. It is not just a question of numbers of devices or numbers of users. Every aspect must be considered, including communications bandwidth, capacity through network devices, data storage capacities, database capacities and, of particular importance, overall realised performance as the system is scaled upwards.

Obviously, performance is important in terms of searching through a large number of records within a one-to-many biometric matching scenario. However, it is also important at every stage within the system and its associated workflow. Even in a one-to-one scenario wherein the biometric is matched within, or in proximity to the device, there is still the question of communicating this result throughout the broader system and writing the transaction to an associated database. Consequently, adding additional points of presence, even of this local one-to-one matching type, will have an effect upon overall systems performance. The broader system will, somewhere, exhibit a bottleneck, which becomes the limiting factor with regard to overall realised performance. It becomes important therefore to understand where this bottleneck resides and how to remediate it. As the broader system scales upwards there is also the question of equivalence of realised performance between operational nodes, and this is a factor which shall be addressed elsewhere in the book.

Factors of scalability also affect the operational process. A process which worked well for a system hosting a few thousand records and a limited number of transactions may break down when asked to cope with a few million records and many thousands of transactions across multiple points of operational presence. Such processes include the training and management of human resources, the physical infrastructure and its workable operation and so on. One aspect of this reality which is often underestimated is the presence of enrolment facilities and the required trained staff in order to cope with large numbers of users. The required infrastructure must be carefully considered beforehand and established in good time to meet the growing demands of the broader system. Such a plan must include all the interactions with different departments or agencies, as may be required, for example, with respect to the checking of credentials. Such an infrastructure also needs operational support and maintenance, just as with the technical infrastructure.

Another aspect of scalability lies in the reality of ever-changing technical specification and the consequent short-lived availability of specific components or software versions. This is a difficult area to cater for due to the unpredictability of systems suppliers and market trends. However, sensible choices may be made with respect to chosen components of both software and hardware and, with respect to hardware, sufficient quantities of spares procured at the time of systems implementation. With respect to software, open source platforms will generally provide a far higher degree of flexibility and interoperability and these should be considered wherever possible.

In conclusion, scalability is something which should be considered not as an afterthought, but rather as an integral part of robust systems design. Indeed, it should form a part of the discussion with respect to almost every component, technical or otherwise, of the broader system. Sadly, this is not often the case in reality and, consequently, some large-scale systems are forever struggling with both their physical and logical operation. Such a situation could easily have been anticipated and allowed for within an intelligent overall design.

Audit Logging

Audit logging and log management presents us with some interesting challenges with respect to systems integration. Many purpose-built log management systems exist, although these systems are generally predicated upon the assumption of specific systems architectures and popular software applications. Consequently, it may not be a simple matter to integrate logs appertaining to the biometric sub-system or even non-standard systems components elsewhere within the broader infrastructure. Log management system suppliers will contend that all such situations may be catered for via the provision of custom 'agents', which may be precisely configured for any eventuality. While this is generally the case, the reality of such configuration is typically complex and often beyond the capabilities of non-experienced administrators. The various components, particularly of the biometric sub-system, may usefully be examined closely for their ability to generate logs of some common format. Of course, much depends upon the activities and events considered important to capture within an audit trail. The configuration of systems components should feature prominently within such an event list, as changes to the configuration of key components may have a significant effect upon both the performance and relative security of the overall system.

If a purpose-built log management system is not available or not desired, there is much that may be achieved within the inherent functionality of key components such as operating systems and middleware, especially among open-source components of this type. It may well be possible to take event log outputs from the biometric sub-system and integrate them into the systems logging capabilities of the host system within a customised design. Indeed, in some respects this may be preferable to using a purpose-built system, as it will enforce a robust understanding of logged events, their relative importance and how they are reported. Sending these logs to a centralised repository will be appropriate in most cases, enabling analysis and report generation accordingly.

In addition to the technical design of such a logging mechanism, there are two other areas which are of paramount importance if value is to be derived from such an exercise. The first lies in the definition of precisely which events should be logged and why. The second is concerned with a robust process to manage and investigate exceptions. If such a process is not in place, the entire logging capability is rendered ineffective. Such a process will typically involve relatively skilled operators trained to correlate related events and correctly infer the implications of the same. Furthermore, they must understand how to remediate exceptions effectively and thus maintain the overall system to a high degree of operational performance and security. Log management is an important factor within overall systems administration and, properly designed and implemented, may provide considerable value to the organisation. However, as with most things of a complex nature, it requires careful consideration, design, execution and ongoing management. With respect to systems incorporating biometric functionality, it assumes a greater stature due to the very personal nature of the data and resultant transactions and, in particular, assumptions made as to the results of such transactions. There may be many occasions whereby a robust and clearly interpreted audit log proves beneficial with respect to the overall application and its attendant orchestration. This is an area which should be accorded significant consideration within the overall scheme of things.

Data Synchronisation

Data synchronisation in this context refers to the alignment of data against synergistic data elsewhere. For example, a biometric aligned against an incorrect personal profile or record becomes relatively meaningless as incorrect assumptions will be made as to the transactions of a given individual. This is an obvious example perhaps, but the issue remains pertinent at multiple levels, especially when data are gathered together from multiple sources within the context of a single transaction. It is an easy matter for an incorrect data element to be perpetuated throughout the system and even communicated to other systems, resulting in incorrect records being maintained, possibly across multiple systems.

At a lower, more granular level, the synchronisation of data as they traverse a given workflow is equally important. This factor is often associated with 'maintaining state' with respect to transactions which traverse multiple elements of infrastructure. If errors are introduced at any point within the transaction, data may be effectively orphaned or delivered in an incomplete state. Mechanisms may be put in place to maintain the integrity of data as they cross such boundaries, although it may still be possible for individual transactional elements to become detached or non-appropriately aligned. Such matters might become complex, especially within a service-oriented architecture which may pass the data between several components within the course of an overall transaction – another matter to take into consideration within our overall systems integration and design.

System Interfaces

The interfaces between system components are of course of vital importance from both a performance and security perspective. Notwithstanding the desirability of standards in this context, there remain a plethora of different approaches to the question. Even if common protocols are achieved, the transferred message content and its inferences may be unexpected or not anticipated between systems. Often this results in custom interfaces being developed for processes considered non-typical. Biometric sub-systems offer an interesting example in this context as the information they are passing is often non-typical with respect to conventional IT systems. Nevertheless, standards have been developed and, no doubt, many devices and components embrace such standards that are available. Nevertheless, one will often find that both logical and physical components throughout the broader systems infrastructure require customised interfaces to be developed.

This necessity for customisation introduces the potential for both performance bottlenecks and compromises with respect to security. For example, will encrypted data pass transparently across such interfaces? Are the data vulnerable at the point of interface? Does the interface introduce capacity limitations in terms of throughput? Such questions, important in themselves, become more so as multiple components and interfaces are introduced or otherwise encountered throughout the broader systems network. In addition, important data are often passed between systems and consolidated into different records. Any errors or vulnerabilities introduced at the interface may have repercussions with respect to the third party system and its particular functionality or application. It may be a trivial matter to ensure that two components are capable of exchanging data, but that function must be undertaken in a manner which is secure, reliable and transparent as far as realised systems performance is concerned. Achieving such a desirable state of affairs may be considerably less trivial and will require an uncommon understanding of such matters. As such, systems interfaces are as important as the systems components on either side of them. They should be considered as an integral component of the whole and provided with due consideration accordingly.

5

Network Considerations

It may be constructive to elucidate our understanding of the network as it applies to our overall application. At the lowest level, it will consist of the copper cable, fibre optics, routers and switches which make up the physical network, plus any wireless segments within the overall local network. It will also consist of any third party network segments, including the Internet where applicable, which provide a transport layer to remote elements of the application. On top of this physical architecture sit the various servers, workstations and other components which, together, constitute the physical implementation of our working application. On these devices sit the various operating systems, middleware and application software components which provide the operational functionality for our application. We may, in some respects consider the whole of this infrastructure as our primary network. Reaching from this network, like the tentacles of a giant sea anemone, are the various connections and interconnections which connect our particular application to other data sources as might be required by the larger operation. We might consider this as an extended network.

When one contemplates matters in these terms, it quickly becomes apparent that we need some sort of mechanism which isolates our particular transactions from general activity upon this network of networks. We generally achieve this via a combination of firewalls and routers, each of which have pre-configured rules as to what network traffic they will allow to pass through them based upon the originating source of that traffic. These rules may be configured as a 'white list' whereupon only traffic originating from explicitly named sources will be allowed to pass, or as a 'black list' whereupon everything except an explicit list of originating sources to be blocked will be allowed to pass. As one might imagine, with respect to a large-scale system or system of systems, the situation can become quite complex. Furthermore, all of these rules must be maintained and managed explicitly by an administrative function. It follows that, if configuration rules may be changed upon these devices, then administrative access must be restricted to known individuals with the necessary permissions to do so. This, in turn, requires another set of rules for each device. And what of shared networks where a common infrastructure may be utilised by more than one application or organisation, such as within a public building for example? What then, when our data must traverse someone else's network in order to complete some transactional function? Clearly, we must establish and maintain a very clear vision of the overall network that our particular application uses, including segments which are outside of our immediate jurisdiction. While undoubtedly a complex undertaking, this is entirely achievable if we embed such considerations early in the systems design stage. This understanding should be explicitly documented with the system names and addresses of every single component. On top of this architectural vision may be overlaid the systems operational dataflow in order to understand precisely which component needs to connect to which other component, and for what reason, within our overall systems functionality. Such an understanding will enable us to draw up a configuration for every firewall and router within our immediate sphere of administration. For those beyond this sphere, we can draw up a precise configuration change request which allows our particular network traffic to access third party systems. There is, naturally, a strong security connotation here as, without such a crystal clear understanding, together with the maintenance of that understanding via managed component rule sets, we shall be introducing additional risks into the overall security and operational stability of our system. Consequently, this is an area which is deserving of considerable care and attention within our overall systems design.

Another aspect of networks is of course relative performance in the form of bandwidth and the sheer amount of data that the network may accommodate. There is an intrinsic dichotomy here between theoretical performance and realised performance. In theory, a network segment may be quoted as offering a given bandwidth. In practice, the bandwidth available to your application on this network segment will depend upon a number of factors including terminating components, whether the network is shared and, in some cases, time of day if network bandwidth is allocated dynamically. The only way of really understanding network performance in the context of your application is to actively monitor the traffic passing through network components. This may be easily achieved via tools and utilities often provided by the component manufacturers, or by purpose-built utilities which may be purchased separately. In the context of systems incorporating biometric functionality, such factors will be especially important if biometric matching must be undertaken against a remote source of reference biometrics within a real-time operational scenario. In such cases, network capacity and performance must be clearly understood and routinely monitored as an integral part of systems support and maintenance. It is outside of the scope of this book to delve more deeply into the finer points of network design and performance; however, suffice it to say that such matters are crucially important with respect to the operational stability and realised performance of a given large-scale system. This importance is accentuated when systems interact with other systems within a real-time transactional scenario.

Systems Testing

Testing is a function which should be undertaken at every stage of systems development and at every juncture of implementation, including when new infrastructure is added or software updated. For any substantial system, a test environment should be maintained which mirrors the live environment exactly, enabling testing without risk of disrupting the live operation. Furthermore, all such testing should be formally undertaken against a documented test plan, with all results logged accordingly. In such a manner, any required remediation may be undertaken and re-tested until satisfactory results are obtained.

Within an overall testing regime, we must of course define what needs to be tested, how such tests should be undertaken and to what degree. We might usefully categorise as follows.

Software

In this context we refer to software developed by the implementing agency or systems integrator which is directly within their sphere of influence. Such software would be developed according to a detailed requirements list, specifying the precise functionality and, where applicable, the user interface.

Testing of this software should be undertaken at various stages. Unit testing should be undertaken by the developers on individual code blocks to ensure that the code functions as intended and does not introduce any errors at run time. Debugging tools can help in this context and are often supplied as part of the development environment. Specialist tools are also available for specific types of development such as web applications for example, and external tools may be employed for penetration testing within a security context. When code blocks are integrated into a functional unit, this should be tested again, including all inputs and outputs to ensure that it functions as intended. Where a user interface is involved, this should be tested, preferably by real users, to ensure the logic and correct operation of the interface. Any external, previously compiled components or services that form a part of the overall software package should also be tested with the new code. This testing should include, in addition to the obvious testing of correct functionality, a degree of performance testing where applicable.

Finally, the completed software must be integrated into the test environment and tested in situ with the broader application, ensuring its correct operation and satisfactory performance. Various utilities may be used to test the software under load, replicating worst-case numbers of transactions and throughput. This is particularly pertinent with respect to databases and database components. Only when all tests have been passed 100% should any production software be moved into the live environment and, if any unexpected issues are found, the live system should be rolled back to the previous stable version of software while such issues are investigated and remediated.

Third Party Software

Of course, where third party software or software components are involved, one rarely has the luxury of having the source code available for internal inspection and testing (unless open-source software is being used – another good reason for adopting it where appropriate). This limits practical testing to functional testing and user interface testing. Functional testing should include testing all inputs and outputs as well as core functions. If anything is not operating as described, or is introducing malfunctions elsewhere within the system, then the software should not be accepted and should be returned to the supplier for remediation. Even when isolated tests appear satisfactory, the software should be installed within the test environment and tested in conjunction with the other software and hardware which constitutes the overall system. All such testing should be properly documented in order to provide feedback to the original supplier, thus aiding and supporting further development.

Hardware

Hardware should of course be subject to the same testing rigour. This includes fundamental hardware such as servers, hard drives, memory and so on, any supplier specific hardware appliances that may be utilised within the system and also network components such as firewalls and routers. Biometric capture devices should also be fully tested before implementation within the system. The precise nature of this testing may vary according to the component being tested. Servers and rack mount motherboards may be easily tested for complete operation, including input, output, configuration and relative performance. Routers, switches and firewalls may be tested for correct operation, throughput, configuration and so on. All of these devices must be tested for integration compatibility as well as overall performance.

Biometric devices may require a special testing regime which, in addition to the obvious functional testing, should include transducer alignment and configuration, ensuring that the device performs to an expected standard under operational conditions. All inputs, outputs and interfaces should also be tested.

Hardware tests, wherever possible, should also take the form of testing in isolation, testing within a sub-system and testing within the whole system within the test environment, with a detailed test plan being run at each stage and any deviations logged accordingly.

Operational Process

Testing should not be restricted to simply hardware and software but should include operational processes and procedures. After all, these have been subject to the same design rigour and are equally important from an operational perspective. All such processes should of course be properly documented and communicated to all those involved. Such documentation should be clear, concise and easily followed in practice. There is no benefit in having overly long, complex documents in this context, no matter how impressive they may appear in themselves. These should be working documents that individuals may pick up and readily understand while engaged in their labours. They may be complemented by diagrams and flowcharts where applicable and should be attractive to the eye.

Having defined and documented these operational processes, they should be tested, preferably, with those individuals who are actively engaged in the operation. This will be partly undertaken during training of course but, occasionally, such processes may be reviewed and revised, causing them to require re-testing, firstly off-line within the test environment and, eventually, within the live environment. In addition, when any item of hardware or software is revised and updated, one of the questions within the associated test plans should be: does the change affect the operational process in any way? If it does, then the processes in question must also be updated and re-tested.

End-to-End Testing

Once all individual components and processes have been tested, both at unit level and in situ within the test environment, then it will be necessary to conduct a thorough end-to-end test of the entire system. This may be undertaken to some degree within the test environment itself. Ultimately, however, it must be undertaken within the live environment, ensuring that the operation is stable, workable and performs as expected in every respect. This may take a little time and should be properly conducted and recorded accordingly. If any one item or process is found wanting, then a decision must be made as to whether to roll back the entire change release to the previous stable version, or whether remediation of that single component may be undertaken off-line and subsequently updated within the live environment. Much will depend upon the observed severity of the situation.

It goes without saying that testing is an important element within any systems implementation and ongoing maintenance. However, it is not always orchestrated with the rigour and precision with which it might be. This is often the case when multiple parties are involved with the provision, implementation and support of various components which, in their entirety, constitute the broader system. In such a scenario, the implementing agency might usefully take it upon themselves to orchestrate and manage all testing activities according to a detailed and robust procedure. Upon one factor of reality we may rely. If a particular component or sub-system is not adequately tested before live implementation, then, sooner or later, that component or sub-system will cause us to lavish an inordinate amount of attention upon it in order to restore it to a satisfactory operational condition. Be warned.

Conclusion

This chapter is concerned with systems integration. From the items discussed we may conclude that true systems integration covers many factors and requires a good deal of attention. Each of these factors, only a typical subset of which are discussed above, must be addressed in fine detail, ensuring a complete understanding of every component of the system as well as the system as a whole. When the system is part of a larger network of systems, as is often the case with respect to large-scale applications within the public sector, this understanding must expand to cover all those systems involved within this network, at least as far as the operation of our system and its data are concerned. Anything less will represent an unacceptable compromise.

Of course, almost anyone of average intelligence could take a biometric device and attach it in some way to an existing system. They may even create biometric identity verification transactions within that system and be able to generate a few impressive-looking reports, no doubt referring to themselves thereafter as a systems integrator. Such a situation, we must contend, is very far from true systems integration. Furthermore, the skills required for true systems integration extend far beyond a familiarity with one or two devices and their operation. Unfortunately, several so-called systems integrators and specialist consultants do not possess these skills. Even among some of the larger organisations who claim such a title, the portfolio of skills often appears rather barren when one looks closely into it. It is foolhardy to make assumptions in this context and, prior to procurement of either technology or services, a detailed questionnaire which explores the presence of such skills should be produced and exercised accordingly. This in itself is a part of good systems design and may be readily documented within the overall design and procurement process. When satisfied that such skills and experience do exist, then true systems integration may begin in earnest.

Review Questions

1. Discuss components and the integration of components within a broader system or network of systems in general terms.
2. How important is the biometric registration process within a broader systems integration context?
3. Where may the biometric matching process be undertaken and how might this vary with respect to different types of system?
4. Where may biometric credentials be stored and how may they be referenced with respect to different applications?
5. Discuss systems security with respect to true systems integration.

Performance Issues

6

Abstract This chapter is concerned with performance issues, the management of which may become complex with respect to large-scale systems and particularly those which incorporate biometric identity verification. In order to understand such issues, we must define the scope of our performance definition, the related metrics and consider how we are to monitor performance overall. This chapter discusses such issues, even from the point of biometric capture, with its related user and technical factors, through biometric operation, including user factors, technical factors, the biometric matching process, common metrics and an explanation of the biometric threshold setting. In this context, the User Psychology Index (UPI) is introduced and examples are given of the distinction between theoretical performance and realised performance. A new metric is also introduced in the form of the average error rate (AER), a single figure which provides for a simple comparison of device or configuration scenario realised performance.

Database performance is discussed in some detail, including factors such as the use of multiple databases, location, network considerations, configuration, database optimisation, query optimisation, read–write performance and other relevant factors. Leading naturally from this topic is network performance, with factors such as bandwidth and latency, associated configuration, network monitoring and the use of third party networks. We then move on to operational performance and discuss functional performance from the human perspective, including the effect upon transaction times and systems throughput. We additionally consider performance monitoring and documentation, including centralised log management for system events and the biometric matching score for biometric identity verification transactions. We introduce the concept of user psychology, as pioneered by the author, and discuss user variables including usability, familiarity, competence, attitude, external influence, disabilities, language, age, ethnicity and well-being, all of which may have a measurable effect upon realised performance. Lastly, we consider the finer points of systems configuration and introduce the concept of total systems performance. This chapter provides a good grounding in the performance of systems which incorporate biometric functionality, from a very practical perspective.

J. Ashbourn, *Guide to Biometrics for Large-Scale Systems: Technological, Operational, and User-Related Factors*, DOI 10.1007/978-0-85729-467-8_6,
© Springer-Verlag London Limited 2011

Introduction

Performance may be defined and understood in many ways from an overall systems perspective, and may depend upon a number of interrelated factors. Managing performance within a large-scale system may necessarily become quite complex and require a careful balancing of factors, especially with regard to the biometric component of such systems and how this functionality interacts with the more traditional systems factors. We might draw an analogy here with realised performance from a motor racing perspective, which, similarly, depends upon various factors including the fundamental design of the racing car, its quality of preparation and maintenance, its precise configuration and gearing, the track upon which it runs, the environmental conditions at the time, and the psychology and behaviour of the driver. They all come together to produce a particular performance. Their object is a sustainable and winning form which delivers their previously identified aspirations. Our objective is no different and will require equal attention if it is to be realised.

In this section, we shall explore performance from various perspectives, introducing some ideas and realities along the way which may not be commonly appreciated. It is hoped that, in so doing, we encourage a broad understanding of realised performance from a systems perspective and, especially, with respect to systems incorporating biometric functionality. This, in turn, may inform competent systems design and infrastructure specification in order to ensure that a given system performs as expected and is both sustainable and manageable.

Defining Performance

It is appropriate at this juncture to define performance in its various guises with respect to the sort of systems under discussion. Of particular pertinence is the performance of the biometric capture device and the associated biometric matching process. However, this is just one aspect among several which serve to provide for a complete operational transaction. For each we may introduce specific measures and associated terminology with which to describe performance. We must also consider, where appropriate, the performance of the supporting infrastructure, such as networks, routers, switches and firewalls, especially in cases where such an infrastructure is shared. Similarly, we must consider database performance and how that performance varies with scale, whether there are additional links and feeds to consider and so on.

In addition to the technical performance of individual components and devices, we must understand the performance of the whole and define our requirements accordingly. Within this broader scope, we must include user variables and even process performance if we are to develop an insight into the real performance of our application. We might also consider aspects such as disaster recovery and what performance we expect to realise under such a scenario. Certainly, there is much more to consider than simply the theoretical performance of a biometric capture device.

Measuring Performance

Measuring performance in real terms can become quite complex. Firstly, we have the dichotomy between theoretical performance and realised performance to consider. Secondly, we have to be clear as to exactly what we are measuring and what effect this has upon realised performance. There exist many measures and techniques that we might employ in this context. Placing them in perspective and understanding where performance bottlenecks really lie will require a degree of correlation and a good deal of operational experience. We shall consider some specific areas for purposes of illustration, although it should be understood that this does not constitute a complete list of measurable components.

Biometric Capture

By biometric capture we mean the reliability with which a biometric may be captured by the transducer within the biometric device. This is often measured in percentage terms and sometimes referred to as a failure to capture rate. There may be many reasons why the device has failed to capture a biometric deemed of sufficient quality to be usable in subsequent identity verification transactions. These might include contamination of the transducer by dirt or condensation, a fault or mis-configuration within the biometric device, an interruption or time-out within the technical workflow or dataflow or other reasons directly connected with the technology. More often, though, it will probably be due to inconsistency on the part of the subject whose biometric is being captured. This may be because they do not fully understand the process. It may be because of external pressures. It may be that the correct procedure has not been properly explained, or it might simply be that the biometric in question is not strongly defined for that particular individual. In any event, failure to capture may lead to difficulties at both the registration stage and for subsequent identity verification. There are various aspects of user psychology which might have an effect in this context and these will be explored later. Failure to capture, as explained, may be simply measured as a percentage of failures within a distinct batch of capture transactions.

The Biometric Matching Process

The biometric matching process is dependent upon a number of factors, some of them purely technical, some environmental and some user-related. Consequently, when measuring performance we require metrics which take such factors into consideration. The most common metrics given are those for the likelihood of a false match and the likelihood of a false non-match expressed in percentage terms. Also popular is the equal error rate which quotes a figure in percentage terms wherein the likelihood of either a false match or false non-match is considered equal. These metrics are also commonly referred to as false accept rates (FARs) and false reject rates (FRRs). Occasionally, a different terminology altogether is employed to express, essentially, the same concepts of measurement. However, the one employed here is considered the most intuitive for general use.

These parameters will be influenced by a threshold setting which is typically configurable at the time of deployment. As a biometric will never be matched absolutely with the reference, we must interpret the match result as a statement of likeness between the two samples. Consequently, we must also define at which point we consider this statement of likeness to constitute a match and at which point it is considered a non-match. This is usually determined by a simple threshold, above which a match is suggested, and below which a non-match. By adjusting this threshold, it is possible to fine-tune the performance of the biometric device. Some techniques employ a slightly more sophisticated approach, but the overall concept of a simple threshold is generally adopted (Fig. 6.1).

However, we should understand that published performance figures from device manufacturers rarely give an accurate impression of performance as realised in the field, due to the impossibility of accurately predicting the non-technical factors involved. Nevertheless, they represent a good starting point for understanding how a given device is likely to perform. In order to develop that understanding further, we must add some weightings for environmental, process and user variables that are likely to be encountered within our particular application. The User Psychology Index (UPI), developed some years ago by the author, provided an insight into how such factors were likely to affect realised performance. The concept has been further developed and refined, with a software utility provided within which various operational scenarios may be explored. The output from this utility consequently provides a much more realistic prediction of the performance likely to be experienced in the field.

The User Psychology Index (UPI) utility, as presented in Fig. 6.2, suggests to us that, given our selected ratings for usability, template quality, familiarity, competence, attitude, environment and external pressure, the quoted FAR of 0.85% is more likely to be 1.9428%. Under the same scenario, the quoted FRR of 1.05% is more likely to be 4.65%. The UPI utility additionally introduces a new single measure for easy comparison purposes,

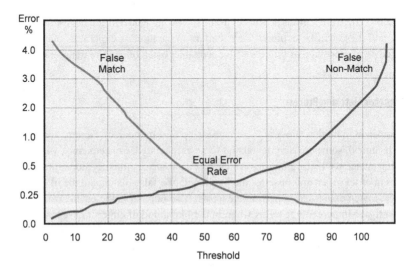

Fig. 6.1 The concept of biometric matching performance in conjunction with a variable threshold

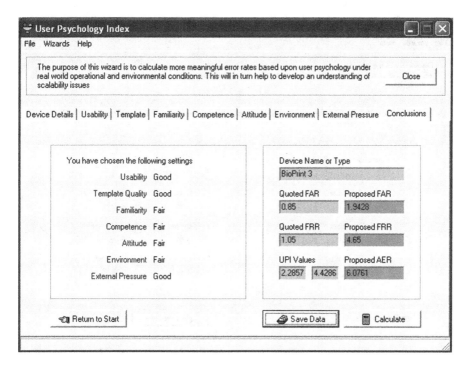

Fig. 6.2   The User Psychology Index software utility

designated as an average error rate (AER). Using the AER, easy and fast comparisons may be made between a number of scenarios as created and stored within the utility.

Perhaps the most interesting factor in the example given is that, notwithstanding the positive ratings selected, which never drop below 'fair', there is still a significant difference between the quoted performance and that suggested within the UPI utility. If more severe ratings were to be selected, then the difference would be even more dramatic.

In the example portrayed in Fig. 6.3, we can see that an FAR of 0.85% has become a proposed FAR of 4.7357% and an FRR of 1.05% has become a proposed FRR of 11.4%. Furthermore, the proposed AER is now 14.869% compared with the previous example of 6.0761%. This fairly dramatic difference arises by selecting poorer-quality parameters, which, nonetheless, may easily be encountered within real-world operational situations.

The use of this utility allows us to vary one or more real-world parameters and observe the likely effect upon realised performance. It is thus an extremely useful tool to have available when designing an operational system.

Integration of the Biometric Transaction

Of course, considerations of performance do not stop with the biometric device. What is important in practical terms is the overall transaction performance. It is this performance which directly affects the smooth running of a given operation. This is especially the case

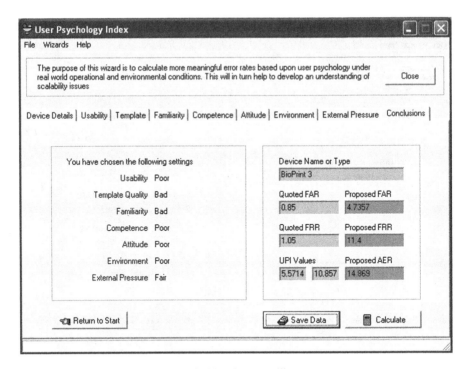

Fig. 6.3 An alternative scenario depicted within the UPI utility

where a large number of individuals are expected to pass through a single operational node or point of presence, such as might be encountered at a border crossing point, for example. In such a situation, a difference of a few seconds per overall transaction has a cumulative effect which may prove to be significant. Consequently, in addition to the time taken to perform the biometric match, other items of workflow necessary to complete the transaction must be taken into account. We can measure this phenomenon in terms of overall transaction time, from the start of a given transaction to the point at which the system is ready to commence a further transaction. The biometric matching element must therefore be carefully integrated into this workflow, which may include elements of both technology and process, in an efficient manner.

From a technology perspective, such integration is reasonably straightforward given modern application development methods and associated interfaces. From a process perspective, things may be less clear, although intelligent and thoughtful design of the operational environment and user interface may make a significant difference to the overall transaction time. Once again, the published figure of a transaction time from the perspective of a device manufacturer will likely be quite different from that experienced in the field.

The transaction time wizard within the UPI utility provides an insight into the proportionality of such differences by applying a weighting according to a set of parameters included within headings such as personal criteria, systems criteria and expected errors. A typical scenario is depicted within Fig. 6.4, whereby a published transaction time figure of 5 s becomes a proposed, and much more realistic, transaction time of 21.63 s. Of course,

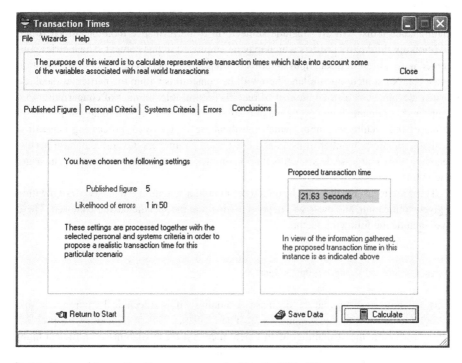

Fig. 6.4 Proposed transaction times as expressed within the UPI utility

individual transaction times will vary according to user variables as discussed later, and so it will be necessary to monitor transactions over a period of time in order to arrive at a representative average transaction time. Furthermore, this approach would also take into account additional system variables elsewhere within the broader application, some of which are discussed below.

Database Performance

There are various aspects of database performance to consider, depending upon precisely how a database is configured and used within the broader application. If, for example, we are simply using a local database to retrieve a reference biometric with a suitable key, then the related performance issues might be relatively straightforward. If, on the other hand, we are passing live biometric data to a remote database to search through millions of records in order to find a match, then there are other aspects of performance to consider. Furthermore, we may be dealing with several databases, whether directly concerned with the biometric or otherwise. For example, we may be writing transactions into a transactions database, while retrieving related data from one or more external databases in order to verify or authenticate the overall transaction. In any event, database performance may have an effect upon our overall transaction time.

6

Many database systems, consisting of the database engine, development tools and maintenance tools, will also include some form of performance monitoring. There are additionally third party utilities which may be employed in this context. The metrics concerned may represent throughput in terms of transactions per second, bits of information per second or something similar. There will be constraints within the particular database system design, such as total number of records permissible, number of concurrent users, supported communications protocols and so on. There will be additional constraints in terms of the architecture upon which the database is deployed, processing capability, available memory, number of users and other such parameters. Overall database performance within a large-scale system is thus a complex matter, both to understand, measure and maintain.

There are measures that may be undertaken in order to optimise database design within a given application, and these will depend partly upon the specific database chosen. These may include the following factors.

System Resource and Architecture Optimisation

This concerns ensuring that the database is running within a technical environment that allows it to perform at its maximum levels of performance. This will include CPU processing optimisation, the availability of sufficient memory, the availability of sufficient high-speed data storage and an architecture suitable for the application. This may include some form of distributed processing and data replication in order to provide acceptable performance in multiple locations. We must also consider where the biometric matching process is best undertaken, whether locally with reference data retrieved from the database or actually at the database with live data provided to it.

Query Optimisation

Query optimisation is something of a specialist skill, especially when complex queries or large datasets are concerned. Many database engines will include a degree of automated query optimisation. However, writing good-quality queries that are oriented towards performance to start with will be beneficial. Database vendors will be able to offer much good advice within their own documentation in this respect. It follows that the underlying table design should also be optimised and streamlined in order to facilitate query optimisation. There are various approaches which may be adopted in this respect, and equally varied views as to the benefits of full normalisation or a more complex table joining paradigm suited to the operational requirements of the database. Similarly, meaningful or abstract keys may have different benefits in different operational situations. Precisely where the query is run and how much data is returned will of course be important. We may decide to execute the query locally or trigger a stored procedure within the database. In any event, query optimisation is a necessary element of performance tuning for a large and complex database.

Transaction Read–Write Optimisation

In terms of reading from or writing to disk drives, we must consider whether to use functions such as data compression or encryption, both of which exert an overhead upon the performance of reading and writing to disk. Functionality such as disk caching when writing data and read ahead pages when reading may also be configurable and have performance implications. Such functions may interact with a database internal buffer with respect to data retrieval and processing. Of course, we also have the inherent performance of the data storage methodology chosen, such as local disk array or network attached storage including any associated control mechanisms, as well as communications to and from such storage repositories.

User Interface Design

It may seem strange to consider the user interface as a component which might affect database performance, but it is possible that a poorly designed interface will seek to drag larger than necessary datasets from the database which, if orchestrated across a network, could affect realised performance. Even simple design features such as look-up combo boxes and lists may be optimised to ensure that they are using data efficiently and not impacting upon overall performance.

In conclusion, overall database performance is quite complex. We have touched upon some obvious parameters and functions which might affect realised operational performance. However, a full treatise on database optimisation is well beyond the scope of this book. Suffice it to say that careful configuration and well-considered design will go a long way towards ensuring that a large database performs as expected. As we will readily appreciate, this is not simply a matter of optimising the database engine in isolation, but taking the entire architecture into consideration and ensuring that each component is specified and configured appropriately. The database vendor's own documentation should be referred to in this context and will no doubt offer good advice with respect to best practice design principles and database optimisation in the broader sense.

Network Performance

There will be some networks, such as closed-loop local area networks, which we have absolute control over and can maintain and tune to our particular requirements. Other networks, such as third party networks, including the Internet, we shall have rather less control over, although we may liase with our Internet Service Provider in order to ensure a reasonable performance. In reality, our wider area network may comprise both these models and be interlinked in quite complex ways. Nevertheless, there are several aspects of network performance that we might understand and monitor in one way or another.

Important factors in this respect are available bandwidth and latency across the network. However, before we can understand such factors, we must define our particular

6

network and what it consists of in the way of infrastructure and associated network devices. There are various network discovery tools which will scan a network and identify devices such as hubs, routers and switches. Many of these devices have integral monitoring capabilities, often via a simple network management protocol (SNMP) agent which may be interrogated via an SNMP manager, deployed on an available administration server. Via this mechanism, various items of information may typically be reported including throughput, discarded packets and so on, providing a view of network traffic as seen by the device. A dedicated and comprehensive network monitoring application will collect such information, identify network segments and collate the whole into various views and reports appertaining to the network in question. However, much can be achieved using the utilities often provided with network devices (Fig. 6.5).

In the context of third party networks, the third party network supplier will be able to provide statistics, reports and configuration details with respect to usage of the network by a particular client. Our primary concerns will be around availability and performance in terms of bandwidth and latency. To ensure high levels of availability, a certain amount of redundancy must be provided including, for critical applications, the availability of parallel segments. However, such a provision will have an associated cost and, in the case of third party networks, such requirements will be subject to negotiation.

With respect to local area networks, things are much more straightforward as we can specify precisely the type of segment required (fibre, copper cable and various bandwidths), its termination and the specification of necessary switches and routers. We can also specify network topology and whatever degree of redundancy we consider appropriate for the task at hand. Having established such a network, we may easily monitor the various devices upon it in order to understand performance and tune this performance accordingly.

In conclusion, there are many aspects to understand with respect to the broader network as it affects our particular application. It is a necessary component of overall performance as an end-to-end transaction will typically make use of it in one way or another. Any latency upon the network will consequently affect the realised performance of our application, albeit usually in a relatively insignificant manner. When designing and implementing

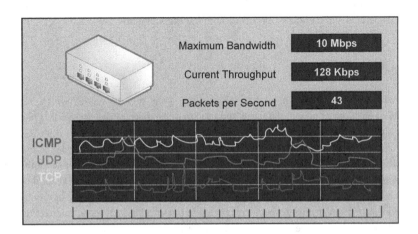

Fig. 6.5 Rudimentary network monitoring tools are sometimes provided with network devices

a large-scale biometric system, we must take the time to understand the associated networks and ensure that they are configured as most appropriate to our requirements. We must also ensure that some sort of ongoing network monitoring is in place, in order to understand where and when performance bottlenecks might be network-related.

Operator Performance

Operator performance may include user and assisted user performance within the context of a live transaction: operator performance in terms of interacting with the system on a day-to-day operational basis and administrator performance in terms of maintaining the system. In all cases we are speaking of the functional performance of a human being and their interface with the system.

In this context, we might usefully separate identity verification transactions from other operational transactions. For the latter, we may not be too concerned with operator performance other than in the interests of training and knowledge of the system overall. For the former, operator performance may have a dramatic effect upon overall transaction time. It is therefore a factor to take into account with respect to overall system performance. There are many factors which might affect operator performance and we shall explore some of these later. We should understand, however, that operator performance overall can not only affect transaction times, but also the quality of such transactions, and in some cases even their legitimacy. If an operator inputs incorrect information, then this will be maintained throughout the workflow. This will be especially pertinent at the time of registration, of course, where poor-quality biometric registration or alignment with incorrect demographic details may have serious consequences later on in the programme.

System Throughput

System throughput is critically important with respect to a smoothly operating overall system. If bottlenecks start to appear, whatever the reason, then the system may quickly fall into a chaotic state. Such bottlenecks might establish themselves due to technical failures or ill-conceived technical architectures. They might develop as a result of unexpected numbers of individuals using the facility. They might also manifest themselves due to poor administration and ill-conceived operational process. It is an easy matter to monitor numbers of individuals passing through the system within a given time period, and this sort of monitoring should really be undertaken on a more or less continuous basis in order to understand trends, peak flows and how the system is performing overall. If difficulties start to develop, the factors contributing to the situation may or may not be obvious. Matters such as insufficient numbers of operational nodes, or points of presence, in order to handle the throughput will quickly become obvious. Factors such as inordinate individual transaction times may be easily investigated as to the primary cause. Slow system response might also be an obvious contributing factor, although pinpointing the cause could be a little more difficult. Inadequate operational processes, possibly causing confusion, could be another contributing factor. The likelihood, in the case of a seriously ill-performing system, is that a combination of such factors will be at play. Consequently, some intelligent investigation will be required in order to understand exactly what is happening and where difficulties may be manifesting themselves.

Much of this particular issue may be alleviated within proper systems design and implementation. A common error is to take a quoted transaction time from a device manufacturer and extrapolate this to the number of expected transactions. The problem with this approach is that there are always external factors which render the average realised transaction time much longer than a theoretical estimate from the device manufacturer suggests. Figure 6.4 provides an idea of the likely magnitude of such differences. When multiplied by hundreds, or even thousands of transactions, such differences may make a significant difference to overall throughput. However, this particular issue may be accounted for within a good systems design. Similarly, technical throughput in terms of communications bandwidth, latency and, where applicable, database performance may also be accounted for within a well-considered systems architecture design. If third party networks must be used, then these may be specified in order to provide the required levels of throughput and availability. System throughput in performance terms should not produce unexpected issues if the overall system, including operational process, is well-considered and properly designed. If bottlenecks do subsequently arise, then a simple process of elimination will suggest the likely cause, enabling remedial works to be undertaken as appropriate.

Documenting Performance

It is difficult to develop an understanding of ongoing realised performance if that performance cannot be documented. In this respect, as before, we need to define those aspects of performance that are of interest to us, and ascertain how they might be documented. For those elements which are capable of generating activity logs, it may be that we might integrate those logs via a centralised log management system and produce correlated summaries of related activity. However, generally, such information as is logged is more concerned with the fact that transactions have taken place at all, rather than any aspect of performance. Such a system is well suited to helping us understand what is happening throughout the system and, therefore, the relative security of our application, but is perhaps not best placed to help us understand and document performance.

As previously mentioned, there are various real-time, or close to real-time, utilities for the purpose of monitoring such factors as network performance, database performance and other infrastructural items. Such utilities will often incorporate a rudimentary reports generator with which to summarise and document performance. The issue herein is the plethora of different utilities, and consequently different reports, which may reside within a large-scale system. Even if we judiciously select a few such reports which we believe will give us an overall representation of overall system performance, there remains the task of correlating this information into some sort of unified, holistic perspective. Such an undertaking requires technical skills that may not readily be found in a typical systems operator or administrator. One must be able to interpret technical information and place it within an operational context. Nevertheless, documented reports such as these remain a useful indicator of how our system is performing and, with regular use, can also help us to spot changes and trends.

When it comes to documenting the performance of the biometric functionality, this will very much depend upon the provided software and its included inputs and outputs. In some cases, it may be possible to output the *score*, or relative likeness, of each biometric matching transaction. This is useful information to have and, when designing a large-scale system, it would be prudent to check that such an output is possible from such devices as are being considered to provide the biometric functionality. By documenting transactional scores over time, we may understand both how the biometric functionality is performing per se and also if trends are emerging as to the habituated usage of the system, or otherwise. This may serve to inform decisions around precisely where the matching threshold should be set. This is an important factor with respect to maintaining an equivalence of performance across nodes, as we shall discuss later. We might also usefully consider throughput in relation to the biometric performance and ensure that we measure and document numbers of transactions per node, as well as in total.

Given the above, it may be supposed that effectively documenting overall system performance is no easy task. However, with a little foresight, it may be perfectly feasible to select a series of pertinent measures which may be reported upon and documented in a regular manner. This will provide both an initial benchmark of overall system performance and a mechanism for monitoring this over time in order to spot trends or unexpected changes. In addition, such documentation will serve a useful purpose in managing scalability in applications which are destined to grow in usage.

System Variables

We have already shown that realised performance is a complex thing to understand in terms of contributing factors and the influence they might exert upon the whole. So much depends upon the precise nature of the system, its architecture and practical operation, including operational process and associated workflows. Among the many variables are those which are related to system components.

As we are primarily concerned with systems which feature biometric functionality, it is reasonable to consider such variables that might affect the biometric capture device itself. Assuming that the firmware and software is stable and inherently error-free, which might in itself be a significant assumption, there remain environmental variables which may affect the reliable operation of the device. These include excess of temperature and humidity which may affect the transducer, for example, condensation upon the lens of a camera or the effect of environmental extremes upon electronic components and circuit boards. If the biometric technique chosen involves physical contact, as is usually the case with fingerprint biometrics for example, then, in addition to natural environmental variables, there is also the question of dirt upon the contact surfaces and even erosion of those surfaces due to prolonged wear and tear. With optical fingerprint readers in particular, dirt and accumulated grease from previous transactions may start to affect performance if not regularly cleaned.

6

Once the biometric has been captured, subsequent processing should be consistent enough although relative performance may still be affected by systems variables along the way. Communications, for example, may be affected by constrained bandwidth at peak times. Database access may be affected by a heavier than usual number of concurrent transactions. Network components may become overloaded or fail completely. Overall processing capacity may be constrained by concurrent demands upon the system, not necessarily from the same application. Third party components or modules may affect overall systems capacity and performance in an unexpected manner. The cumulative effect of such system variables may conspire to degrade overall transaction performance for our particular application. Less obvious, but nonetheless important, variables include factors such as the user or operator interface. If automated points of presence are deployed within the system, whereby the user effectively self-serves according to a user interface and attendant workflow, then this needs to be as intuitive as possible. It also needs to cater for multiple languages and needs to be able to handle exceptions in a manner which seems logical and expedient to the user. If the operation is more of an assisted one, then the same rules apply to the user interface for the operator. If such user interfaces are ill-conceived in this respect, they may well introduce significant variations into the transactional workflow, according to the understanding or habituation of the users and operators at a given point in time and geography.

Such system variables measured in isolation may not seem significant. However, if we take their cumulative effect and multiply by the number of transactions at a given point of presence, then a subtly different picture may emerge. In any event, it is good to be aware of, and understand, such system variables and their potential effects upon the performance and reliability of the system overall.

User Variables

If system variables conspire to have a significant effect upon realised performance, then user variables may have a *very* significant effect upon the same. The reality of this position was researched and understood by the author almost two decades ago, although it was not popularly understood at the time. With the advent of the UPI, conceived and introduced by the author, such realities are now more widely appreciated, although not always fully taken into account within systems design and implementation. A comprehensive dissertation on user psychology with respect to the interaction with technology would fill more than one book. Of necessity therefore, in this volume, we shall provide a brief overview of a cross section of user variables and how they might impact upon realised system performance.

Usability

Usability refers to the user interface with the technology and to what degree this is attractive and intuitive. A well-designed user interface can make a significant difference to how the user sees the system and how easily they are able to navigate through it to perform the required functions. Items like colour and tonal balance, the use of readily understandable symbols, the relative logic of the workflow and of course a slick and timely operation all serve to influence the appreciation of the interface, and therefore the system, in the eyes of the user. The same holds true for operators of the system and how intuitive their interface is perceived as they navigate the workflow. A poorly designed interface can create a negative impression of the system, even when otherwise functioning perfectly. Such a negative impression may be translated directly to realised transactional performance as users struggle with the interface and lose any enthusiasm for undertaking a smooth transaction.

Familiarity

For many, the use of such a system will be a new experience. Furthermore, with certain types of large-scale applications, such as border control systems for example, usage will for many individuals be irregular and infrequent. Consequently, even though the operation may have been carefully explained at the time it was first used, the likelihood is that the user will interact with it in an inconsistent manner, at least for a period of time, if not indefinitely. Such inconsistency of use will be directly reflected in transactional performance for that particular user. Furthermore, certain technologies have an ability to learn by updating the stored reference upon every successful transaction, thus tracking either minor physiological changes or changes in the way the user provides the live sample, to the degree to which usage is habituated or otherwise thus becomes an important factor with respect to realised performance. Within a large-scale system, which may have many tens of thousands of users, there will naturally exist some significant variation in transactional performance as different users become habituated to the use of the system at different rates. Some individuals may of course never become habituated users.

To a lesser degree perhaps, the same applies to operators who, as they become more familiar with the system, will be able to better advise users and more readily understand exceptions, their likely causes and how to remediate them. This is typical for any systems of course, although the addition of biometric functionality presents some particular issues which tend to accentuate this factor somewhat.

Competence

Competence may seem like an unfair factor to include in this list of user variables, but the fact remains that, as individuals, we tend to have aptitudes in different areas and, consequently, some are more comfortable than others when interfacing with technology. What may seem to be perfectly logical and intuitive to one individual may seem quite the opposite to another. Therefore the degree to which an individual becomes competent in the use of the system will vary from one such individual to another. However, there is no doubt that competence will go a long way towards consistency and expediency in use. This will translate directly into both transaction times and the consistency of transaction times between instances. If we multiply this factor by the number of individuals at a particular point of presence, we can readily appreciate that a significant variability may exist among our user population and the efficacy of their respective identity verification transactions. Of course, we may achieve much by virtue of proper explanation, good-quality user training and equally good-quality guidance at the operational point of presence. Even users with little interest or natural aptitude in using such technology may improve their relative operational performance if everything is clearly explained and they do not feel intimidated by either the system or the process.

Attitude

Perhaps one of the most elusive, but nevertheless interesting, factors may reside under the general heading of attitude. Even skilled users can become remarkably inconsistent if they have a negative attitude towards the process being followed. In the case of public sector systems, this is entirely predictable, understandable even, given the connotation with law enforcement and what may be perceived as *big brother* policies implemented by government agencies. Furthermore, there is a perception in some countries that such policies are being enforced against the wrong people, effectively criminalising the innocent while the real criminals enjoy celebrity status and seem to be almost protected by the state. However distorted such a view may appear, in certain countries, there exists little will to demonstrate otherwise. Inevitably, such a state of affairs will result in many citizens resenting what they perceive as unnecessary levels of control upon their rights as citizens, including freedom of movement. Where such attitudes exist, even among the educated and informed, there will be little incentive for the individuals concerned to interface either correctly or consistently with the system. They will make no particular effort in this direction and, as a result, their transactional performance will be variable.

Much of this particular factor may have been diffused if the situation with public sector systems, notably identity documentation and border control, had been handled with a little more understanding and intelligence. Unfortunately, government agencies have not always been forthright as to how these systems are actually operating and how personal information is shared between them. In effect, certain government agencies have broken every principle of their own in place of data protection and privacy instruments. As citizens come to understand this, their perception of both the system and the operating authority may be unnecessarily tarnished, leading to the creation of negative attitudes as described. The situation could of course be very different. If citizens were to perceive that, actually, the system is performing a worthwhile societal function, and that the operating agency is being forthright and open about how the system is being used, then the prevailing attitude is more likely to be positive. There may be much that can be achieved in this context, with some sensible and honest communication, coupled to responsible systems design and ethical policies. When user attitudes are positive and enthusiastic, transactional performance may increase significantly. This is a factor which typically receives little consideration within the context of contemporary systems design and implementation, and yet is very significant in relation to performance. It is equally significant in relation to the creation of fraudulent identities or fraudulent identity credentials, an undertaking which, sadly, is not at all difficult within certain administrations, notwithstanding the widespread use of biometrics.

External Influence

Of all the user variables, external influence, or pressure, can have some of the most dramatic effects upon realised transactional performance. Imagine an individual who, by nature, is rather shy and who is not particularly comfortable when interfacing with technology. Imagine that this individual has nonetheless expended great efforts in striving to understand the system and its operation and has paid particular attention to the training they have been given when registering their biometric with the system. Imagine that this individual feels quietly confident that they will be able to use the system effectively under real operational conditions. Now imagine that, when the user arrives at the operational point of presence for the first time, it is discovered that the system interface is different from that shown during training. Imagine that signage to this point of presence is poor and that the individual is now behind schedule. Imagine that the environment is unusually noisy and extremely busy with many other individuals queuing to use the system. Now imagine that our individual attempts to use the system, but the transaction fails, for no reason that our individual can understand. Imagine that other users are becoming visibly impatient. The individual tries again, but by now is quite flustered and is not being consistent in the way they present their live biometric. Consequently, the transaction fails again, to audible disapproval of those waiting to use the system. The probability that our individual will successfully negotiate the system and undertake a valid transaction has now reduced considerably. The effect upon realised performance has been dramatic, if not devastating. The individual will almost certainly require assistance in order to be able to complete the transaction.

We have simply described one of many potential scenarios whereby the confidence that an individual has in the system and their own ability to interface with it has been significantly reduced, leading to a negative impact upon transactional performance. There exist many other factors which might conspire to exert such influence: some environmental, some due to other events which have served to confuse or agitate the user, some in the form of the presence or attitude of other users, some perhaps caused by a perceived attitude among system operators, the possibilities are almost endless. Of course, certain individuals will be more hardened against external influence than others, but most will be susceptible to a certain degree. Furthermore, the likelihood of such external influence existing will vary according to location and even between points of presence at the same location, creating a rather complex overall landscape as far as this particular factor is concerned. Once again, much may be achieved by intelligent systems design and well-considered operational processes, in order to ensure that the operational environment is as conducive to a relaxed and consistent operation as possible.

Disabilities

It is important to cater for users with disabilities, ensuring that they are able to interface with the system without undue difficulty. At automated points of presence, this includes the provision of an interface at a height suitable for those in wheelchairs, and enough space for them to operate the system effectively. Similar attention should be paid to signage, ensuring that it is clearly visible for such users. Those with very poor eyesight or who are registered as blind will no doubt require an assisted operation and this should be catered for accordingly.

However, not all disabilities are immediately obvious. Those who suffer from deafness live in a different world which can seem confusing at times, especially if others do not understand their difficulty. In large-scale systems, such exceptions should be catered for with the provision of trained operators who are able to sign and thus communicate with those suffering from deafness. There are other disabilities which are even less obvious. There are various degrees of autism, for example, which, while not necessarily obvious to others, may cause the user to have difficulty when interfacing to a technological system which they may not fully understand. In addition, there exist various forms of learning difficulty which manifest themselves in different ways and may cause an individual undue difficulty in maintaining a consistent use of the system. The same may hold true for those with personality disorders, which may make it difficult for them to interface with the system in the expected manner. Such disabilities which are not visibly obvious are nonetheless real to those harbouring them and we should be sympathetic to this reality. In proportional terms, such users may be more than anticipated within the context of a given large-scale system. We must be cognisant of this possibility when planning and implementing the system and ensure that our operator training and associated processes cater for every reasonable eventuality. Those with disabilities should, as far as possible, not be considered as exceptions, but should be accommodated within the overall design of the system and its operational processes. If this is not the case, the effect upon overall realised performance could be significant, especially with respect to those disabilities which are not obvious. This is an important factor within the broader sphere of user psychology and we should strive to understand the situation in depth and how we might best accommodate those with disabilities of all kinds in a respectful and helpful manner.

Language

Language is a factor which would seem obvious to cater for in any public sector system and, in general, we see evidence of this in items such as signage and printed documentation, although the precise choice of languages may be a contention in some areas. Within system interfaces, the situation is sometimes quite different, with either far fewer languages catered for or, in many cases, a single language. Clearly, it is difficult to accommodate every language and, if two or three are chosen, there will always be a proportion of users who will not be supported. In many cases, the situation may quickly be retrieved via an assisted operation. However, this may not be very practical in the context of a large-scale busy system with a number of automated points of presence. Moreover, even multilingual operators will be restricted to their particular set of languages. Another approach may be found in the use of logical symbols and icons which have a universal meaning. Much more could be made of this approach; indeed, it would be informative to design a user interface entirely using logical symbols, and then complement it with textual descriptions as appropriate. While this is the reverse of what usually happens, its effect upon consistency of use throughout a large-scale system may be very worthwhile. Furthermore, it might serve to reduce the costs inherent in managing exceptions. Such an approach could usefully be standardised among national administrations, creating a universal sign language appropriate to user interfaces within public sector systems. In some respects we are close to this ideal, as several industry sectors have implemented something of the sort, albeit in a piecemeal and often inconsistent manner. There exists an opportunity therefore for some department or agency to take the lead, design such a system and actively promote it internationally. In the meantime, we shall have to accommodate language as best we can in a world where we rely increasingly upon automation and information technology. Naturally, if a given user is having language-related difficulties, their transactional performance and consistency will be affected.

Age

Age is an interesting factor from several perspectives, and one which can have a dramatic effect upon realised transactional performance. We may anticipate that, among the elderly, a proportion of individuals will develop physical characteristics that will render them less able than they once were. Such developments may restrict movement within individual joints, which makes it more difficult to interface with systems. Furthermore, such developments may be accompanied by deteriorated eyesight or hearing, rendering the individual less able to function as the system might expect them to. They will typically require a little extra time to complete the identity verification transaction.

In addition, within a fast-moving world of technological change, those who have been on the planet for an extended period may find it difficult to understand and relate to new concepts which were not contemporary with the majority of their time on Earth. There are exceptions of course, but as a generality, we must expect that the elderly may not hold the same perception of a system and its operation as those significantly younger in years. Furthermore, with the onslaught of physical frailties, the ability to interface with such a system in a consistent manner may be impaired. Again, we must be sympathetic to this reality and accommodate the elderly and infirm within our overall deliberations.

Another interesting factor is the effect upon a biometric with age. It is generally held that biometrics do not alter with age. However, this is an oversimplification. In the case of fingerprints, for example, the fundamental characteristics of the fingerprint may not change significantly, but the skin will certainly change, possibly rendering the fingerprints less distinct and harder to read in an automated manner. Furthermore, shape and size of the fingertips may change slightly with age. Naturally, the same is true at the other end of the spectrum as children become adolescents and, finally, adults. The iris is considered stable throughout an individual's lifetime, but it may become more difficult to read with age if the eyes become occluded by facial characteristics or even cataracts and other symptoms of failing health. An individual's face will be subject to change with age and, furthermore, the degree of change will be variable among a given population. These changes may render the comparison with a biometric reference captured much earlier increasingly difficult. A sensible approach to this issue would be to recapture the reference biometric periodically in order to track natural age-related change within the individual. Certain techniques allow for this, even to the extent of updating the reference at every valid transaction if required. If no such adjustment is accommodated within the design of the system, then it is likely that increasing age will result in transactional errors and reduced performance for a given individual. Extrapolated across the user population and geographic distribution of the system, this factor may have a significant effect upon realised performance.

6

Ethnicity

Ethnicity sometimes becomes a contentious issue when discussing biometrics – something the author finds interesting as there clearly exist ethnic characteristics which will translate into biometrics. In one respect, this does not matter, as our systems and processes should be absolutely transparent, and certainly, as far as an automated biometric comparison is concerned, this is indeed the case. However, there remain two interesting avenues to explore in this context. Firstly, an often asked question is whether ethnicity may be determined from a biometric. Many are sensitive to this question from a human rights perspective, although the author has no knowledge of any system ever attempting to do this. From a scientific perspective, with certain biometrics it might be possible to infer ethnicity to some degree, based upon understood characteristics, but such a process would, in all probability, be rather tenuous due to inherent variability. The larger question would be why would anybody wish to do this via a biometric check when such information is already generally available.

The second avenue of exploration is concerned with whether ethnicity might have a bearing on biometric characteristics, in such a manner as might have a bearing upon matching performance. This is an interesting question for which ongoing research may provide an insight. Some hold, for example, that the proportionality of fundamental fingerprint types differs among certain ethnic groups. Others maintain that the amount of textural detail within the iris varies among certain ethnic types. We are aware of course that anatomical and facial details vary to some extent between ethnic groups. The question is whether one particular set of characteristics is more or less distinct than another and whether this has matching performance implications. If it were to transpire that this was the case, then that would make the setting of matching thresholds an interesting exercise as the relative probability of errors would be different for different groups. In addition, the combination of ethnicity with other user factors may provide an interesting operational context. However, this is an area where further research is required before we may draw meaningful conclusions. It may become increasingly pertinent as large-scale public sector systems proliferate.

Well-Being

The notion of well-being is a complex thing in relation to human beings. It is easy to understand how extremes may affect our everyday behaviour and interactions with the world at large. Between these extremes, however, resides a complex graduation of relative well-being, influenced by an equally complex web of internal and external triggers, both biological, environmental and relational. Each of these degrees of well-being will have a corresponding behavioural expression. Behaviour is directly linked to the consistency and efficacy of a biometric identity verification transaction. When personal well-being is at a low ebb, it is natural that the individual will behave in a subtly altered manner, their thinking will be slightly different, their reaction to external influence subtly diverse and their physical stance and body language changed, all of which contribute to a change in the manner in which they interface with an external system. If we overlay onto this perspective the equally complex area of emotions, then we have an additional factor in that emotions can translate directly to physiological change, directly affecting the physical interaction in combination with the behavioural interaction. The combination of these effects will have a direct impact upon realised performance with respect to the biometric identity verification process. The effect in isolation may be more or less subtle; however, in combination with other user factors, it may grow in significance.

The interesting thing about user factors and user psychology in relation to realised performance is the degree to which they can influence that performance. In technical and theoretical terms, we discuss transactional performance in fractions of percentile points. The influence of user factors may be measured in whole percentile points or, in some cases, tens of percentile points. It follows that such factors should be paramount in our understanding of biometric-enabled systems and their operation. Historically, this understanding has been somewhat variable in both its depth and reach, although, as we move forwards with this technology, one might expect this situation to change. In any event, user factors and user psychology should form an important part of our overall systems and operational process design.

Systems Configuration

With respect to systems configuration, we need to be clear as to which system components are in scope and why. It is easy to focus too much attention upon the biometric device and its configuration, yet this is only one of the many components which, together, constitute our system, its practical operation and, consequently, its overall performance. As previously stated, the whole will be no better than its weakest link with respect to realised performance.

Starting with the biometric device, there may be various configurable parameters according to the type of device in question. Perhaps most fundamental will be the threshold setting for the biometric comparison, if indeed matching is being undertaken within the device and not remotely. If the device has an optical sensor, then this may be calibrated according to the prevailing environment, although a degree of automation may be in place in this respect. Indeed, for some devices, there may be no readily available user configurable parameters whilst, for others, it may be assumed that the commissioning engineer will configure the device ready for use. However, where there are configurable parameters, they will almost certainly have an impact upon performance in one way or another.

The biometric device will be connected to the first external processing point, often a computer, even if subsumed into some sort of appliance, via a communications channel. This may be a simple serial connection if part of an overall physical local node. If the first processing point is remote from the device and communication is via a network, then this communication channel must be configured to be both secure and to offer a suitable performance. From here onwards, every systems component, from servers to individual network routers, firewalls and other devices will have its particular configuration. If such configurations are unknown, or have never been checked, then the system will almost certainly exhibit a less than ideal performance and possibly be more vulnerable than it should be from a security perspective. As part of the overall systems design, every such component should be subject to an appropriate, documented configuration which maximises both performance and security. With respect to large, complex systems, this may be a considerable undertaking if not tackled at the time of installation. There are available tools with which to centralise and manage such configurations and their use might be appropriate for wide area networks under the jurisdiction of a single agency. Where third party networks are concerned, the picture becomes more complicated, although one might usefully ask about configuration management for such networks.

Suffice it to say that systems configuration and the management thereof is an important factor with respect to overall performance. It is a little like tuning a motor car. The car will no doubt run, even in a decidedly poor state of tune, but when properly tuned, it will run much better and more reliably. The same is true of large-scale systems. A little attention can make a useful difference to realised performance. Those who never lift the bonnet may not realise the potential of their investment.

Total Systems Performance

We have discussed various factors which can have an effect upon the performance of a system incorporating biometric functionality. Some of these are purely technical, many are not. Ultimately, it is the end-to-end operational performance of the whole system which is important to us. The phrase Total Systems Performance was coined by the author many years ago in order to define this importance. There are various ways of thinking about total systems performance.

From a transactional perspective, total systems performance may be considered as the end-to-end transaction, including all aspects of the workflow, touching every applicable systems component, until the transaction is completed and the system is ready to start another. The performance of every component and process within this chain is therefore in scope and of some importance. This naturally includes communications channels, database access, the matching process and the interface between the user and the technology, including the user variables previously discussed. The sum of these component parts and their operation represents total system performance from a transactional perspective.

Total systems performance is also highly pertinent from a systems administration perspective. Those supporting and maintaining the system must be able to do so efficiently via whatever tools they have at their disposal. Furthermore, the use of such tools must not impact upon the operation of the live system. Factors such as database administration must be as transparent as possible. Similarly any maintenance of network components such as firewalls and routers should not impact upon the normal operation. The tools used in this context will naturally have a bearing upon how seamless and efficient such maintenance may be. There is also systems administration from an operational point of view, in maintaining records, producing reports and other day-to-day tasks, all of which will have a degree of performance associated with them. Report generation, for example, will typically rely upon database queries, which may or may not be optimised, and the formatting capabilities of the report-generating mechanism. Such routine operational functions will have a time element which will, in turn, absorb the time of a human operator, which is another aspect of operational performance.

In short, total systems performance refers to the overall performance of the entire system and its operational processes, all of which may be optimised in order to realise the best performance obtainable given the component parts employed. In this context, we include operational processes as well as physical systems components. All of the variables discussed within this section are pertinent within the context of total systems performance; hence the requirement to understand these variables in some depth and design the system in such a manner as to accommodate every foreseeable operational eventuality. In such a manner, we may effectively manage the performance of our system.

Review Questions

1. Consider aspects of biometric device performance and optimisation.
2. Explain the relevance and operation of the biometric matching threshold.
3. Discuss the purpose and potential value of the User Psychology Index.
4. Identify potential network performance issues and their remediation.
5. Discuss user variables in relation to realised performance.

Equivalence of Performance

7

Abstract An equivalence of realised performance across operational nodes is a highly important factor with respect to large-scale systems, indeed for any system. In this chapter, we explain equivalence of performance and why it is so important. We also explain how it is never achieved within the majority of deployed systems. This additionally leads us into a discussion of equivalence of process across both operational nodes and, where applicable, between systems. We then consider the importance of equivalence of performance from the system operator's perspective, including the visibility of errors and the balancing of error rates against perceived risk. The potential for denial of service and perceived discrimination is discussed, as well as the potential for fraud within a system that has no integral equivalence of performance management and reporting.

The APEX concept and system is introduced as an example of how equivalence of performance may be addressed. The APEX architecture is discussed and overviews are given of the APEX Node software and the APEX Device Simulator and how they may usefully be utilised. The APEX Host software is discussed in some detail, including the directory of nodes, transaction monitoring, real-time alerts generation, the generation of reports and how the host software provides for a complete view of the entire system, whether it consists of a collection of nodes at one operational location, several nodes at several locations within a national context, or multiple nodes at multiple locations within an international context. APEX is the only system to date which provides such functionality. From here we discuss the management of equivalence of performance, including the setting of the performance criterion in relation to the perceived level of risk and how this may be dynamically controlled. We also discuss security factors, systems integration and possible next steps for developing and implementing an equivalence of realised performance functionality for large-scale systems. As such, this is a very important chapter as attention to these issues may provide a very significant operational improvement for relevant systems, in addition to the potential for equally significant cost savings with respect to support and maintenance.

J. Ashbourn, *Guide to Biometrics for Large-Scale Systems: Technological, Operational, and User-Related Factors*, DOI 10.1007/978-0-85729-467-8_7, © Springer-Verlag London Limited 2011

7

Defining Equivalence of Performance

When we use the term *equivalence of performance*, we refer to the equivalence of *realised* performance across operational nodes or points of presence. For example, if a particular user passes through an automated identity verification point at location A, and subsequently passes through an additional identity verification point at location B, he has a right to expect that the technology will perform in an equivalent manner and produce the same result. There may be several operational nodes at a given point of presence, presenting a choice of channels for the user who should expect that they will all perform in precisely the same manner. There may be additional nodes that the user is required to interact with throughout the course of an overall transaction. For example, automated border crossing points at either end of a journey or multiple access control points within a given facility should all perform in an equivalent manner. Even biometric identity verification nodes within systems administered in different locations should ideally perform to an equivalent standard. Thus, if an individual provides his live biometric sample in a consistent manner across multiple nodes, they should all provide the same result within a reasonable tolerance.

The reality is that this is rarely, if ever, achieved due to variables in installation, configuration, environment and ongoing maintenance. This is especially the case where the installation and maintenance of the equipment is undertaken by subcontracted third parties at different locations. Factors such as the biometric matching threshold may be configured differently, or not configured at all, effectively rendering each node as a distinct entity with its own particular performance profile. Even if the technical configuration at individual nodes were to be identical, the realised operational performance from each will be different due to environmental and user factors, as previously discussed. The challenge is therefore to align the performance of disparate nodes, at least within a reasonable envelope of equivalence. This is a factor which is rarely understood with respect to large-scale systems featuring multiple points of presence and multiple operational nodes.

We may extrapolate this concept to additionally, and very usefully, embrace equivalence of operational process across nodes and across systems, especially as operational process may itself impact upon realised performance. The reader will notice the emphasis upon *realised* operational performance, as distinct from theoretical performance or measured performance under test conditions. This is a very important point to take into consideration.

Why Equivalence of Performance Is Important

There are several reasons why equivalence of realised performance is important. These may be subdivided into those pertinent to the operator and those pertinent to the user.

From the Operator's Perspective

Assuming that the object of the operation is to verify the identity of users and identify any fraudulent claims to an identity, the operating agency needs to understand how robustly the identity verification check is being undertaken, according to the level of risk that they have previously identified and accepted. As a part of this operational profile, they will also have defined an error rate which they believe appropriate and acceptable, given the context of the application. For example, in the context of a very high security application, perhaps in the military or government sectors, it would no doubt be considered appropriate to configure the biometric matching threshold towards a very low probability of false acceptance, at the expense of increased errors of false rejection. For an application where such a high level of security is inappropriate, the operator might prefer a more relaxed threshold setting whereby the probability of errors is roughly equal or, perhaps, set to favour a probability of lower false rejection errors, thus promoting flow through the system while inconveniencing as few individuals as possible. In any event, having made such decisions, the operator must have confidence that the realised performance at each node throughout the system is equivalent. If the situation is otherwise, then there is a very real danger that either effective security has been compromised or operational efficiency has been degraded. Consequently, if the operator does not have a close to real-time view of the realised performance, and associated error rates, at each and every node on the system, then they have no understanding of how the system is actually functioning from a performance perspective. Given the relative importance of some of these systems, this is not a good position to be in.

Furthermore, if the operator is challenged by a user, or group of users, as to the equivalence of performance across nodes, claiming perhaps discrimination at certain locations, where, for example, certain users seem to be regularly rejected, then how is the operator to prove such an equivalence in the absence of such an understanding? The answer, of course, is that they will not be able to. There may, in some cases, be legal implications around this factor, especially if such challenges claim an unfair denial of service or discrimination on unfair grounds.

Given the variables already discussed affecting realised performance, it will be appreciated that a mechanism with which to monitor and control equivalence of performance across operational nodes would be desirable, particularly in situations where the collection of nodes in question is administered by a common agency.

From the User's Perspective

From the user's perspective, it is equally important to have confidence that the performance, and therefore the user experience, at each node throughout the system is equivalent. If a user is continually rejected at a particular node, while not having any difficulty at others, he will likely not understand the reason for it. He may wonder whether it is something to do with the way he is presenting his biometric, in which case, attempts to do so differently may simply worsen the situation. He may assume that the equipment is malfunctioning, despite protestations from the operating agency to the contrary. In any event, such a user will be inconvenienced by what they perceive as an incorrect and unfair rejection of their claimed identity. If this level of inconvenience were the only manifestation of such degraded performance, that would be serious enough. In certain cases, however, the inconvenience may be of a substantially more serious nature, possibly leading to an unwarranted arrest and interrogation by law enforcement agencies. If such an experience is repeated, one can imagine that the user will not be best pleased and may seek compensation. In other situations, different forms of unfair denial of service may arise due to a poorly configured and poorly performing operational node. If this only occurs at certain nodes, then, clearly, there is a form of unintentional discrimination at play.

Of course, the reverse could also be the case. Fraudulent users may discover that, at particular nodes, they are always able to fool the system as the biometric matching process seems to recognise almost anybody when aligning a particular biometric. Another possibility might be collusion with a systems administrator or support engineer in order to ensure that this is the case. Legitimate users would not notice and it would therefore be unlikely that such a mis-configuration would be easily noticed. If the operating agency has no means of monitoring such a situation, then what confidence will they have that disparate nodes on the system are performing to an equivalent level? The concept of equivalence of performance may therefore be very pertinent to certain systems, especially those in the public sector.

Facilitating Equivalence of Performance

There may be several ways in which an equivalence of performance may be realised for a given system. By way of example, we shall describe a capability conceived and developed by the author some years ago in order to provide a possible solution for typical large-scale systems. This capability, named APEX, consists of software at each node and at a host control position in order to provide an active monitoring and control system, as shall be described. It utilises an output matching score from the biometric device and integrates with the matching threshold via a feedback loop based upon realised performance at each node. This enables a desired level of performance to be set centrally and downloaded to every node on the system immediately. Each node will then automatically and dynamically adjust its own configuration in order to remain close to the desired performance criteria. This will ensure an equivalence of performance at each node, regardless of the influence of external factors. Furthermore, such an approach enables the performance of the entire system to be adjusted, for example in relation to special conditions or events, from a centralised control position. It also allows for detailed reports to be produced around the performance of both individual nodes and the entire system, thereby providing auditable evidence of maintained equivalence of performance.

The APEX node software, as depicted in Fig. 7.1, sits upon a computer platform at the node position and performs several functions. Firstly, it connects directly to the biometric device and matching engine and takes an output score (degree of likeness) from each transaction. It batches these transaction scores according to a defined sample size and then averages them to produce a representative score at that position. Because it is dealing with actual likeness scores, external factors such as environment and user factors are automatically accommodated. The sample size may be adjusted according to system throughput and the desired granularity of operation. At every batch cycle of sampled transactions, the average is communicated back to the host software where it is written into a transaction database, thus providing an audit trail for every node on the system. This average performance is compared to the desired performance criterion as downloaded from the controlling host software. The biometric matching threshold is then adjusted dynamically in order to approach the desired level of performance. This is undertaken via a sophisticated algorithm which acknowledges the proportionality of any such disparity between realised performance and

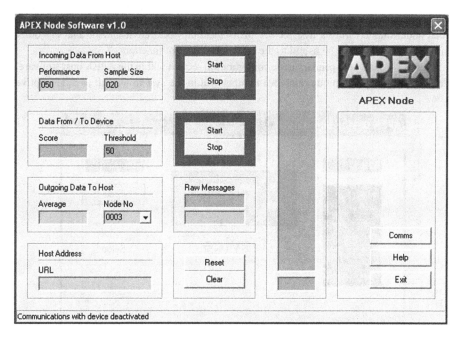

Fig. 7.1 The APEX node software application

desired performance and chooses one of several adjustment factors accordingly. The node software features a graphical interface which enables a commissioning engineer to monitor activity from the node, configure the software and confirm reliable communications across the network. It also enables communications from both the host and the biometric device to be stopped and started if required during the commissioning phase. Once configured and cut over to live operation, the node software will be controlled by the host. In order to verify communications and aid configuration, a device simulator is provided which may be used in isolation from the actual device. This can be useful when a new system is being established and the commissioning engineers wish to prove the network and overall functionality.

The APEX device simulator, as depicted in Fig. 7.2, enables full communication to be tested with the host before live transactions are available. Furthermore, it additionally tests the functionality of the node software as it creates random transaction scores representative of an actual device. It then transmits these scores in the correct protocol to the node. It also has the capability to receive the dynamically adjusted threshold setting and display this for the commissioning engineer, confirming that the node is functioning correctly. In conjunction with the APEX node software itself, this approach enables the entire communications chain, from the centralised host right down to the biometric device, to be tested and verified off-line, that is, in the absence of live transactional data.

At the centralised control position, individual nodes may be configured and brought into the system as they are commissioned and activated. At any time, the operator may force a download of the desired performance criterion and sample size, and a log of all such transactions is maintained within the system. These parameters are common to all nodes and thus ensure an equivalence. The facility exists to add free-form comments about each node, thus creating a true picture of its location, local environment and any other information which may be useful to the centralised control function.

Figure 7.3 shows the primary node configuration section within the APEX host software. Each node is given a unique reference number within the system as well as a descriptive

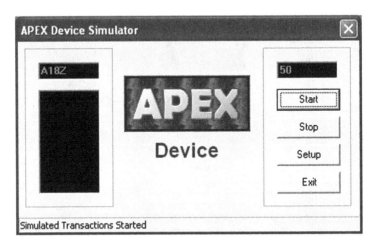

Fig. 7.2 The APEX device simulator

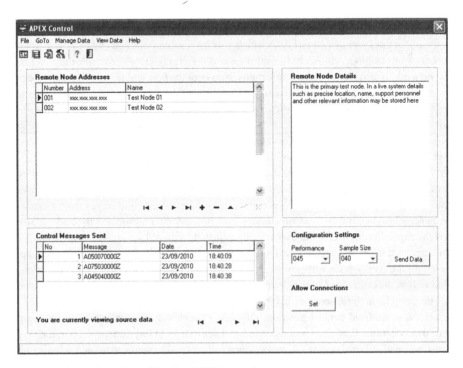

Fig. 7.3 Node configuration within the APEX host software

name, both aligned with a unique network address. Additional information may be added in a text file associated with each node entry within the system. Within this dialogue, the operator may activate the connection and send the performance and sample size data down to the remote node. All such configuration transactions are logged in a format which allows an audit trail of what parameters were sent and at what date and time. The host software is actually quite simple and intuitive in usage, yet also quite powerful in terms of its inherent functionality and the element of control it introduces with respect to realised performance across the entire system (Fig. 7.4).

As previously indicated, each node also communicates back to the host every time its transaction batch cycle is completed, thus providing a date and time stamped audit trail of realised performance at every point within the system. An operator at the control position may therefore see at a glance, and in close to real time, how the overall system is actually performing. In addition, alerts are created in the event of the realised performance at a given node deviating from the desired performance by a significant amount, indicating a possible fault or some other exceptional condition which might warrant investigation. This is a powerful function which is typically not provided for within large-scale systems. The combination of standard messages and alert messages provides for an uncommon and comprehensive understanding of the system and its overall operation from a realised performance perspective. Naturally, all of these messages are additionally being written to an integral database against which reports may be generated. The Manage Data menu item within the host software enables straightforward database backup facilities and the

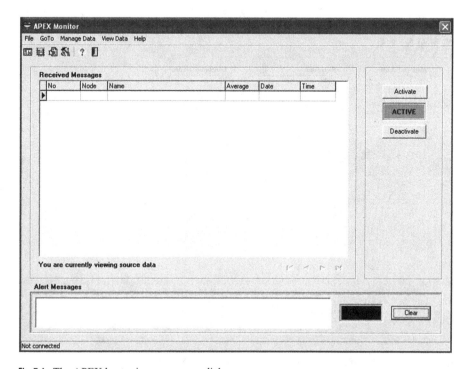

Fig. 7.4 The APEX host primary message dialogue

reloading of data if required. This would allow, for example, transactions from a defined time period, perhaps annually, to be archived and retrieved if ever required. An operating agency might maintain a second copy of the host software upon a separate unconnected platform, specifically to view previously archived data in this manner.

Figure 7.5 shows some additional parameters within the host software. These allow for an operator password to be set or reset and for the alert threshold level to be set, this last setting representing the level of deviation between realised performance and desired performance. It also allows for the number of concurrent nodes for communications purposes. This setting may be useful for very large systems with many nodes if there are communication constrictions of any kind. It simply specifies the number of nodes which may be communicating with the host at precisely the same moment. If a greater number of nodes are attempting communication, their messages will simply be queued and handled sequentially. Lastly, the Allowed Connections list provides a convenient check on all communications network addresses currently active within the system. This can be very useful when verifying the connection to a particular node or, for security purposes, in providing confidence that other connections have not been opened. The host software will only recognise connections which have been explicitly configured as part of the system. All other connections or connection attempts will be blocked. In some ways, this may be considered as a rudimentary firewall functionality, although it does not obviate the necessity for a proper network security architecture to be established.

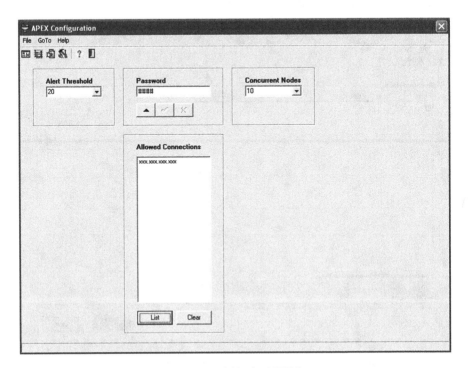

Fig. 7.5 Additional configuration parameters within the APEX host

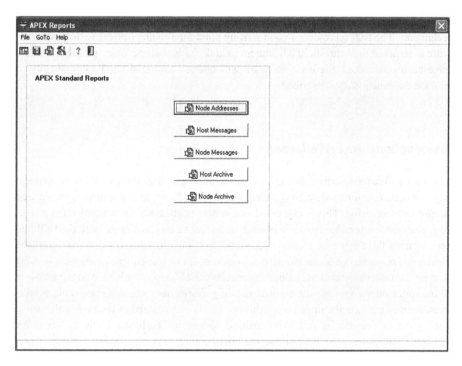

Fig. 7.6 APEX provides an integral reports functionality

As indicated, it is possible to query the APEX database and create various reports (Fig. 7.6). This may be undertaken via a separate purpose-built reports generator if one is used within the operation. However, APEX itself provides some ready-made reports which may be simply generated with a single mouse click. These reports may then be viewed on-screen, printed on any connected printer or saved in a variety of formats for subsequent analysis or distribution within the organisation. Within the context of an actual deployed system, further custom reports may easily be developed and made available within the APEX host software.

These few screen shots demonstrate the elegant, yet powerful, functionality of the APEX concept for providing an equivalence of performance across operational nodes. In fact, it provides for much more than this. It provides for a level of centralised control over the pertinent infrastructure and its performance that is simply not available within contemporary systems. Furthermore, it provides transaction logging, archiving and reporting for all nodes on the system, including for operational performance. Consequently, reports can show unequivocally that an equivalence of performance has been delivered across the system overall. Such reports provide useful evidence in situations whereby equivalence of realised performance may be challenged.

In order to facilitate equivalence of realised performance across operational nodes as described, the biometric devices must be integrated and aligned with the controlling software at the node position. A Biometric Operability Index (BOI) was introduced by the author many years ago in order to align the relative performance of different biometric techniques. The BOI represents a good starting point for aligning devices to the node software in terms of their threshold adjustment granularity and scope. Once these parameters have been established, the node software will operate seamlessly and automatically to provide the functionality described.

Managing Equivalence of Performance

The host software described in the previous section provides the capability to manage equivalence of performance across nodes. The primary factor in this respect is the desired performance criterion. This is expressed as a simple number which corresponds to a level of performance attainable from the biometric devices in use, as aligned with the BOI and representing the degree of likeness score. By manipulating this performance criterion figure, it is possible to bias the biometric devices more towards either a probability of false matches or false non-matches. As this criterion is defined and downloaded simultaneously to all nodes on the system, the equivalence of performance, within a reasonable performance envelope, is maintained across the system. This is assured as the node software at each point of presence is recording realised operational performance as the basis for dynamic adjustment. The operator at the host position may also define the transaction batch size upon which the node software will operate. This provides for an adjustment according to throughput, whereby systems with a low typical throughput may be configured to use a smaller batch size.

The host software described within this illustration thus provides for a very simple, yet very effective, management of the entire system with respect to realised performance and the equivalence thereof across nodes. Furthermore, as the operational parameters are simply downloaded to the nodes across a network, this management capability functions in close to real time.

Security Considerations

Within such an infrastructure as described, it is naturally important to maintain security between the host and node software, ensuring that changes to the performance criterion may only emanate from the host and that reported transactional performance only emanates from bona fide nodes. In addition, we should have confidence as to the integrity of all such data passing back and forth across the network.

There are various approaches and measures which may be taken in this respect. The most fundamental is to secure the network in order to ensure reliability of the transmitted data. This may be undertaken by the provision of a virtual private network and data encryption techniques. The operational nodes all have distinct network addresses and these are the only addresses recognised by the host. Infrastructural firewalls and routers may also hold white lists of these addresses ensuring that no other sources may transmit over the network. Operators and commissioning engineers must also be subject to operational security policies as appropriate to the system at hand. These policies may be reflected in both physical and logical access control procedures. Clear policies should also be established with respect to the desired performance level of the system in relation to operational situations.

Security in this context is really just an extension of the security measures one would ordinarily take with respect to large-scale systems. In most cases there will be existing policies in place which may be reviewed and updated as required to incorporate the biometric functionality and the equivalence of performance mechanism employed.

Systems Integration

Systems integration from the broader perspective remains important, as previously described within these pages. However, there is another layer of systems integration if a sub-system to provide equivalence of performance is implemented. The first item to be considered is the biometric device itself and the interface between the device and the node software. The physical configuration of many nodes in such a system consists of the biometric capture device, a computer, often in the form of a motherboard within an overall enclosure, a local data storage capability and the necessary power supplies. The computer motherboard provides the network communications and any local processing which may be required. The biometric device will often be connected to the motherboard via a serial connection, either a USB connection or RS232 port. Within the computer, in addition to the operating system and communications drivers, will reside any local processing software for the biometric functionality. The motherboard may, in some cases, be a minimalised device as is available from certain suppliers, with an integral processor. Data storage may be provided in the form of a traditional hard disk drive or, increasingly, a solid state drive which typically consumes less power and offers higher performance. As, in this case, all that is required is a minimalised operating system and some local software to facilitate the biometric functionality, a solid state drive is a sensible option.

Onto such a physical platform, we shall also load the node software, and this must communicate with the biometric device, both to receive transaction scores as to degrees of likeness and also to manipulate the threshold setting within the biometric matching engine, which may be integral to the capture device or initiated in software upon the local platform. In any event, we shall need to establish this integration in such a manner that the inherent performance of the biometric device and matching engine is aligned with the node software and the range of the performance criterion to be set centrally. This may require a small amount of work from the biometric device supplier, depending upon the standard configuration of the device in question. Once this integration has been established, the node software may simply be configured with a local network address and the address of the central host, after which communications will occur via the inherent facilities of the on-board computer.

If a local computer is not supplied, for example if the biometric device has all the necessary functionality and communications processing integrated within a single appliance, then a separate small format motherboard and storage capability may easily be established. However, this would probably be an exceptional situation.

7

Having integrated successfully at the node position, a location must be established for the central host software. Typically, within a large-scale system, such an operational administration position, as distinct from localised operational positions, will already exist and it will be a simple matter to load the host software and configure it accordingly. If such a centralised administration does not exist, it is a simple matter to establish a workstation within a suitable location and load the host software onto this workstation, perhaps as a dedicated machine for this particular function. It need not be anything too sophisticated or powerful as the host software will typically consist of a small footprint application with relatively limited resource requirements. Given the points made about security, integrating an equivalence of performance sub-system into an existing system, or designing it into a new build situation, is a relatively straightforward undertaking and should be easily accomplished within most scenarios.

Reporting on Equivalence of Performance

The ability to report upon equivalence of performance within a large-scale system is one of the primary benefits of establishing such a functionality. It is curious that, in many implemented systems employing biometric functionality, there is actually no possibility of reporting upon realised biometric matching performance at each operational node. Given the ramifications of different types of errors, this is somewhat surprising. However, such factors are easily overlooked if the emphasis has been upon other factors within the broader application. Even the simple example sub-system described in this book provides for some very useful reporting upon realised performance across the entire system. This capability may be summarised as follows.

Architecture

Among the useful information obtainable at the host position is that appertaining to systems architecture. All nodes on the system are instantly visible, and identified by name, unique identifier and IP address. Furthermore, for each node, additional information may be recorded as appropriate: for example, details of specific local environments, who is responsible for local technical support and maintenance, date of installation, or any other information which might be useful to understand centrally. In addition, it is possible to see at a glance the IP addresses of all actively connected nodes and, naturally, nodes may be added or disconnected from the central administration position. This functionality alone provides a valuable overview of the scope of the overall system and its connectivity.

Individual Node Performance

The transactional performance of individual nodes is additionally relayed back to the centralised host for every batch sample cycle. We can therefore understand the averaged realised performance at that node in terms of biometric match likeness, as well as precisely how the matching threshold has been set. This enables us to monitor an individual node over time and understand the realised performance at that particular point of presence and how this may have fluctuated and been allowed for via the matching threshold adjustment. From this information we may be able to spot trends, for example at peak throughput periods, or perhaps associated with seasonal variations. We may query this information by date and time in order to provide very specific details for a particular node.

System-Wide Performance

We also have a centralised view of every operational node on the system, providing a complete picture of overall system performance. This may be reported upon in its entirety, or we might group certain nodes together, perhaps by geographic location, in order to understand performance and associated settings by region. This could be extremely useful with respect to systems operating upon a national or international scale and which encompass various user groups. By defining such groups, we can understand where the most significant variances occur. Again, we may query this by date and time in order to provide very specific information according to our particular focus within the broader system. These broader reports may additionally be utilised to demonstrate an equivalence of realised performance across the entire system, or within any part thereof.

Alerts

The ability to immediately understand precisely where and when exceptional conditions have escalated to the point whereupon very large variances are occurring with respect to realised performance will prove invaluable within any large-scale system. As one may define the point at which such variances generate an alert, this represents a valuable functionality within the system overall. Furthermore, all such alerts are logged and may be cleared by a system operator after investigation, providing a valuable audit trail. This capability is generally absent within contemporary large-scale systems.

Configuration

Configuration changes, in terms of desired performance level and sample size sent to all nodes, are logged and date and time stamped. Consequently, we will be able to report upon all such occurrences and which operator made the changes. These reports may then be aligned with the associated policy decisions. Furthermore, we may also align these changes with realised performance experienced at every node on the system, enabling a deeper understanding to be developed as to the effects of changing these parameters. This intelligence would be very pertinent to any decisions made to relax or tighten the biometric matching process according to prevailing conditions.

7

Next Steps

We have shown unequivocally within this section that there are ways in which an equivalence of realised performance across operational nodes may be established. The performance at each node, while not being identical, as this would be impossible, may nevertheless be brought within a fairly tight envelope in order to guarantee an operational equivalence. Depending upon the precise methodology employed in order to provide such a capability, it may be possible to realise many additional benefits associated with this functionality. Furthermore, the technical and practical effort involved in the establishment of such a capability may be relatively trivial in many cases. The necessary components are available; they just need a coherent integration and configuration, aligned with operational policy.

We have additionally shown that there are many good reasons for establishing such a capability. Some of these are directly systems-related, some more related to higher-level operational considerations. In addition, there may be very distinct economies to be realised in this context, especially with respect to larger-scale systems featuring large numbers of operational nodes. Consider, for example, a nation-wide system with installations in several states, deployed within existing infrastructures. The cost of sending commissioning engineers to each point of presence to make local adjustments in order to fine-tune the system would soon become significant, not to mention the timescales involved in scheduling and undertaking such remedial maintenance. With a centralised system as described, such adjustments may be made once and instantly downloaded to every node on the system. In such a manner, the entire system will be operational with the new settings, faster than the time needed to fill out a single work order. Furthermore, not a single engineer will need to be dispatched to site. One can easily imagine that there are significant savings to be made in this area. If and when a particular node is malfunctioning so badly as to generate alerts, the node in question may be precisely identified and, if required, taken off-line pending repair or replacement. Having this level of centralised control would be a boon for many systems. The granularity of such control may be varied. It could be implemented regionally, nationally or even internationally, with nodes grouped accordingly.

Having demonstrated and discussed the potential benefits of such a capability, the next steps for an interested implementing agency would be to perhaps run a pilot system in order to place the idea firmly in an operational context. Such a system might be more or less as described here. For example, another manner of implementation might be with respect to multi-modal biometric systems wherein more than one biometric technique is employed. In such an instance, an equivalence of realised performance between the disparate techniques could be maintained as well as an equivalence across operational nodes. There are many potential variations upon the common theme. The design and implementation of such a pilot system may be relatively straightforward and would provide an additional opportunity to revisit and refine many areas of operational significance. Indeed, significant improvements might be made in the way we implement biometric technology within large-scale operational systems, especially those within the public sector. It is recommended therefore that the concept of equivalence of realised performance across operational nodes be revisited and realigned with future aspirations around the use of biometric technology.

Review Questions

1. Define the equivalence of realised performance as a concept.
2. Discuss the example sub-system described and its potential benefits.
3. Discuss and explore the potential operational reports which might be provided within such a capability.
4. How might the concept be applied to systems featuring multi-modal biometrics, from both an operational and technical perspective.
5. Discuss how operational nodes might be grouped within a system of international scope.

Aligning Biometrics with Data

8

Abstract This chapter is concerned with the data records which are aligned with biometrics. It therefore focuses strongly upon data management and the personal profiles which are constructed and maintained with respect to each individual. It starts by confirming what a biometric identity verification transaction really is and how conclusions are reached with respect to degrees of likeness between two biometrics, based upon a predefined threshold. We discuss the accuracy of the source data appertaining to personal profiles and the unrealistic assumption that, somehow, a successful biometric check validates such information. Consequently, we revisit the registration process and stress the importance of validating any source data at this point, highlighting the ease with which fraudulent identities may be created as a result of weaknesses in the registration process. This leads us to the importance of training for registration facility personnel and, similarly, the importance of an equivalence of process between registration facilities. We discuss the concept of biometrics as simply an additional security feature within existing methodologies and stress that it is the authenticity of the associated data record which is of primary importance, as it is upon such information that transactional decisions are made. Policies around access to such information and how they are enforced in everyday operation are of considerable importance in this context and are discussed accordingly.

Information security is of course vitally important with respect to large-scale systems handling personal information and we discuss the importance of understanding system's infrastructure and associated data flows, as well as factors such as encryption, systems component configuration and the concept of information security embedded into operational processes. Identity theft is becoming widespread and is likely to become even easier with the wider proliferation of personal information. We discuss how a general disrespect for the privacy of both citizens and personal information, coupled to ineffective legislation, is generally exacerbating the situation and we call for a more ethical approach to data management in general.

J. Ashbourn, *Guide to Biometrics for Large-Scale Systems: Technological, Operational, and User-Related Factors*, DOI 10.1007/978-0-85729-467-8_8,
© Springer-Verlag London Limited 2011

8

Introduction

The association between a biometric reference and the data that is aligned with that reference is very interesting. This also represents a very important area for which assumptions are often made, sometimes in error. It is an area which should be at the very heart of any systems design, especially with respect to operational processes. It is also an important factor with respect to the relationship between system users and system administrators. Within a world increasingly focused upon information and the sharing of information, such issues adopt an increasingly important profile. It is as well that we consider them carefully within the context of any planned system, whether within the private or public sectors. In this context, we should also consider associated infrastructural trends such as cloud computing and virtualisation, and what this means from a data management perspective.

What Does a Biometric Check Prove?

In the early days of automated biometric identity verification, a common claim was that a biometric check proves that you are who you say you are. Of course, this is simply not the case; a biometric check proves no such thing. We need to remind ourselves of what exactly is happening when a biometric is compared with another biometric. Usually, but not always, this is a matter of a live biometric being compared either with a single reference sample, or being compared with a collection of reference samples within a database. In every such instance, we are effectively saying, here is a data item, we wish to compare it with this other data item and analyse how closely the two are alike. From this comparison we shall derive a metric of likeness, let us refer to it simply as a percentage of likeness. We define a threshold, above which we consider the comparison a match, below which we consider it a non-match. In simple terms, let us imagine that our threshold is set at 80% and the comparison yields a likeness result of 82%. We may thus consider this a match. If the comparison were to yield a likeness result of 69%, we shall consider it a non-match. All we are doing is comparing two sets of data and, according to predefined criteria, reaching a conclusion as to whether they are alike enough to be considered a match. When searching through a database of reference biometrics, we may find that our search returns several possible matches. This is purely a data processing exercise. At this juncture we have no idea as to the source of the biometric.

By aligning a particular biometric reference with a unique identifier and a set of associated data items, we create a personal profile. The accuracy of this profile will depend very much upon how the associated data was gathered and to what extent it has been independently verified. The personal profile may be completely accurate, completely false or somewhere in between as a result of confused processes. To assume that the personal profile must be accurate because the biometric check has returned a match is somewhat disingenuous. We must bear in mind what the match result is actually telling us, and combine this intelligence with other factors in order to reach a reasonable conclusion. There exists a good deal of misunderstanding around this point, and such misunderstandings may lead to complications with respect to operational process and the granting of privileges or denial of service, based upon incorrect assumptions. We should not consider a biometric as a replacement for our usual rigour with respect to managing personal data in a secure and responsible manner. We should certainly never consider a biometric as positive proof of identity.

The Registration Process

The registration process with respect to an application which features biometric identity verification will consist of a combination of capturing a reference biometric sample and creating a personal profile with which to align it. Capturing the biometric is simple enough, although care should be taken with respect to the quality of the created reference. Some registration software allows for a quality metric, ensuring that, if the captured sample is poor, an opportunity to recapture and recreate the reference exists. This is actually quite important as a poor quality biometric reference will cause many problems in subsequent live comparisons. For some individuals, the process of providing a good quality biometric reference may be complicated for reasons beyond their immediate control. It may be that their particular biometric trait is less distinct than is usual. It may be that, due to disabilities or illness, it is not easy for them to interface with the biometric capture device. For example, those suffering with arthritis in the hands may find it difficult to consistently provide a fingerprint. Those who are wheelchair bound may find it difficult to align with a camera device for a facial recognition or iris recognition image capture. Those who are poor sighted may find it difficult to interact with any such system. Exceptions such as these should be acknowledged and catered for within the overall registration process (Fig. 8.1).

However, perhaps the greatest issue with the registration process, is verifying the identity of the individual by documentary means and thus creating an accurate personal profile with which to align with the biometric. This is a particularly serious situation with regard to the creation of national identity documents containing a biometric. Organised criminals will not have been slow to realise this weakness, as well as the potential for a documented identity authenticated by government, that may be verified automatically via a biometric. Indeed, with a little forethought, it would be possible to create multiple fraudulent identities of the kind. The same may be said for illegal immigrants seeking to authenticate a fraudulent identity and subsequently claim benefits to which they are not entitled. Consequently, the vigour with which associated claims of identity are verified prior to registering the biometric and associated personal profile becomes paramount if we are not to unwittingly create a plethora of fraudulent identities. This situation is exacerbated by the illogical assumptions we make around the validity of a national identity document when it contains a reference biometric. This is a serious factor with respect to identity management and the use of biometrics overall, and one which is rarely given enough attention. The ease with which breeder documents may be created in order to create a fraudulent identity, especially within our contemporary digital world, facilitates the possibility of such a fraud for almost anyone who chooses to pursue such a strategy (Fig. 8.2).

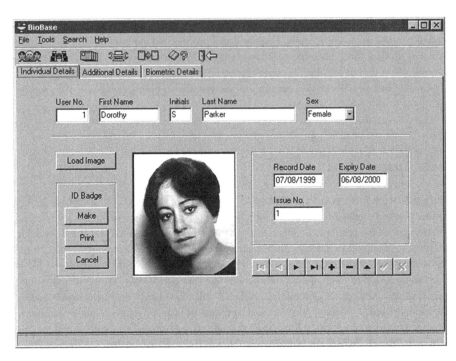

Fig. 8.1   The registration process may be more or less sophisticated

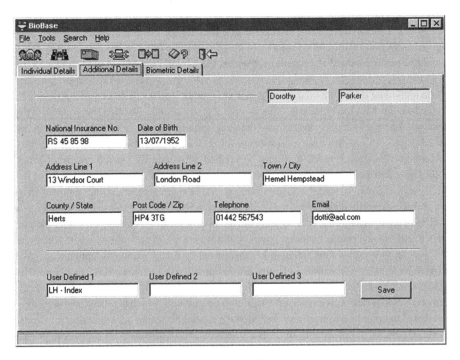

Fig. 8.2   What level of additional detail may be captured?

Those officiating at a registration facility should therefore be especially trained to detect such attempts and, if they are in the slightest doubt, should refuse the application and refer the individual for further investigation. Furthermore, the type of acceptable documentary evidence should be chosen very carefully and cross referenced with other sources in order to verify its validity. This should be a rigorous and well-defined process which is adhered to without exception. Unfortunately, especially in the early days when relevant agencies where in a rush to issue such documents, such a rigour was rarely practiced, and still may not be in many cases. The reader may perhaps appreciate how vitally important the registration process is and how we must beware of making assumptions around the validity of a claimed identity, simply because a biometric is involved. If the registration process is not especially robust and delivered by properly trained individuals, who themselves have been properly vetted, then problems will undoubtedly arise, as has been demonstrated within the national identity document issuing offices of several countries, including those claiming to have advanced systems in place.

The same applies, albeit in a slightly different way, to operational systems within the private sector. Having established a fraudulent identity, for whatever purpose, if the presence of a biometric, and a successful biometric check, is assumed as positive verification of this identity, then the acquisition of such an identity becomes an attractive proposition for fraudsters. Organisations operating such systems should therefore be just as diligent in their registration processes and take particular care over the issue of any associated tokens, documents or the creation of stored identities. The addition of a biometric to any such token should be viewed simply as the addition of another security feature, among many such features, all of which should be checked at an operational point of presence. It does not in any way lessen the requirement for a comprehensive check and verification of any documentary evidence produced to support the claim of a given identity. If the associated process is less than robust in any respect, then there is a possibility of fraudulent identities being inadvertently or, with collusion, deliberately created. This need not be in the form of a brand new identity, but could simply be beneficial attributes added to an existing identity in order to obscure the truth. In any event, once this has occurred, the likelihood that such fraudulent identities will ever be discovered is very slight indeed. The assumption that the addition of a biometric somehow prevents this is a seriously flawed one. The registration process is therefore a critical element with respect to any system providing identity management functionality, with or without the addition of a biometric. Indeed, if a biometric is involved, one might posit that the registration process becomes even more critical. Our operational processes should reflect this reality.

With respect to large-scale systems upon, for example, a national scale, it is likely that a number of registration facilities will be required. Depending upon the size and geography of the country concerned, the requirement might be numbered in tens or hundreds. The issue then becomes, in addition to all that discussed above, one of equivalence across these disparate registration centres. Equivalence, indeed, in all things, from equivalence of process to equivalence of staff training, to equivalence of technical infrastructure, to equivalence of security. It follows then that the model employed for the first such facility must be easily replicated. It also follows that if serious errors are present within the operational processes of the first facility, these might also be replicated, at least until their discovery and remediation. This brings us back to good systems design, part of which involves planning and ensuring a logical scalability. If the original registration facility is properly conceived, designed and implemented, it will be a simple enough matter to use this as a template and create copies wherever needed. A little like retail franchises perhaps, although the importance of maintaining an equivalence of operational quality is more pronounced. Good documentation can go a long way to ensure that such replication is practically achievable, and in an efficient manner. This includes documentation of the technical architecture, the technical configuration, the physical design, the operational process, exception handling routines and all other aspects of the facility and its operation.

With respect to large-scale systems of international scope, things become a little more complex as, with rare exceptions, one country will typically not be in a position to define and enforce the operational processes of another. Certainly, intelligent agreements based upon friendly cooperation may be in place. However, this places much on trust and the reality may be more difficult to align. Then there is the question of countries who, while considered perhaps as friendly nations, actually have little in common when it comes to official processes, especially those around identity management and national identity documentation. There are of course many agreements and many standards, with equally many variations upon how these are interpreted. The question comes down to the level of trust that one administration may have in the registration processes, and therefore the quality of national identity documentation, of another administration. Practical experience in this context may sometimes find itself at odds with binding legal agreements, creating a rather confusing overall picture. Nevertheless, if a clear understanding is not in place, this factor renders any theoretical advantage of embracing biometric technology rather weaker than anticipated. In this respect, it would be well to return to first principles and develop a certain clarity of purpose at the highest level, before drilling down to the design of a system for practical implementation. As with many aspects of biometrics and identity management, we must sometimes step back a little in order to appreciate the broader picture in its entirety. There exists a temptation, and indeed a tendency, to focus too closely on the biometric technology itself while failing to set it firmly in context. This is an avoidable error.

Associated Data Records

There are various data records which may be aligned with a particular personal profile, some of these will be in the form of static information and others in the form of recorded transactions. In all cases, such records are subject to manipulation in the form of information updates, corrections and appended information. As the data are shared between agencies and commercial organisations, such potential manipulation increases in scope. Consequently, if a data record contains errors, or is deliberately falsified, such errors may be compounded across many systems and even geographic boundaries. A biometric identity verification transaction will serve to bind the individual to whatever data is available at the particular point of presence. This may be fine for the majority of occasions, if there is nothing indicated in the data which might effect a denial of service or, conversely, bestow a privilege to which the individual is not entitled. Such decisions tend to be made in light of the available information, once the biometric has been verified. Data accuracy therefore plays an essential part within any operational system wherein identity management is a key function. We are in effect not managing a *real* identity, but managing a *digital* identity which is itself a composite of many items and associated transactions. Furthermore, this *digital* identity may reside in numerous disparate systems, each of which appends a particular complexion to the stored identity, an identity of which the individual in question may be completely unaware. A simple error may therefore cascade and be amplified through numerous links to the point at which it is accepted by the organisation or agency in question as the truth. A successful biometric identity verification transaction will often serve to confirm this truth in the eyes of the implementing agency, regardless of its basis in fact (Fig. 8.3).

The reality is that information is constantly collected in relation to a given individual at almost every turn, building into a composite digital identity or personal profile. However innocent such transactions might be, they may, when aligned with other data, serve to create a false impression. In many cases, for example when an individual incorrectly gets a poor credit rating, this can be difficult, or even impossible to correct. Depending upon exactly when such an error is noticed, the individual in question may be able to get the record corrected in one place, but will typically not even know how many other places this information has been cascaded to. The result is a far from unified personal profile existing across a plethora of systems and services. A more extreme example occurs when an individual obtains a criminal record incorrectly. This can occur for a number of reasons and through no fault of the individual. Once such a record has been established, even if subsequently cleared at source, it may taint the personal profile of the individual for ever more and may, under some scenarios, lead to serious denial of service, without perhaps the individual understanding why.

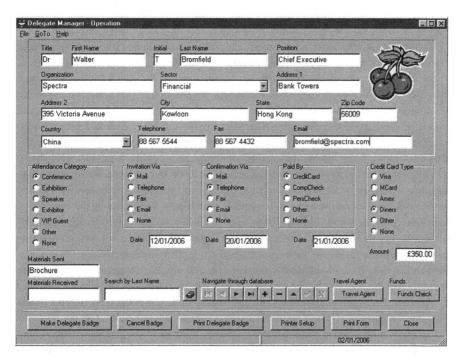

Fig. 8.3 Information being collected in everyday transactions

The inclusion of this section serves to emphasise the reality that, irrespective of the identity management technique employed, it is the underlying data within the associated personal profile which informs transactional decisions at the point of presence. We must beware of falling into the trap of supposing that, because a biometric identity verification check has been successful, this in some way validates the data held in relation to a given individual. There may be all sorts of reasons why such data is, in fact, incorrect and should not form the basis of any such decision. This may work for or against the interests of both the individual and the implementing agency. The establishment of a new system, which incorporates biometric functionality, may provide an opportunity for data cleansing with respect to such personal profiles. In any event, we should be careful in how associated data might be related to our own systems and their resulting transactions.

Access to Information

Given the discussion within the previous section, it follows that access to such information is an important factor. Controlling access from an everyday operational perspective may be easily accomplished via contemporary methods, although these do vary in their overall security. A simple password, for example, is easily compromised and passed between individuals. A logged on administrator may leave the terminal unattended for a period of time. A systems or database administrator may effectively have access to all such personal information unless specifically blocked from doing so. These are all security weaknesses which are understood and may be remediated via the implementation of robust controls, coupled with an equally robust logging, and alerting system, creating an effective audit trail.

However, of greater concern perhaps are the policies which define who may have access to such information and under what circumstances. Ideally, no one should have access to any of this information unless it is explicitly required within the context of an operational transaction, in which case, it may be accessed for the duration of that transaction only. No one should be able to browse through such information randomly, or be able to generate reports or copy it to other locations. Furthermore, the information should be encrypted wherever stored and also encrypted in transit if it is referenced remotely for legitimate transactional purposes. Such fundamental controls would seem logical enough, yet it is surprising how often they are not in place. Often, the reason for this is to be found either in inadequate operational policies, or a disconnect between policies and system configuration. This reality is often reflected within the organisation hierarchy, whereby those defining the operational policy are completely removed from those responsible for configuring, operating and maintaining the system. Operational policies are, in themselves, worthless if they do not flow down into systems design and systems configuration. Furthermore, an effective log management and alerting system should be enabled and aligned with the operational policy in order to ensure that the policy is indeed reflected within the day-to-day operation of the system.

The situation becomes complex when personal information is shared between systems and between agencies. Even if reasonable access controls are in place within the host system, there is no guarantee that the same applies to third party systems which are able to access the data. As data is replicated throughout these systems, any such lack of control is accentuated accordingly. As many such data sources are shared or otherwise connected internationally, the situation quickly becomes out of control as no one assumes overall responsibility for access to information. The situation is further exacerbated as data often flows through third party networks and infrastructures with various levels of inherent trust. Who knows who is maintaining such networks and infrastructures, what access rights they have and what potential control they may exercise over the data as it passes through? The advent of cloud computing and virtualisation will further confuse this picture. An implementing agency should understand completely the end-to-end systems network and be able to account for the data at every point, ensuring that access to information is absolutely controlled at every juncture. While this may indeed be complicated due to the technical and operational architecture of typical large-scale systems, anything less will result in the potential for compromise. As we have witnessed only too often, such comprises are readily translated into serious data loss, data misappropriation and data corruption. The public sector in particular does not enjoy a very good record in this respect and this is an area which should be given particular attention.

Verifying Information

An interesting phenomenon exist within the broader information technology paradigm as to the relative trust placed in available information. When a record is first created which contains personal information, we are reliant upon the quality of the external information and associated evidence, used to populate the record. We are also reliant upon the integrity and competence of the system operator who created that record. Any errors, whether introduced deliberately or as a result of incompetence, will be embedded into that record. When the record is subsequently accessed from an operational perspective, it is generally assumed that the data it contains is correct. As this record is shared between agencies and replicated across systems, this assumption is similarly proliferated. As previously discussed, other information may be appended to these records, based upon the assumption that the original data is correct and, this additional information is also of course subject to errors. As the data proliferates, the probability that it is harbouring inaccuracies increases proportionally. Yet, we place an unwarranted confidence in the integrity of this data. It might be as well to verify the data periodically, especially if it is being used with respect to important transactions.

Of course, the first place at which to verify data is at the registration stage. Whatever documentary evidence is presented at the time should be subject to subsequent verification, even if this is conducted off-line, before a given record is regarded as complete. Operational personnel will no doubt argue that, given the number of applications, especially in relation to public sector applications, such verification is impractical. However, failure to properly verify information at this stage will simply lead to further issues downstream which may absorb a great deal more time and effort in the long run. The degree to which such verification takes place must of course be sensibly aligned with the perceived risk at hand. However, no verification at all is a practice which would seem hard to justify under any scenario.

Once data has become operational and is subject to all the manipulation previously referred to, it may become systematically detached from reality. It would seem sensible therefore to periodically verify the accuracy of data as aligned with a particular biometric. There are various ways in which this might be accomplished. One way would simply be to take advantage of any interaction with the individual concerned in order to check the validity of data, at least from their perspective. Another would be flag each record according to the date it was last verified and systematically re-verify information which has aged beyond a certain threshold. Yet another approach might be to undertake random checks upon records, verifying the information therein against external sources wherever possible. If any potential errors present themselves, these may be discussed with the individual concerned and updated accordingly. In any event, some sort of systematic data verification would benefit most large-scale applications. It is curious to consider that this rarely seems to be the case. Consequently, and especially with respect to deliberate fraud, a record created in, or containing serious errors, may never actually be discovered. With regard to large-scale systems and applications, it would be worthwhile to maintain a small team whose express purpose is to verify the accuracy of information aligned with a biometric within personal records.

Information Security

Popular definitions of information security often include factors such as confidentiality, data integrity and availability. Confidentiality in so far as preventing unauthorised access to information, data integrity with respect to ensuring that the data cannot be modified and availability to ensure that the data is available where and when it is needed. These fairly high-level definitions, while useful enough, do not provide much of an insight as to where potential problems may exist and how we might remediate them. Furthermore, there are various facets of information security which cut across these broad definitions. Identity theft, for example is a particular concern where we are managing large and interconnected databases of personal information. Web security, especially with respect to the use of web browsers as front-end interfaces to operational systems, is another area with which we should concern ourselves, as is wireless technology. In short, there is no all-embracing panacea for information security. We must understand our broader system and its potential vulnerabilities in some detail and ensure that best practices are followed with regard to the associated configuration and operational process.

A good first step is to understand how data flows throughout the system. This includes its operational state both at rest and in transit. For example, is the data encrypted in storage? If so, at what point is the data decrypted and what exactly is this mechanism? If certificates and keys are used, then how are these managed? As the data flow across the network, it will pass through various system components, all of which should be configured properly in order to allow only legitimate communications, with everything else blocked. These components include database and application servers, routers, firewalls and terminal devices, whether personal computers or some other interface. In each case, unused ports should be closed and strict access control maintained throughout. Operating systems and middleware should have the most recent security patches in place and a system should be established in order to maintain currency in this respect. Links and feeds to others systems often represent vulnerabilities in themselves, depending upon which protocols are used and how exactly the information flows between one system and another. These are all straightforward information security factors appertaining to the physical infrastructure and are easily attended to.

Just as important as infrastructural security, indeed, some would say of more importance, are the operational processes which govern how a system is used, including how information is accessed and processed. Ensuring that only the right people may access personal information, and only when it is absolutely necessary to do so in order to perform their operational function, is paramount. This may be achieved via logical access control using directories, groups and permissions. However, such an access control methodology must be carefully managed and, it is often in this area that vulnerabilities creep in. In particular, we must be very careful as to how administrator privileges are assigned and we must establish segregation of duties in order to ensure that administrators cannot access personal information in plain text form. The technology exists with which to implement these controls and yet, it is astonishing to find how often inappropriate access is granted to personal information, especially within public sector systems.

We must also think logically about factors such as identity theft and how personal information may be systematically gathered with respect to a given individual, building up a profile which, with a little imagination, might be abstracted for criminal purposes. This will become easier as social networking via the web proliferates and, to some extent, as individuals are encouraged to diverge more and more information about themselves. However, often the key piece of information that an identity thief needs in order to successfully hijack an identity, can be provided by public sector systems. It is therefore in everybody's interest to ensure that such personal information is properly protected, both from an infrastructural and process perspective. Strong information security does not happen automatically, we need to design it into the very fabric of our systems. Furthermore, having established it, we need to maintain it over time and ensure its ongoing efficacy.

Another interesting area in this context is that of web security. Apart from the reality that the Internet itself is a third party untrusted system, web technology has many inherent flaws which might compromise the security of information. Chief among these is the web browser, and while it is true that advances have been made in recent years, the web browser is still a cause for concern from a security perspective. This is ironic in a way as application development has veered towards using browser-based user interfaces, even for systems which are running entirely in-house upon dedicated infrastructures. Many such vulnerabilities may be ameliorated by good design and web developers may like to follow best practice as described, for example via the OWASP initiative, which also publishes a list of typical vulnerabilities. Factors such as injection flaws, for example, are particularly pertinent as a bogus SQL injection could result in the misappropriation of data upon a large scale. Cross-site scripting could allow malicious script to be executed within a browser interface, effectively hijacking a session, perhaps temporarily and without the knowledge of the user, and manipulating the data accordingly. There are many well-known vulnerabilities in this context which seasoned web developers with an understanding of security will be able to protect against via good coding practices. Similarly, a sensible configuration of web browsers can go a long way in protecting against such eventualities. Whether the same rigour is applied to the interfaces of identity management systems would be an interesting question to ponder. Security of information is an important factor with respect to any IT system. For public sector applications dealing with the personal information of citizens, it is of particular importance. The use of third party networks and, with the advent of cloud computing, third party infrastructures, accentuates this importance to the degree where it should be of primary concern at the design, implementation and operational phases, as well as being embedded within operational policy and associated processes. Anything less will represent a vulnerability in itself.

Data Protection and Privacy

Ever a thorny issue, the reality of data protection and privacy has become far removed from the popular notion held by many. Most would defend privacy as a basic human right and would include in that definition the privacy of their personal data. Most national administrations have data protection instruments of one sort or another which they like to quote when expedient to do so. However, these are riddled with so many exceptions, mostly on behalf of government agencies, that they become practically worthless. The notion that your personal information should not be used for purposes other than what it was collected for, should not be passed to third parties without your express consent and should not be bought and sold without your knowledge or consent, is effectively trashed by our contemporary government agencies who do all of these things routinely. After all, they can always claim that it is in the interest of national security or the collection of taxes, for which purposes they may effectively do anything they like with your personal information. The problem is, having demonstrated such disrespect for the privacy of citizens and their personal information, government agencies have set a precedent which commercial organisations have been happy to follow. It matters not whether you tick little boxes on forms or websites to opt out of such shenanigans, your personal information is bought, sold, shared, divulged and generally manipulated completely outside of your knowledge or control. Furthermore, as an individual, you have absolutely no idea of exactly where this data is actually stored, to what extent it has been replicated and who is using it for what purpose. The situation has become deplorable, mostly as a direct result of government probing increasingly into the private lives of citizens under the guise of national security and law enforcement, creating a precedent for the private sector to follow. This is evident in many interactions with the financial sector, for example where the divulgence of personal information which has absolutely no bearing upon the transaction at hand, is often insisted upon or the service denied. Whether all of these measures have made the world a safer or better place may be open to debate, but they have certainly created a mess with regard to both the amount of personal information in circulation and to its relative security. From this situation, questions must also arise as to the accuracy of such information.

In recent times, national data commissioners and similar agencies have, in some areas at least, acquired stronger powers of enforcement in relation to data breaches. While there will undoubtedly be some high profile cases of imposed fines for serious neglect, it is unlikely that such agencies will have an impact upon the routine disrespect for personal information that currently proliferates. However, attitudes may change over time. In any event, from a systems implementation perspective, we should ensure more than just a token adherence to place data protection acts with all their ambiguities. We should recognise and respect the principles of information privacy, whether or not expressly articulated within an official act. In particular, we should forbid, and take steps to prevent, the sale of information held in trust within our systems to third parties. Similarly, such data should not be used for any purpose other than that for which it was expressly gathered, with the consent of the user. Furthermore, we should publish a clear policy which sets out precisely what data is gathered and why, how it is to be used, how and where it is stored, how it is backed up, what links exist to third party systems and why, what the data retention policy is and how the data is destroyed when no longer required or pertinent to the function or transaction for which it was collected. Individual users must also be able to check the information held within their profile and ensure that, if incorrect, it is updated accordingly. The provision of this service should be straightforward and without cost to the individual.

It is only by adopting ethical practices such as described above at the local agency or organisation level that the situation might gradually improve with respect to data protection and privacy. While it is outside the scope or remit of this work to document proposed best practice in this respect, it will not be difficult for implementing agencies to do just this, at least as far as their particular application is concerned. Such a document may then be openly published, thus setting an example which others might follow. In such a fashion, improvements may be effected over time. There is an inherent responsibility here not just for current practices and held records, but for the future understanding of the relationships between citizens and state, citizens and commercial organisations and the general efficacy, and therefore levels of trust inherent in such systems. Indeed, it is a question of social wellbeing within a technological age. To date, we have not distinguished ourselves in this area. It is time for a change.

Review Questions

1. Define and discuss exactly what a biometric identity verification transaction actually tells us.
2. Discuss the registration process and identify the most important factor thereof.
3. Discuss logical access control for the purposes of systems administration, where it might be implemented and why.
4. Discuss information security, both from the broader perspective and, in particular, with reference to biometric sub-systems.
5. Define and document a best practice advisory with respect to data protection and privacy which improves upon current practice.

The Mobile World

Abstract Within our deliberations around large-scale systems, we cannot ignore the mobile world and the impact that mobile technology is having upon everyday transactional activity. This chapter acknowledges the phenomenal growth of mobile phone technology and its acceptance worldwide, discussing both the scale of this growth and the attendant growth in the development of device form and functionality. It witnesses the veritable technology explosion, fuelled by commercial gain and the opportunity to change what had been a largely social telecommunications service into one of the most lucrative business opportunities of contemporary times. Such dramatic technological change necessarily imposes an equally dramatic cultural change, especially with regard to younger generations and their understanding of technology and social interaction. Such matters are discussed, along with the development of mobile devices for payment purposes and how personal identification is weaved into this overall framework.

We then consider how biometrics may be used in relation to mobile devices, whatever their form factor, and predict a rise in interest in biometric technology as the mobile world becomes all-pervasive. Such rapid development introduces many new challenges, particularly from a security and personal identification perspective and it may be that biometrics can perform a useful function in this respect. We ponder the situation as mainstream applications seek to catch up with the rapid developments in mobile technology, increasingly offering services which exploit mobile functionality. This, in turn, will introduce yet more security-related challenges. Lastly, we consider mobile futures, including the relationship with cloud computing, cloud-based services and cloud data storage. The mobile world and biometric technology may be destined to embrace each other in a significant manner within the near future.

Introduction

There has rarely been a technology that has developed as rapidly as that of mobile devices, especially mobile phones. It was not that long ago, 1983, that the first commercially viable mobile phone was demonstrated. These early devices were large, relatively heavy instruments which were fairly expensive, had little coverage and quickly lost their power. Indeed,

J. Ashbourn, *Guide to Biometrics for Large-Scale Systems: Technological, Operational, and User-Related Factors*, DOI 10.1007/978-0-85729-467-8_9,
© Springer-Verlag London Limited 2011

in the early days, car based units, or car-phones as they became popularly known, were more practical as they could draw power from the car's electrical system and also make use of a proper antenna. Nevertheless, as cellular networks became established, the mobile phone was destined to become increasingly popular, with around 12 million or so cellular subscriptions by the year 1990. Today, it is estimated that there are more than 4.6 billion subscriptions world-wide. In less than 30 years, an idea which seemed at best impractical, has enveloped the world and created a user base of staggering proportions, even if one allows for users holding multiple subscriptions.

The form and functionality of mobile phones has also changed dramatically since those early days. Devices which were akin to a house brick in their weight and proportions can now sit almost unnoticed in a shirt pocket. Initially, the novelty of being able to make a phone call from almost anywhere was enough to ensure popularity of the concept. Nowadays, such functionality would be considered trivial, as most devices have the ability to also send and receive images, browse the Internet and much more.

A Technology Explosion

The situation described above has attracted the world's largest and most powerful electronics and telecommunications organisations, as there are significant profits to be made from the mobile revolution. Little wonder that competition is fierce and both device suppliers and service providers are constantly striving to introduce new capabilities, whether for fashionable or more practical purposes. The ability to send text messages was in itself quite revolutionary, but this quickly expanded to full-blown email capabilities and, perhaps inevitably, the ability to access the Internet. Such capabilities caused the form factor of the devices to change, in order to include a miniature high resolution display. Thus equipped, it was an easy matter to incorporate a camera device which, as expected, has become popular for all sorts of reasons. Modern devices typically also include the ability to play music files via earphones, to act as a radio or even a GPS device. Indeed, contemporary high-end mobile phone has capabilities not far removed from a personal computer, but in a package which weighs just a few ounces and is truly a marvel of miniaturisation.

Such a technology explosion must necessarily impact upon contemporary technologies. The mobile phone has effectively killed the Portable Digital Assistant (PDA) market, as many phones incorporate similar capabilities. In a sense, this is unfortunate as the concept of a well-designed PDA was found useful by many. The concept of very small personal computers, also being redefined as hybrid mobile devices, replace conventional netbooks or even notebook personal computers. Such comparisons of capabilities have also served to raise the cost of high-end mobile phones to a level which is almost bizarre, far eclipsing any notion of material worth. Currently, it would be possible to purchase two very capable netbook computers for less than the cost of some of the popular mobile phones. However, the impact is not only upon contemporary technology. The provision of communications services has also been severely impacted. Having found that subscribers will pay more for their mobile communication service, the service providers have tended to also increase charges for landline subscribers, forcing up the cost of communications for everyone. Furthermore, the traditional telephone boxes which have served communities well for many decades are disappearing rapidly in many countries as service providers cannot be bothered to maintain them while such huge profits are to be made from both mobile and fixed communications. We have indeed witnessed a cultural revolution as well as a technological one. Such is progress. And such progress introduces both benefits and challenges. Among the challenges are the security of information, the misappropriation of device presence by third parties and identity verification, a topic we shall explore later. There exist additional concerns from a health and well-being perspective, although these are currently debatable and are, in any event, outside the scope of this particular work. There is also the interface between mobile devices, whatever their form, and other systems to consider, including the security of the same.

Functionality

The functionality of mobile devices has developed in many directions and supported other modern digital phenomena as mobile devices entwine with popular culture. For example, social networking via the Internet has readily spilled over to mobile phones which may be used to view blogs, post messages and interact with web-based content in a variety of ways. Online gaming and community gaming represents a popular usage of such devices and, no doubt, other activities such as online gambling. Interaction with the Internet, logically extends to online purchases, undertaken from a mobile device. Increasingly, payment may be made for low value transactions, such as train fares, for example simply by presenting the mobile device to a near field communications point. This payment by phone capability introduces several interesting issues, especially around the legitimate use of the device for such a purpose. Consequently, in addition to administrative controls associated with the mobile communications contract between subscriber and service provider, additional measures have been introduced in order to identify individual devices. Most mobile phones, for example, incorporate a SIM card which incorporates details of the subscriber and associated service and of the device itself. In addition, many devices have an embedded unique identifier. SIM cards may of course be exchanged between devices, enabling subscribers to change devices, maintain multiple devices with different functionality, or perhaps maintain multiple subscriptions for different types of usage. Such identification measures become important, not just for the purposes of communications service charging, but with respect to the broader functionality of the mobile phone which, in many instances, may be functioning more like a personal computer in connecting to networks, accessing and downloading information and so on. Then of course we have devices which are portable personal computers but which have wireless connectivity capabilities, including the ability for voice over IP telecommunications. These come in a variety of guises from netbooks and notebooks to tablet like devices with touch sensitive screens. These devices may be identified by IP address and, occasionally, other unique identifiers and some also accommodate SIM cards. In short, we now have a massive global wireless capability with a huge subscriber base and functionality which seems to be increasing every day. As functionality increases, the need to identify both devices and subscribers becomes increasingly pertinent. A potential issue in this respect is being able to identify who is actually using the device for a particular transaction. It may or may not be the subscriber.

Personal Identification

Identity verification in relation to a wireless transaction is important from several perspectives. From a network perspective it is important to understand who is using the network services. From a host system perspective, it is important to understand who is logging on to the host system and to have confidence that access controls are not being abused. From a payments perspective, it is important to understand who has purchased a service and may be charged accordingly. From a users perspective, it is important to have confidence that, should they misplace their mobile device, a stranger will not be able to easily impersonate them and undertake spoof transactions. This last point is especially important in cases of dispute as to precisely who has accessed a host system, conducted a purchase, used an online service or conducted some other transaction. However, many unique identifiers have been incorporated into the device or removable configuration cards, we cannot be absolutely sure as to who has conducted the transaction.

The concept of biometrics will naturally appeal to many in this respect. After all, if one can simply provide a fingerprint via a touch sensitive interface, or even a dedicated fingerprint sensor then, surely, this must prove who made the transaction? Or maybe use face recognition via a built-in camera device? Or iris recognition? Or voice verification for telephone calls? Or perhaps a combination of such methods? Certainly, in theory at least, there are many possibilities. However, practical reality requires many factors to be in place before such a methodology may be relied upon. Firstly, there is the question of where the reference biometric is stored and where the biometric identity verification takes place. If it takes place on the device itself and the device is simply outputting a binary pass or fail tag across the wireless network, then how easily might this binary message be spoofed? Even if we implement a password and a biometric as a two factor function, if the output result can be spoofed, then our efforts are to no avail. However, there may be measures we can take from a network security perspective which make this quite difficult and thus render such a likelihood as a relatively low risk. Alternatively, if we capture the live biometric locally and match it against a reference stored remotely within the host system, then we shall have to have a suitable technical infrastructure in place, including a high performance database and communications channel. Moreover, we shall have to have some manner of trusted registration process which provides confidence as to who the reference biometric really belongs to. And of course, in either case, we shall have to define a biometric matching threshold which we consider suitable according to the balance of perceived risk and usability. Whether this threshold is going to be suitable for every user, whether we allow it to be varied and whether it may be maliciously varied are questions which we shall have to ask ourselves with respect to such a systems design and implementation.

Nevertheless, the concept of using a biometric on a mobile device for certain wireless transactions is bound to be of increasing interest. It may be, for example that ways could be found to place the biometric and biometric functionality firmly in the control of the user as simply another personal identifier to be used whenever the user or service provider consider it appropriate. Such a concept is not far removed from the random number generators, used with a password, which have become popular for remote connections to corporate networks and some online services such as banking. The reference template might be registered under supervision onto a SIM card or other token which would then be effectively owned and maintained by the user. Such a token could then be destroyed by the user upon the termination of a service contract, ensuring that orphaned biometric data is not residing upon third party networks. There may be many possible variations on such a theme. In any event, personal identity verification for wireless transactions remains an important factor, and the future use of biometrics in this application sphere may become quite interesting. It also might uncover some equally interesting technical and operational challenges.

Application Catch-Up

As discussed, the available functionality via mobile devices has mushroomed in recent years, providing all manner of interesting possibilities with respect to using the mobile device to conduct transactions via remote hosts. Indeed, the potential functionality of many contemporary mobile devices exceeds that offered by many service organisations. Consequently, there is a degree of catch-up as large organisations strive to incorporate mobile technology options in their interface with customers. Existing web functionality is often ported to specific mobile types, allowing access to services in a format to suit. Interactive real-time messaging between supplier and consumer allows transactions to be tracked or advice to be given, for example on flight status for airline passengers. The physical location of the mobile device may additionally be tracked, facilitating the provision of location-based pertinent information. Such capabilities may suit the provision of some services better than others. They may also raise some interesting questions around the user's ability to opt in or out of such provided functionality. Clearly, the possibilities are broad and no doubt many organisations in both the private and public sectors will be considering how they might exploit this ever developing functionality.

A potential issue in this respect is that, in the rush to provide such functionality, factors such as security might not receive the attention that they deserve. The interface between the wireless device and the host network may be a particular concern, and this should be provided for within the overall network architecture. Once a connection has been made from a wireless device to the network, it should be subject to rigorous access control in order to ensure access to only the functionality legitimately on offer. Identity verification should of course form a part of this information security rigour. It may be that, when allowing wireless connectivity to existing applications, those applications should be completely redesigned in order to ensure that the enhanced functionality does not also introduce enhanced risk. If biometric identity verification is anticipated within this functionality, then it should be properly conceived, designed and implemented, together with robust operational processes being in place and properly communicated. Indeed, ideally, this should be driven from the application side, not from the mobile technology side, although one suspects that the reverse is often the case.

Mobile Futures

The rapid rise in mobile device development and the attendant adoption of wireless technology from a consumer perspective have brought substantial changes to the use of technology in society. The younger generation in particular are growing up with a completely different understanding of the computer age and the uses to which computers are put in everyday life. Indeed, the concept of the personal computer as originally understood may already be dead. For many, both at home and in the workplace, the personal computer had already largely been replaced by the laptop computer, which offered the added bonus of portability while sacrificing nothing in terms of processing power and local data storage. Laptops have themselves tended to be supplanted by smaller, lighter notebook computers and, with the advent of even smaller and lighter netbook computers, the opportunity to use computing power almost anywhere at all has been realised. While netbooks are perhaps a little too constrained for business level computing functionality, a new breed of device, somewhere between a netbook and a notebook seems to be taking over for corporate use and for many in the home. Such a rapid transformation is interesting indeed. However, with devices which we tentatively call mobile phones increasingly offering similar powers of Internet access and interaction, plus built in computing applications, the line between a small portable computer and a high level mobile phone is becoming increasingly blurred, opening up a space for tablet devices which offer the functionality of both. Given this lively carousel of technology development wherein the effective life cycle of a leading edge product may be measured in months, one wonders what the situation will look like in 10 years from now. Bearing in mind also the drive towards virtualisation, cloud computing and cloud storage, it may well be that personal computers will be completely supplanted by mobile devices of various forms, allowing both individuals and organisations to manage their data processing requirements via wireless devices connected to services via the Internet. Such an infrastructural model will also have new data security requirements and the associated requirement for personal identity verification will become increasingly pertinent. In this sphere, biometrics will no doubt have a part to play and we should be thinking about robust architectures and operational processes in order to support such a model. The future for identity verification is going to become quite interesting.

Review Questions

1. Discuss the rapid development of wireless technology and mobile devices from a global society perspective.
2. Discuss the relationship between the Internet and mobile devices.
3. Why might personal identity verification become increasingly important in this context.
4. Define ways in which biometric identity verification may be incorporated into mobile technology and associated devices.
5. Discuss data security in relation to wireless technology and host systems.

Human Factors

10

Abstract The importance of understanding human factors is stressed as we commence this especially important chapter. We introduce the concept of user psychology in relation to biometric identity verification, and the effect it has upon realised operational performance, noting the development of the User Psychology Index, the Biometric Operability Index and the associated User Psychology Index software utility. We acknowledge the depth of human emotions and how they may be linked directly to physiological change. Human factors such as age, ethnicity, health, disabilities and general variability are discussed in this context and several examples are given of human behavioural types and associated effects upon operational performance.

We ponder the subject of inherited behaviour, acknowledging the part it plays in evolution within the natural world and align it with the human condition where a mixture of inherited and learned behaviour creates varied attitudes and behavioural types. Such behaviour is influenced partly by societal developments and we should strive to understand how and why this happens. There is a direct link between this discussion and the reality of how we are deploying biometric technology. We then move to a discussion around human rights issues and how certain fundamental rights affecting both privacy and human dignity have been seriously eroded in recent times under the pretext of national security. This leads into a warning around the provision of ethical processes with respect to the deployment and usage of biometric technology. A call is made for the creation of a Biometric Constitution as a framework within which proper guidance may be provided for both systems developers and implementing agencies as to the ethical and sustainable use of biometric technology. The Biometric Users Charter is mentioned and a first draft of a possible Biometric Constitution is provided within these pages. The relevance and scope of human factors in relation to the interaction with technology, is wider and more important than many suppose. This chapter establishes a starting point from which readers may develop their understanding accordingly.

J. Ashbourn, *Guide to Biometrics for Large-Scale Systems: Technological, Operational, and User-Related Factors*, DOI 10.1007/978-0-85729-467-8_10,
© Springer-Verlag London Limited 2011

10

Introduction

Human factors become particularly important with regard to automated biometric identity verification, as the interface between the individual and the technology is a particularly personal one. More so perhaps than might at first be imagined. This has a direct bearing on how individuals interact with and use the associated technology and, therefore, the realised performance of any such transaction being undertaken. This in itself is fascinating enough, but these same factors can give rise to emotional responses and the development of societal attitudes, both within implementing agencies and user bases, which have a deep effect upon the very fabric of our society. It is an area which we should strive to understand properly in all of its dimensions and to which we should give every consideration and respect.

It would be possible to write an entire book on any one of the user factors outlined below if we were to align it with the use of contemporary technology, however, we have limited our discourse to the obvious factors which have a special relevance to biometric identity verification. It is perhaps outside the scope of this particular work to reach more deeply into the subject, although future works may do so. In the meantime, this section may at least serve to highlight the importance of user factors within a large-scale systems context.

User Psychology

The author first coined the term 'user psychology' in relation to biometric identity verification almost 20 years ago, when it became evident that a user's physiological and emotional state had a significant effect upon the interaction between the user and the technology. In turn, this had an equally significant effect upon realised transactional performance. Since that time, the author has undertaken much research into the phenomenon, both under laboratory and live conditions and has formulated a distinct understanding of user psychology under operational conditions. While it is hard to impose very precise metrics upon the situation, trends were observed which made it possible to generalise with enough precision to predict the effect of various user psychology factors upon transactional performance. Consequently, the author pioneered the development of a User Psychology Index which applied metrics in the form of performance weightings to specific factors. Following on from this advance, the author also developed the concept of the Biometric Operability Index which offered a mechanism for device manufacturers to align the performance of their devices with a common datum. A few device manufacturers embraced the Biometric Operability Index in the early days but, as the supply chain for biometric devices and associated systems design has changed over the years, this useful tool has been largely forgotten. That is a great shame as it would have proved extremely useful for system architects and implementing agencies. However, it may yet be revived if, perhaps, one of the larger global suppliers were to pick up the thread.

The User Psychology Index has however been widely used and has undergone one or two revisions since its original inception. An important step forwards in this respect was the provision of a software utility which enabled the creation of various operational scenarios and their effect upon realised performance to be visualised. The tool included visualisation of the popular metrics of false accept rates and false reject rates. It was further developed to include proportional performance figures and introduced a new metric of average error rate. The most recent implementation includes the ability to save an unlimited number of named scenarios into a database and an easy reporting function. It also introduces new sections to measure transaction time, to understand architectural requirements and much more. At the time of writing, the author is considering the creation of a third generation User Psychology Index which will advance the science significantly.

A primary factor within user psychology is the emotional state of the user at the time of a given transaction. Emotions not only have a direct effect upon our actions and interactions, both with technology and those around us, but they can also have a direct physiological effect. Hands can sweat and swell, pupils may become dilated, facial countenance will alter and so on. The combination of these physiological and behavioural factors can create significant variances between the way one individual might interact with the system compared with another, and also between individual transactions undertaken by the same individual under different circumstances. The proportionality of these differences far outweighs the minor performance differences which might be encountered across similarly configured technical points of presence, although these too have an influence upon realised performance. In this context, our previous discussion around equivalence of realised performance becomes highly pertinent.

In addition to fairly transient factors which might affect our emotions and therefore our operational performance, there are a brace of fixed or slowly changing factors which also play a part in shaping our overall ability to interact consistently with technology and associated systems. In each case, there is a combination of physiological and emotional condition which creates an overall effect. Furthermore, several of these factors may occur in relation to a given individual, and may fluctuate in intensity in relation to one another. This reality serves to create an interesting yet potentially complex situation. The User Psychology Index tool is thus extremely useful as a means of taking all such factors into account and developing a conclusion as to the probable effect upon realised performance. Some of the individual factors are discussed below.

Age

Age is an interesting factor from several perspectives. As we grow older, our general dexterity may weaken and we may become increasingly detached from technological wizardry and its various implementations, causing us to take a little additional time in our interactions with the system. We may also of course become physically infirm in one or more areas, perhaps with the onslaught of arthritis or similar conditions which affect our physical ability to interact smoothly with a technological point of presence. We may also, by degrees, lose our mental faculties, thus affecting our speed of comprehension or general understanding. All of these things are predictable and must therefore be taken into account when designing our systems and operational processes. However, there is another age-related factor to consider and that is the effect of ageing upon the biometric trait in question. Purveyors of different biometric capture devices typically claim that their chosen biometric is not affected by age. However, this simply is not the case. Even if the raw biometric trait is reasonably constant with age, its physical expression and our ability to capture it consistently may well be affected.

For example, whether or not the fundamental characteristics of a fingerprint have changed, there is little doubt that our skin changes with age and that, typically, the skin at the fingertips becomes more brittle and the fingerprints themselves rather less distinct. The iris texture may not change significantly over time, but eyelids may become more occlusive and the physical expression of the iris often becomes clouded to a small degree. In some cases, the iris itself may actually become obscured by disease. In addition, as sight weakens, the ability of the individual to focus properly without spectacles may affect their ability to interact with the technology in a consistent manner. The face naturally changes with age and, although certain features may be in more or less the same juxtaposition with each other, some faces change significantly and may confuse facial recognition systems if earlier reference templates are being used. Furthermore, the physical attitude and bearing of the individual will also likely change which, combined with changes in the face itself, can create very different vistas of light and shade when viewed from a common point. The human voice, while retaining many of its characteristics, can also change both in its timbre and, significantly, in its dynamics, making voice recognition a difficult prospect over an extended time period. There are of course several other biometric traits which we could consider, but, in all cases, the combination of changes in the trait itself, associated changes which render measurement more difficult and behavioural changes in the individual, all conspire to ensure that ageing can have a fairly dramatic effect upon the realised performance of a biometric identity verification transaction. At the other end of the age scale, we have the rapid physiological change of adolescence to contend with. In some individuals this occurs over a longer time period than with others and must be allowed for accordingly.

Given the above, it would be a good policy to ensure that biometric reference templates are periodically updated. This is quite possible from a technical point of view although one wonders how often such a policy is enacted with respect to actual, operational systems. When public sector systems are checking fingerprints against criminal databases, no doubt such variations are simply absorbed. However, for systems whereby the reference is stored on a portable token such as an identity document, periodic template updating might be a sensible option, providing that proper operational controls and processes are in place to manage such an operation. In conclusion, there is no doubt that age is a significant factor with respect to biometric identity verification, both from a physiological and behavioural perspective. There are many dimensions to explore and understand in this context and the development of such an understanding should be an integral part of our systems design. If ageing is not accommodated within our overall operation, then we may expect a disproportional amount of errors from the proportion of our user population who are undergoing rapid changes associated with age.

Ethnicity

Ethnicity in relation to user psychology and the interaction with technology and systems may be considered in various ways. Firstly, there exist concerns among citizens that ethnicity may be derived from a biometric and that this information may subsequently be used to categorise and discriminate among individuals. While systems operators tend to vigorously deny such claims, actually, there is something in this depending upon one's point of view. From a strict biometric perspective, certainly it may be possible to observe trends among ethnic groups. While more research is needed in this respect, it is clear that the physical expression of certain traits may be grouped, to some degree at least, in this respect. But of course, it is quite likely that ethnicity information would have been gathered and stored as part of the registration process, and may consequently by absolutely aligned with the biometric via the associated data record. In such a case, the determination of ethnicity by association is a very real prospect. One might of course posit that it matters not whether ethnicity can be determined or otherwise from an identity verification transactional perspective as this has no direct bearing upon the transaction in question. However, if the information is gathered and stored, it may be used in a myriad of data search and analysis scenarios, orchestrated via a variety of agencies and commercial organisations for their own purposes. This is certainly the case and ethnicity is often used as a parameter within such scenarios. However, it must be remembered that this is simply one of the several factors by which a population of users may be grouped, segregated and discriminated by. If we are concerned about ethnicity data being used in this way, we should be equally concerned by age, gender, location, health and all the other parameters which are used by government agencies and commercial organisations in their data mining activities, for whatever purpose.

The other area where ethnicity becomes interesting is that of whether or not ethnicity has a bearing upon the distinctness of biometric traits, and consequently, the relative performance that might be expected from a matching perspective. Some early research suggested that this might be the case and found some generalisations and trends in respect of both fingerprints and irises. However, to date, this has remained rather inconclusive. Nevertheless, it is a topic which might warrant further research. Once again, this has a bearing upon equivalence of realised performance across operational nodes, particularly when the user population profile differs from one area to the next.

Ethnicity is also an interesting factor from a social evolutionary perspective. Broader studies in genetics and evolution confirm the mechanisms of inherited behaviour among all organisms, including humans. From a societal perspective, there is additionally a more immediate factor of inherited attitude and behaviour, sometimes dependent upon social conditions, sometimes upon family, sometimes as a result of external influence. Sometimes this has little to do with ethnicity, and sometimes not. Witness, for example the often extreme religious polarisation or perception of societal values between such groups. Such perceptions and attitudes may well have an effect from a user psychology perspective and therefore impact upon realised performance. While politicians are afraid to even think about such matters for fear of being branded as politically incorrect or

10

biased in one direction or another, from a scientific perspective, it would be ridiculous to disallow such discussion. It may turn out that ethnicity is of little consequence in this context, but at the moment, we are not in a position to make such a claim. It is an area which deserves more attention within an open, honest and sympathetic framework of scientific research.

Health

The general status of health and well-being with respect to any individual will certainly have a psychological effect to some degree. We instinctively feel this when we are run down, suffering from a temporary infection or are over-tired. We notice that our reactions might be slower, the manner in which we interact with others may be affected and we shall no doubt entertain a generally less optimistic view of the world. When we have recovered, our spirits are lifted, our energy levels are higher and everything starts to look a little brighter. If we consider this obvious example, we may readily acknowledge that the consistency with which we interact with technological processes is likely to be impaired. This is particularly the case where such processes are non-habituated in nature, as might be the case with public sector identity verification systems.

If we imagine now a more serious medical condition which might also be more persistent, it is clear that our general demeanour and even deportment may be significantly affected. This, in turn, will have an effect upon the manner in which we interact with the technology and possibly the process. From an operational performance perspective, this will result in a change of one sort or another. There may of course be health issues which have a direct physical effect due to damage of a limb, scarring or other condition which makes biometric capture almost impossible. In some cases, the individual may be able to re-register their biometric and create a new reference, but this may not always be possible. We must acknowledge such possibilities when designing and executing our system and its attendant processes.

There is another aspect of health to consider with respect to biometric identity verification and that is that changes in the relative well-being of an individual can result in direct physiological change. Our hands and feet might swell slightly. Our eyes might water or become bloodshot. Our facial expression and colouring may be affected. We might break out in an allergic rash. Such changes might be triggered by actual infections or maybe by a more subtle combination of conditions. Furthermore, our emotional response to such conditions may further affect the overall situation, leading to something akin to a positive feedback loop of relative well-being. This will certainly affect the way in which we interact with the technology and the resulting realised transactional performance. It goes without saying that variations in mental health, which might also trigger physiological reactions, may have a similar affect upon our interaction with the system and the resulting performance thereof. In short, health and well-being constitute a very real human factor within the context of biometric identity verification.

Disabilities

Some individuals have disabilities which are immediately obvious. When someone is wheelchair bound for example, we can see straight away that they may need assistance of a different kind in order to successfully negotiate an automated identity verification point of presence. Similarly, if someone has a limb in plaster or is on crutches, their predicament is obvious and we can make allowances accordingly. Indeed, the physical design of the locations where our system is deployed may incorporate special facilities to help the disabled. These may include wheelchair access, signage and displays at different heights and controls within easy reach. Having provided a limited number of such facilities, we may consider that we have accommodated the disabled within our system. In fact, we may have just scratched the surface in this respect and not have provided adequately for all of the exceptions we may encounter due to individuals with disabilities.

Those with diminished senses also have special needs. Those who are very poorly sighted or completely blind will not easily be able to use such a facility and will almost certainly require assistance. We should be prepared for this and ensure that an adequate number of properly trained personnel are available on a given operational site. Being completely blind presents many difficulties when negotiating everyday situations which the properly sighted do not think twice about. However, there are degrees of blindness. There are many individuals who, with the aid of powerful corrective spectacles, may be able to see just enough to enable them to move around unaided in public places. However, the same individuals might find it almost impossible to use an automated terminal, or to read any signage or instructions at such a terminal. Consequently, they will struggle with such a process. Those with slightly better sight may be able to manage to interact with such a terminal, but will doubtless be inconsistent in the way that they provide their live biometric sample, with consequent results upon transactional performance. Even less extreme conditions, such as colour blindness, for example from which a sizeable proportion of the world's population suffer, may render operation extremely difficult if care has not been taken with factors such as display tonality and contrast. These are the sort of factors that typical technology suppliers and systems integrators will not have considered for themselves, and which need to be explicitly defined in relevant terms of reference or requests for proposals.

Deafness is another condition which, while not necessarily obvious to third parties, can make life extremely challenging for those thus afflicted, particularly with respect to public interactions and transactions. We should allow for this in particular at the point of registration, ensuring that trained personnel are on hand to assist with signing as required. Similarly, at operational points of presence, trained personnel should be available to work with deaf individuals as required. As with blindness, there are of course degrees of deafness. There are plenty of people who are hard of hearing and, in the bustle of public places, understanding what is said to them, particularly by unfamiliar voices and perhaps accents, may be quite difficult. Furthermore, they may not wish to draw attention to their condition which, being non-obvious to others, may lead to misunderstandings. Clear visual signage and unambiguous on-screen instructions at terminals can go a long way to ensuring that problems do not arise unnecessarily. These should be complemented by sympathetic and properly trained staff at operational points of presence.

10

Physical disability or loss of one of the senses, once understood, may be accommodated within the operation without too much difficulty, provided we have built such an accommodation into our overall systems design and operational process. However, there are other disabilities which may not be easily noticed or, indeed, may not be noticed at all, which are nevertheless very real to the individual and may cause them some difficulty in the interaction with technology and the system overall. Mental illness, for example, can manifest itself in many forms within individuals who, outwardly show no signs of disability. Some individuals may be intellectually impaired and may simply not understand at all the process they are being required to follow. Explaining why the system is in place and how they should interface to it may mean absolutely nothing to individuals with such an affliction. In severe cases, they will probably be accompanied by a carer who will steer them through the process and who will answer questions on their behalf. In less severe cases where the individual is unaccompanied, misunderstandings could easily arise and these may place the individual under higher levels of stress than might be imagined, making it increasingly difficult to complete the transaction. Such instances should be managed sympathetically by properly trained administrative personnel. Other conditions simply result in individuals who might see the world through different eyes. Autism and its various strains, for example, may have a variety of effects upon an individual, ranging from noticeable disability to simply a different way of looking at things. Once again, those with severe difficulties may be quickly noticed and assistance provided for them. However, autism, like many other conditions, may be manifested by degree. An individual with slight tendencies may, in almost every respect, appear completely unaffected and yet, when confronted by something which appears to them illogical, incorrect or maybe even frightening, will probably react rather differently than expected. The interaction with technology represents an interesting case in point which, to some affected individuals, will present absolutely no difficulty, and yet others may find it almost impossible to complete the transaction as required. We could discuss many other medical conditions and even personality traits, such as extreme shyness, for example, which make it difficult for some individuals to undertake everyday transactions, especially in public, which for others present no such difficulty. We should be sensible to this reality and make every effort to provide sympathetic assistance wherever and whenever required. Furthermore, we should understand that, especially with border-line cases, the realised transactional performance with respect to such individuals is likely, through no fault of their own, to be erratic and probably rather poor in terms of biometric matching accuracy. We should also understand the proportionality of such afflictions within typical populations which, in many instances, is probably higher than most would imagine. Needless to say, such matters should be given careful consideration when designing and implementing large-scale systems.

Variability

Variables are always interesting, both as atomic factors and in their relationships to each other. In nature, there are many variables and their complex interaction is partly what renders the natural world such a fascinating place. They exist in every organism, including human beings, and they also exist in systems, both natural and man-made. From a human factors perspective, we may consider variables in many ways. Within a given individual there are variables such as those appertaining to health and well-being as previously discussed. There are variables of mood, variables triggered by relative tiredness and variables triggered by environment. All such variables will affect the way we are thinking and behaving at a given point in time. This, in turn, will affect the way in which we interact with systems, processes and technology. As the interaction with biometric technology is such a personal affair, it follows that these variables may have a larger than anticipated effect upon the resulting transactions.

Within populations there are of course variables among individuals. This applies to populations of almost anything and especially applies to humans. Thus we have variables within the individual and variables between individuals. Consequently, not only will an individual's transactions be variable, but those of different individuals will be similarly so. Layered on top of this reality will be variables arising as a consequence of the interaction between individuals and between individuals and their environment. When everything is entirely as expected and operating smoothly, such variables may not be significant. When things are not as expected or conflict occurs, variables may become very significant. Variables triggered by external events or influence may have an amplitude in general proportion to the event, or may be out of all proportion, depending upon the individual– another variable. Overall, it is a complex picture which is not easily perceived in its finer detail. To what extent such variability is materialised from an operational performance perspective is perhaps open to debate. However, it is a factor which we should be sensible of within our broader portfolio of human factors.

Human Factors and Operational Performance

From a systems perspective, the main point about human factors is the effect they can have upon realised performance. Biometric vendors and systems integrators tend to speak of variations of false match or false non-match in terms of fractions of a percent. Indeed, some claim theoretical performance figures to two or three decimal places or more and, no doubt, potential implementing agencies compare such specifications and draw conclusions as to which device or matching algorithm is the better, based upon such information. Whatever these small variations in specified theoretical performance, they all pale into insignificance when the performance variations due to human factors enter the picture. While we might have been concerned over the difference between a small fraction of 1%, we may now contend, not only with whole percentage figures, but possibly tens of percentage points. Associated error rates in some cases might vary between multiples of percentage points to an incapability of completing the transaction at all. It follows then, that human factors are somewhat important from a systems performance perspective. In order to illustrate the point, let us consider some possible scenarios.

10

Shyness and the Self-conscious User

Some individuals suffer terribly from shyness, which can have a devastating effect upon their whole lives. It may be difficult for the confident or bombastic to understand this, but it is nevertheless a reality for those affected. Interacting with systems and other people in a public environment can be especially trying for such individuals. Imagine the shy person who, with some difficulty, has managed to register their reference biometric under controlled conditions and is now about to use the live system for the first time. Imagine that this is a particularly busy day and that queues are forming at point of presence terminals. Imagine also that the signage is inadequate and that the system is slow to respond due to the load and that, in any case, the presented instructions differ from those expected. As our shy person waits patiently in the queue, their anxiety levels are steadily increasing. They notice that someone ahead of them seems to have experienced difficulty with the system and that, behind them, people are becoming vocal about the delays. By the time our shy user finally gets to the terminal, they are in a state of heightened anxiety and hope that they can remember the correct procedure and slip through without incident. As they approach the terminal and present their portable token, nothing happens. They try again and a message appears asking them to present their token. They do so once more and are prompted to supply their biometric via a reader interface which looks particularly grubby. They diligently do so and the system rejects them. They try again but nothing happens. They try once again and the system times out, prompting them once more to present their token. By this time, our shy user is feeling extremely self-conscious. Their anxiety level may well have translated into a physiological response of some kind and, if that was not enough, the queue behind them is becoming impatient and vocal. They present their token once more and supply their biometric, this time with some exaggeration. The system rejects them once more. By now, the probability that this user will be able to supply a live biometric sample of good enough quality to represent a match via this terminal has receded dramatically. If they do manage to scrape through, the resulting score will be very low and not representative. In any event, it has been a very unpleasant experience for this user and, the next time they have to undergo the process, they will be feeling extremely apprehensive before they even begin. Our previous discussion around equivalence of realised performance is highly pertinent to such cases.

The Under Protest User

These users have registered their biometric, under protest, simply because they have been required to do so by the laws in force in their particular country, or perhaps a country which they are visiting. At the registration process, they were deliberately not very helpful and it is likely that their reference biometric will be of relatively poor quality. When it comes to the live process, they will certainly not approach the situation with any enthusiasm. Indeed, it is likely that they will deliberately try to give either an incorrect or poor quality biometric sample. After all, they have absolutely no interest in the system working correctly or as intended by the implementing agency. It could be that they disagree most strongly, on what they consider to be ethical grounds, in the entire process, and that they will be quite happy to see the system fail completely. Depending upon their particular strength of feeling, they may deliberately fail the process, ensuring that manual intervention will be required, thus causing as much chaos as possible within the live environment. An under protest user with a slightly milder disposition may simply try giving a deliberately poor quality sample and, if need be, slowly increasing the quality, in order to discover how tolerant the system might be in this respect. If they can get away with consistently providing very poor quality biometrics, then they will be happy to do so. If on the spot disputes arise, these users will probably be extremely vocal, making their views heard to as many around them as possible. They will enjoy creating some controversy that they can subsequently recall for the benefit of private audiences after the event. They will also be very difficult to reassure as to the ethical use of the system at hand. The under protest user falls broadly into two groups. The first group will protest at almost anything and will never be satisfied with any official response. They will be forever an under protest user. The second, and more significant group, are those who sincerely believe that the system is ill-conceived and is not being operated along what they would consider to be ethical lines. For the first group, little can be done other than helping them through the process as expediently as possible. For the second group there is much that should be done. First of all, if many individuals feel this way, then something is very wrong, either in the system and its administration, or in the way in which it has been communicated. In either event, the administrating agency should take great pains to address the issues in question and then re-communicate to all users and prospective users accordingly. From the operational performance perspective, any under protest user is going to create errors. If there are many such users, there will be many errors.

The Technical Sceptic User

This user probably has no particular political or ethical perspective in relation to the system overall, but is nonetheless very cynical about technology in general and biometric technology in particular. Their wish, more than anything, is that the system will be shown not to work. They will be very happy when their live biometric fails to match as this will prove conclusively that the system is ill-conceived, poorly designed and that the technology interface is the worst that mankind has ever had the displeasure to observe. Such a failure will also provide the opportunity to offer an opinion to all those within earshot as to how much better a manual system would be, or, perhaps, that the system might have worked had they chosen a different type of reader or a different biometric. They will probably be quite good natured about the whole thing, jocular even, as they prove repeatedly how useless the whole process really is. After a few failures, this user, when assisted and made to use the system properly, will reluctantly provide a good quality biometric sample and complete a successful transaction, until the next time, when the entire pantomime will be re-staged for a new and willing audience. Of course, the effect of these shenanigans upon realised operational performance will be quite dramatic, ensuring that there are many unnecessary failed transactions. The overall effect may even be to goad the local administration to reduce the matching threshold in order to realise less errors of this kind. This may especially be the case if the local administration does not enjoy a robust technical understanding and has a sneaking suspicion that the technical sceptic may even be right, especially if they have encountered sizeable numbers of the species. Alternatively, if maintenance and support is provided by a sub-contracted third party, the party in question may be called in to tinker with the system and may possibly leave it in a somewhat compromised position. Here again, is where our chapter on equivalence of realised performance and how this might effectively be managed, is of some importance.

The Late Arrival User

The late arrival user is the one who typically knows better than anyone else the operational processes in place at this particular location, and knows for a fact that it is pointless to allow for the amount of time recommended as he or she will simply march through the various processes on a just-in-time basis. They are probably the ones who have a plethora of mobile devices and other technology with which they manage their very important lives and with which they receive up to date information that is unavailable to mere mortals. On the other hand, they may simply be one of those hapless individuals with whom fate conspires to associate every conceivable event destined to delay them in their progress, although fate usually reserves such a sentence for those who are hopelessly unprepared in any event. With either specie of late arrival, of course, the cause of their tardiness is never really their fault and they are usually quite indignant about the whole thing. The result is often that they are quite flustered and have probably forgotten the niceties of how to interact with the biometric technology and associated system. If a token is required from which to read the reference biometric, they will not be able to find it immediately as they sift through all of their other paraphernalia while holding everybody else up. Finally, they will be ready to give their live biometric and will do so hurriedly and, almost certainly, incorrectly, necessitating two or three attempts before they are accepted and can continue through the process. Mostly, the late arrival is of little significance to the administrating agency, other than something of an operational curiosity. However, there is of course the possibility that the late arrival is a deliberate attempt to confuse the system and fraudulently acquire the associated benefit. Consequently, such events should be viewed with caution and, on no account, should the late arrival be rushed through the process for reasons of operational expediency. From an operational performance perspective, these individuals will probably be inconsistent with respect to biometric matching transactions, and for reasons which, at least technically, will remain unclear.

The Tired User

In a world as nature intended, when we become tired, we would stop and rest. In the man-made material world, we are often obliged to continue with our various activities, whether tired or otherwise. Consequently, many of us are functioning occasionally in a very tired state, while some enact their bustling lives under a weight of perpetual tiredness, the condition simply varying by degree. However, any organism, when tired, will be functioning in an impaired manner. Their powers of observation reduced. Their reactions slowed. Their attention span limited. We know when we are tired, but we often try to disallow it, carrying on in what we believe is a normal manner. The reality is that we are simply not able to function in a normal manner. As we become more tired, the effects become more pronounced. Such conditions, in extremis, often lead to serious accidents. In a less dramatic scenario, they lead to mistakes being made or individuals performing in a limited manner. A biometric identity verification transaction is, as we have previously stated, a very personal event. Therefore, if our performance is impaired due to tiredness, there is a likelihood that this condition will be reflected in the manner in which we interact with the system and, consequently, in the resultant transactional performance. The tired user will often forget the procedure which should be followed. They may not present their biometric token properly if and when required, and they will almost certainly present their biometric in a non-consistent manner, leading to a poor matching result or, perhaps, a failed match. If the cause of the failed match is obvious, they will probably not see it. They may well need assistance when, ordinarily, this is not the case for that individual. Overall, such random episodes of extreme tiredness will result in an overall inconsistent performance record for a user prone to such conditions. Tiredness may also bring irritability, causing the user to quickly become exasperated with the whole process if they experience a failure. As they become increasingly exasperated, the probability of a good, successful biometric match recedes. If they have the presence of mind to stop, take a deep breath, and summon an increased concentration for the task at hand, then they will probably succeed. However, such clear thinking is uncommon among the very tired. In applications such as automated border control for example, this phenomenon might manifest itself for those arriving after a particularly long journey or, perhaps, a journey where excessive delays have been experienced. Those with heavy loads or young children in their care may carry an additional burden, as might the elderly and frail. It is a factor to take into consideration where such users might be encountered.

The User on Medication

It is a fact of contemporary life that almost all medication has some sort of side effect associated with it. Strong medication exhibits more powerful side effects. Furthermore, these unwanted side effects often manifest themselves differently in those with varying constitutions. Medication which might have but a minor effect for one user might have a devastating effect upon another. The effects themselves might also vary in both their character and intensity as complex biological reactions take place and, possibly trigger other, unexpected reactions. The result can be very confusing. The impact upon the individual equally so. Such effects might induce drowsiness, disorientation, nausea and other conditions to limit the effective mental acuity of the individual. They might also have a direct physiological effect, making it near impossible to provide a representative biometric sample. In extreme cases, the individual's behaviour may be significantly affected, causing them to react in unexpected ways that even they themselves would be surprised to learn of after the event. The truth is that, these days, strong medication is routinely prescribed for a number of common conditions. In addition, the supply chain for prescriptive drugs is itself variable and there is no guarantee that one batch will have precisely the same effect as another. As a result of the supply and demand situation within a society conditioned to rely increasingly upon medication, drugs are also often deployed in the market with inadequate testing. The result of these combined realities is that those destined to rely on medication enter into something of a lottery as far as side effects are concerned. The individual may have no expectation of any such effects and, when experienced, no understanding of their reach. Consequently, they will be ill-prepared to cope with the effects and, quite possibly, a little worried about them. Under such conditions, their ability to interact with the system in a consistent manner may be severely impaired, although this may be not at all obvious to the system operator. The transactional history of such users will probably be quite varied, depending upon their condition and its relative permanency. For those afflicted with a condition which involves persistent deterioration until a point of total disability is reached, their own relative performance and consistency will be similarly subject to persistent deterioration and, it may be, that their medication is increased in strength accordingly. We must acknowledge that it will typically not be obvious that individuals are suffering in this way, and that we must find ways of taking such situations into account within the design and operation of our systems.

The Angry User

Some individuals are better able to manage anger than others, and some have a different threshold at which anger manifests itself in relation to a given situation. We see this all around us, on the roads, in the workplace, in public facilities, at social gatherings and when individuals are confronted with a process that they must interact with in order to proceed through a particular transaction. Some have the patience of a saint, some the disposition of a devil, and many more inhabit a land somewhere between the two. In any event, once the threshold has been crossed and anger manifests itself, the individual in question is subject to some dramatic change. Actually, this is a perfectly normal phenomenon and is nature's way of providing a response to extremes of danger. At least, that is what it should be and often is within the animal kingdom. Humans seem to have distorted this natural trait into something far less rational and less predictable. Some individuals explode into a fit of anger at the slightest provocation however irrational. Others may let their anger simmer for a while before, if the provocation continues, it finally boils over. Yet others will simply walk away and not be affected at all. Furthermore, the provocation may be something which, to most, seems entirely insignificant and yet, to one individual will become an insurmountable obstacle, and so their anger erupts. The physical implementation of anger may vary quite a lot among individuals. Many will try to control it and not allow it to become visible at all, others will control it and yet will show clear signs of its presence. Some will simply lose control over it, hopefully temporarily. The effect that anger will have upon an individual's ability to successfully conduct a biometric identity verification transaction may be dramatic. If they do not successfully complete the transaction the first time around, they are likely to become increasingly irritable, entering into a vicious circle wherein the more irritable they become, the less probability will exist of them completing the transaction. As might be imagined, the consistency of their performance in this respect may leave a little to be desired, and this will be reflected in the overall performance of the system at that particular node.

The User with Something to Hide

The user with something to hide may or may not be a hardened criminal, but may nevertheless have reservations about the system and its interconnections. This may make them rather nervous and cause them to function in an erratic manner. It may be, for example, that an individual has identity documents which have been fraudulently issued, or perhaps correctly issued but against fraudulent information. Such an individual may not be sure of the result of the biometric check and what it means in this context. Alternatively, the individual might have authentic documentation but is aware of a transgression which would render them ineligible for the privilege being sought, if it were revealed to the controlling authority. Such an individual may appear somewhat furtive in their behaviour. Herein lies an interesting aspect of the dichotomy between automated and manual systems. In a manual system, such behaviour is likely to be noticed by an experienced operator who will doubtless initiate an additional layer of investigation. In an automated system, providing the biometric matches, the individual will be considered bona fide, even if he is a complete fraud. Such an eventuality stresses the importance of the registration process, as previously discussed within these pages. It will be difficult to infer that an individual has something to hide, purely on the basis of their transactional biometric verification history, however erratic it may be. However, if an individual repeatedly fails the biometric match, even though their credentials would otherwise appear to be in order, then such an occurrence probably warrants further investigation. The operational process aligned with our system must allow for such eventualities under all conditions of operation. Furthermore, it must allow for a distinction between those with something to hide and those subject to other human factor variables. Such a paradox serves to remind us that computers and automation cannot replace intelligence and diligence.

The Disabled User

We have discussed disabilities and it is clear that such conditions will have an effect upon realised transactional performance. Just as disabilities may be varied in their manifestation, so will be the effects that they confer upon operational performance. For extreme disabilities, we may make special allowances and ensure that the transactions of those involved are handled as exceptions and therefore do not impact unduly upon overall transactional performance. It is the many and varied non-exceptional disabilities which are likely to affect the transactional performance of both the individuals concerned and the system overall. We have discussed how disabled users are likely to encounter difficulties when navigating their way through the process of a biometric identity verification transaction. Such difficulties may fall into two groups. Within the first group, individuals may find it extremely difficult to undertake the transaction at all, which will typically take much longer in its execution than for that of a non-disabled user. Within the second group, individuals may be able to successfully undertake the transaction, but will be very inconsistent in the manner in which they do so, leading to equally inconsistent results. Consequently, we are likely to see some quite variable and inconsistent matching scores among the transactions of disabled users. As many such disabilities are non-obvious and unlikely to be advertised by those harbouring them, this presents an interesting picture with respect to overall systems performance. The proportionality of those with disabilities may also vary from region to region, or from time to time with respect to operational transactions. We must strive to understand this phenomenon.

From the few examples offered above, and we could offer many more, it is clear that human factors may have a dramatic effect upon realised performance. When combined with environmental factors which, in turn, might serve to trigger further human factors, we may readily appreciate that the overall realised performance of a given system is only partly informed by considerations of a technical nature. At this juncture, the author refers back to the concept of equivalence of performance across operational nodes and the importance of accommodating human factors into this broader scenario.

Inherited Behaviour

Those who have studied evolution will understand that, in addition to the genetic imprint passed down through the hereditary tree, there is also an inherited behaviour pattern. This pattern is complemented throughout the lifetime of the individual by learned behaviour, some of which is taught by family associations, some of which comes from direct experience. The next generation thus benefits from the same inherited behaviour, tuned slightly to match the contemporary environment. We see this vividly in animals: the manner in which salmon and certain turtles return instinctively to a specific location for breeding purposes, the migratory flights of birds, often with great precision, the way in which young spiders know precisely how to spin their webs and have inbuilt defensive behaviour patterns which have been learned and refined over countless generations. In fact, the insect world in particular relies heavily upon inherited behaviour traits. It is hardly surprising therefore that humans are subject to the same phenomenon of inherited behaviour traits. It is well known that certain types of family perpetuate their particular values, beliefs, attitudes and often even professions. The popular phrase, 'like father like son' has an equivalent in almost every human culture. It is for such reasons that, within a family steeped in criminal behaviour it is often difficult for a child to break free of this trend. Similarly, one often finds families with a long line of doctors, farmers, engineers and so on.

The interesting point here is that behaviour and attitude can play a significant part in the way in which an individual interacts with both technology in general and biometric technology in particular. We cannot expect that everyone will see things in the same way that we do. We cannot expect that, even when carefully explained, users of our system will have a common understanding of it or a common attitude towards it. In addition to all of the human factors so far discussed, there will be an element of inherited behaviour and attitude which will shape the individual's perception of the system, why it is there, and how they personally interact with it. We shall therefore discover some notable variances among individuals in this respect and shall not be able to make blanket assumptions about our user population. This factor may not be especially material with respect to the day-to-day operational performance of our large-scale system, but it is one which deserves our understanding and which may explain variances unaccounted for by other means.

There is another aspect of inherited behaviour which is most interesting. Each new generation grows up with a contemporary world around them, which, to them, is accepted as normal as this is all they know. Those from the previous generation might decry certain developments and be very reluctant to accept them, based upon their own understanding of the world as it previously existed. When Aldus Huxley wrote his Brave New World, the general reaction was one of horror. People could not imagine how awful it would be for humans to exist under such conditions which would seem to deny everything that was special about the human constitution. It is a sobering thought to ponder upon how close we have come to some of the ideas expressed in that volume. What was absolutely horrifying to one generation may become acceptable to another. Politicians may make great store of this reality, knowing that once accepted, certain practices will be tolerated and future generations will not even question them. However, there is a fly in this particular ointment as, sooner or later, even the most dumbed down and downtrodden population is likely, at some point, to wake up. And when it does, the environment is created for revolutionary change. We shall explore considerations of a political nature elsewhere in this volume.

Human Rights Issues

We live in interesting times wherein nothing seems to be quite as expected. Human rights represent a case in point. On the one hand, the newspapers are full of stories of people claiming, quite unrealistically in many cases, that their human rights have been violated by some petty offence and that they are therefore entitled to compensation in the form of monetary awards. In that respect, human rights issues have become a good business proposition. On the other hand, *real* human rights are often eroded by government actions and legislation introduced under the pretext of national security or some other national concern. The right to privacy has, in particular, been almost completely eroded on the pretence that giving up this right is going to somehow facilitate the fight against terrorism and organised crime. Of course, as any 5-year old of average intelligence could have predicted, the destruction of this particular right has had absolutely no impact whatsoever on terrorism and organised crime. How could it? Such a development is not addressing the root cause of these ills. Indeed, serious crime is generally on the increase in most societies, joined by new waves of terrorism which did not exist when we had our right to privacy. The right to a reasonable level of dignity is now also being eroded with the introduction of intrusive searches for no particular reason in public places. Laws have been enacted in some societies which endow individuals with a criminal record the moment they have any interaction with the police, eroding the age old right to be considered innocent until proven guilty. One could go on. Suffice it to say that these are very serious developments from a societal perspective. Governments have been guilty of hoodwinking citizens, under the pretext of national security, in order to exert increasing levels of intrusive control over the lives of normal, law abiding citizens, often while real offenders are allowed to bypass such controls. Such developments do not go un-noticed. Consequently, if we wish our user population to harbour a cooperative understanding of our large-scale system, we should take great pains to ensure that we do not violate their fundamental human rights within the context of this system. Indeed, we should pay particular attention to privacy and the operational processes with which we interact with user population. Commercial organisations have been equally guilty in riding roughshod over the privacy and dignity of individuals who, like the government, they seem to believe exist purely to be exploited. If we continue down this path, we shall be creating a society where a general lack of respect will create problems upon a scale never previously imagined. It is time for a change of attitude and we can support such a change with robust and sympathetic systems design, coupled to well-conceived operational policies.

A Biometric Constitution

Given the various issues we have uncovered under the general heading of human factors and, indeed, these have by no means been comprehensive, it would be a good thing to develop and put down in writing an ethical framework with which to offer guidance to those developing systems that incorporate biometric functionality. Similarly, a framework for users can be developed which sets out a policy of how biometric data may be used in an ethical and responsible manner within different scenarios. Something akin to the latter was developed some years back by the author and named The Biometric Users Charter. It is perhaps a good time to bring these ideas up to date and develop something which all might understand and to which all might subscribe, at least as a starting point. Such a framework would provide a reference point against which different perspectives and operational processes may be aligned. For now, we shall call this a Biometric Constitution, and offer a rough outline below which, hopefully, a responsible organisation might take and develop further.

The Biometric Constitution: A First Draft

Scope

The scope of the Biometric Constitution is primarily around the use of biometric data within systems. This inevitably touches upon the use of personal data and, in particular, the personal data aligned with a particular biometric. The objective of the Biometric Constitution is to provide guiding principles for both systems designers, implementing agencies and users themselves, in an open, easily digested manner to which all may subscribe. It is deliberately minimal in its content, in order to maintain clarity. Users may expand upon the fundamental principles outlined within the Biometric Constitution, in the context of their own particular situation.

Registration

The registration process is vitally important in that it is the first point at which the biometric is captured. Any weaknesses at this point will undoubtedly be magnified as associated data proliferates throughout the host system and possibly beyond. The following principles are recommended for purposes of biometric data registration.

The biometric data may be saved in a master database together with a unique identifier which may be used to align the biometric data with a personal identity profile. This master database must be heavily secured from a network perspective and all data must be encrypted. Access to the database must be strictly controlled and limited to a few individuals whose access processes must be documented and limited to exceptional conditions such as when operational biometric data is lost or corrupted. Systems administrators must not have the capability to decrypt or otherwise access any data within the database.

The operational biometric reference data should, wherever possible, be maintained on a portable token such as an electronic identity document, from where it may be extracted temporarily for comparison purposes within an identity verification transaction. After a comparison has been made, the biometric reference data must be deleted immediately from the system. If, from an operational perspective, there is no alternative but to maintain an operational database of reference biometrics, then the biometric data must not be stored together with personal data about the individual in question, but may be stored with a single, unique identifier which may be used for data alignment purposes, only when absolutely necessary. In the case of an automated identity verification transaction, the unique identifier may be input from a token for the purpose of a one-to-one biometric check. In the case of a one-to-many biometric check, in most cases, there will be no reason to refer any personal data associated with the biometric.

The particular systems architecture, including how and where biometric data is stored, under what circumstances it may be aligned with other personal data within an operational context and exactly how biometric data is used in the context of a live identity verification transaction, should all be clearly documented and provided to the user at the time of registration. The user must be able to discuss any such points if desired with a responsible representative of the implementing agency at the point of registration. If the use of a biometric is not compulsory for the application at hand, then this should be explicitly documented and the user offered the option to opt out of the biometric element of registration.

Clarity of Purpose

For a given system and associated application, a Biometric Charter document should be published and provided to every user of the system, stating clearly the precise purpose of the system, why it has been established, who the implementing agency is, and who is maintaining and administering the system on a day-to-day basis, together with full contact information for any issues arising out of usage, or general enquiries. In addition, this document should explain precisely how the user's biometric is used for transactional purposes and what other personal information may be aligned with it.

The implementing agency must be absolutely clear as to the purpose and day-to-day operability of the system. The Biometric Charter document for each system must also detail any third parties with whom personal information might be exchanged, why this is the case, under what circumstances might such exchanges take place and what data protection is in place with respect to third parties.

The Biometric Charter document must be defined and published before users are registered into the system. For applications in the public sector, the document should be published at least 3 months before the system is implemented and a mechanism provided under which prospective users may question or challenge any provisions of the document. Any such questions must be answered and resolved in full before the implementation date and, if the Biometric Charter document is modified as a result, this must be re-published and the process repeated.

Having clearly defined the purpose and scope of the system within the Biometric Charter, the operational scope must not deviate from this definition in any way whatsoever. If a change of scope is desired, a new Biometric Charter should be prepared and distributed to all users for comment. Only after a successful consultation with users, resulting in a majority acceptance of the proposed changes, should such changes be implemented. In the absence of a majority acceptance, such proposed changes may not be implemented.

Ownership of Data

It must be clearly established that ownership of biometric data lies with the individual to whom the data pertains. Implementing agencies using biometric data do so only with the express permission of the individual. Similarly, biometric data may not be shared with any third party without the express permission of the individual. Furthermore, implementing agencies may not insist upon the use of a biometric, except where the application is in place solely and unequivocally for the purposes of national security. For any other application, users must be given the option to opt out of providing biometric data. Biometric data must not be used for any purpose outside of the system or application for which the individual has given their permission.

At all times, biometric data is owned by the individual and must not be tampered with in any way by implementing agencies. Implementing agencies are required, upon request, to notify the individual of exactly where and in which systems their biometric data resides. Such requests must be responded to at no cost to the user. If a reference biometric becomes practically unusable for any reason, either the implementing agency or the individual may request a re-registration of the reference biometric. Any such re-registration transactions will be logged, together with the reasons for re-registration, and the process subject to at least the same rigour as the original registration from a security perspective.

Accessibility of Records

The individual to whom the biometric data belongs must have access to any other personal information which may be aligned with or otherwise referenced to the biometric or an associated identity verification transaction. Upon request, the implementing agency must provide a full listing of all such personal information and this must be provided at no cost to the user. This listing must include information held by third parties where the implementing agency has shared personal information about the individual with such third parties. In such cases, the implementing agency has a duty of care to ensure that any such information is provided securely and only to the individual in question. There may be various mechanisms for providing such a service, any of which must be operated with great care and in a responsible manner.

If an individual finds that information held about them and associated with a biometric is in error, they may request that this information is updated accordingly. Under such circumstances, the implementing agency must satisfy themselves that such errors are real and that any supplied updates are genuine and verifiable. If this is the case, then the implementing agency must provide confirmation that the records in question have indeed been updated.

Repudiation

The individual must be able to repudiate any false assumptions made due to the use of their biometric. Such assumptions may arise due to the misalignment of data within systems or perhaps due to an incorrect biometric match. In such cases, the implementing agency will provide an immediate response and the facility for the individual to discuss the reasons of their repudiation with a responsible representative of the implementing agency and within a non-confrontational environment. Such reasons must be investigated promptly by the implementing agency and a detailed, documented response provided to the individual.

In the case of a suspected fraudulent repudiation, the implementing agency must be seen to have undertaken all the correct steps with respect to interviews with the individual and the proper investigation of associated claims.

Third Party Connections

Third party connections and the reasons for them must be documented within the Biometric Charter for any given system or application. If, for any reason, these third party connections change, then this must be reflected in a new Biometric Charter and reviewed accordingly. In all cases and at all stages of development, the implementing agency must take appropriate steps to satisfy themselves that the third party is operating responsibly and with due diligence with respect to the security of personal information. The third party must provide a written assurance that the data shared with them will not be used for any purpose other than that specifically defined within the Biometric Charter. Such assurances must be appended to the Biometric Charter accordingly. The implementing agency will provide all relevant third parties with The Biometric Constitution as a reference document.

If the individual has any questions or concerns with respect to the use of personal information as a result of such third party connections, they may discuss the same with the host implementing agency who will provide relevant information accordingly. If the individual were to liaise directly with the third party in this respect, such a liaison will be at the discretion of the parties involved.

Life of Data

Biometric data may only be stored and used within the context of the originating system or application and only for the lifetime of that application with respect to its applicability to the individual. When the application becomes no longer applicable to the individual, the biometric will be removed immediately from all storage points within the system. Historic transaction information, if required for legal purposes, may be retained but all biometric data must be removed.

In such cases, the individual may request confirmation from the implementing agency that biometric data has been removed from all systems components, including those concerned with data backups. The implementing agency, in turn, must request the removal of biometric data to any third parties with which it may have been shared.

Data Backup

Within the context of a given system, it is reasonable that operational data will be backed up in order to facilitate business continuity or recovery from simple data media failures. Biometric data collected at the point of registration may also be backed up in this manner, although all such backups must be encrypted and no additional personal information must be stored together with the biometric data. When a new data backup is taken, any previous data must be destroyed in accordance with robust data destruction principles.

The data backup process for a given system must also be described in the Biometric Charter for that system. If a third party organisation is employed for data backup and business continuity purposes, then that organisation must not have access to any of the operational data involved. Furthermore, the third party organisation must provide a written statement of their backup and business continuity process to the implementing agency, a synopsis of which must be appended to the Biometric Charter.

Data Destruction

When biometric data is no longer needed by a specific application, then all instances of that data must be destroyed. Similarly, when data backups are replaced, the previous data must be destroyed. On a live system, the removal of biometric data may be accommodated by file deletion followed by a sophisticated data overwrite procedure to ensure that the data may not be recovered. For instances where the storage media itself has become redundant, due to replacement for example, or because it has exceeded its planned life cycle, then the media must be wiped clean and then physically destroyed. The destruction mechanism employed should be such that it is impossible to retrieve the remains and rebuild the media. This will typically involve fragmenting the physical media. If such destruction is undertaken by a contracted third party, then the organisation involved must provide a written statement of its data destruction process to the implementing agency, a synopsis of which must be appended to the Biometric Charter.

Conclusion

As explained, the above is simply a rough first draft of something which might usefully be developed by consensus and then widely published for the common good. There will of course initially be disagreement with respect to certain points depending upon perspective, but such disagreements may be resolved and a framework developed which, thereafter, will prove invaluable to both implementing agencies, third party contractors and users themselves. Indeed, we have been waiting for such an instrument for some time now. Let us grasp the opportunity to re-think how biometric data is used and publish these guiding principles accordingly.

Review Questions

1. Discuss the importance of human factors with regard to real-time systems operation and associated performance.
2. Define the term User Psychology in broad terms.
3. Discuss ageing and the likely implications for biometric identity verification.
4. Discuss disabilities and the various ways in which they may affect consistent biometric data capture.
5. Discuss human rights in association with biometric identity verification.

The Politics

11

Abstract We start this chapter by explaining why politics are so important with respect to large-scale systems. The relationship between technology and politics is discussed, including the use of technology to support political agendas and how information technology in particular has fulfilled this role, with biometric technology continuing the trend by serving many agendas. We consider the supply chain with respect to politics and discuss how an over-reliance upon technology often leads to a weakening of responsibility and initiative within government agencies and elsewhere. Technology should never be considered as a substitute for managerial responsibility, and yet this is often exactly how it is perceived.

We progress to a discussion around the use of biometric technology in law enforcement and the relationship between citizen and state. Serious crime and terrorism is discussed with an emphasis of getting to the root cause of such ills, rather than supposing that technology can solve such deep seated issues. This leads us to consider scope creep for political reasons with respect to large-scale systems, and how such systems may consequently become misrepresented to the public as to their clarity of purpose. We also consider societal development in general and the associated impact of technology.

Introduction

Within the context of any large-scale system, one is likely to encounter politics of one kind or another. Sometimes these are interdepartmental within the design and development phase, and revolve around technologies and techniques. Sometimes they are more to do with subsequent usage and perceived requirements, including interactions with other systems. Sometimes they emerge after the event and develop among and between user groups. When such a system is deployed within the private sector, such politics tend to be contained and industry-specific. However, when such a system is deployed within the public sector, things become very different indeed and the politics often take on a national or even international complexion, in addition to those centred around procurement and development. This is a complex picture and one which is often difficult to comprehend. In any event, the politics around a given system will be as significant, if not more so, than either the technology or functionality. Indeed, without the politics, the

J. Ashbourn, *Guide to Biometrics for Large-Scale Systems: Technological, Operational,* and *User-Related Factors*, DOI 10.1007/978-0-85729-467-8_11, © Springer-Verlag London Limited 2011

system would simply not exist. It would therefore seem reasonable to include a section on politics within this work, and discuss at least a few of the pertinent parameters. Such discussion will serve to inform our understanding of why systems are as they are, and where they might be going in the future.

Politics and Technology

There exists a perennial relationship between technology and politics in the broader sense. Technology is always of interest to politicians, especially if it can serve to support political agendas. And there are many such agendas, from education, to administration, to law enforcement and many more besides. Furthermore, in many cases, the technology need not even exist in a practical implementation, so long as the promise of the technology sounds plausible. If the technology looks as though it might provide a shortcut to the realisation of such agendas, or maybe replace the onus of responsibility for a given department or function, it will be especially welcome. This is not a new phenomenon and has existed more or less in parallel with the advent of modern politics itself, albeit with different types of technology. For example, the advent of the printing press, the development of modern weapons, transportation and communication technologies and others have all had a part to play in political activities and associated developments. Furthermore, political developments often drive technological research and, in so doing, shape the direction that technology follows. In this context, information technology has had a significant impact and may yet prove to have a bigger impact than any technology, at least in living memory.

Biometric technology in particular has served many political masters as it has provided a promise of positive personal identification which may be utilised and manipulated in many directions. While governments were initially slow to understand its potential in this respect, a huge step change was introduced when the technology was embraced by border control and law enforcement agencies. As was to be expected, the associated political rhetoric has hardly been reflected in the actuality of deployment, and we have witnessed many false starts and about-turns in both policy and related projects. Such a situation is also quite expected within a political context as a technology evolves and is brought into play with respect to various political ideals. However, there is another factor with respect to biometric technology, due to the binding of biometrics with individuals and the distinctly personal interaction between the individual and the technology. This factor, together with political aspirations for the use of the technology, introduces a strong societal element into the overall mix. In a sense, this accentuates the politics with respect to this particular technology.

The Supply Chain

Given the political aspirations around the use of biometrics, it is hardly surprising that the politically inspired supply chain has been especially active in this area. It is interesting to note that almost all major suppliers within the IT industry have a dedicated government or public sector department. A part of this function is simply to sell technology and associated consultancy into both central and local government agencies. Another is to lobby government agencies and plant ideas which would favour the use of certain technologies. With regard to an emerging technology, as biometrics is sometimes still regarded, wonderful opportunities present themselves as technology suppliers can effectively sell an idea, and then worry about the development after they have secured the contract. Even better, they can fish for the aspiration and then align their ideas with it, whether or not the technology or particular configuration has ever been tested under equivalent real-world scenarios. This has the added benefit of guaranteeing some very substantial consultancy business. When things do not work out according to plan, as is often the case, the whole process may simply be repeated. It is perhaps no wonder that government has such a poor record with respect to the implementation of large-scale IT projects, when one considers this supply chain model.

With reference to the biometric technology supply chain, initially, this was primarily in the hands of specialist, pioneer companies who had developed biometric sensors and matching algorithms. Such organisations understood the biometric functionality but were often rather less experienced in the broader area of systems integration. This led to a situation whereby the larger systems integrators and consultancy firms would act as project leads and bring in the services of the specialist biometric organisations as required. Nowadays, such lines have been blurred somewhat as many of the larger IT organisations have some sort of biometric capability. However, levels of expertise seem to have also diluted in some cases and it is interesting to see questions arising within new projects which, actually, have already been resolved a decade or more earlier. This situation is partly exacerbated by the fact that government agencies like to work with a small number of known suppliers, often the larger organisations within a given industry, who have become known to them as a result of constant and successful lobbying. The result is sometimes a less than perfect understanding of the technology within both the commissioning agency and the technology supplier. Of course, this is not always the case, although politics can certainly muddy the water and lead to complications in this context. A better approach would be for government agencies to maintain their own specialist technology design departments, who might then design a robust system and produce the necessary specifications to be met and fulfilled via a simple procurement exercise. In some cases, this is happening by default as government agencies develop their own expertise and practical experience with respect to the use of biometric technology. This, in many ways, is a good thing, although it would be nice if such centres of expertise could reside in isolation from political agendas and therefore appreciate the broader picture. In some countries, something akin to this model does exist and has produced some worthwhile research.

Roles and Responsibilities

Another aspect of the use of technology within public sector systems revolves around roles and responsibilities. Technology may be used to support an existing role, in which case its cost may be justified in a political sense. It may even be used to create a new role or, more usually, a brace of new roles. It is thus an effective vehicle for growing public sector departments and creating jobs. Such an activity is, of course, readily aided and abetted by commercial consultants and technology suppliers who will be only too pleased to recommend any number of systems, each with their own support and maintenance contracts. Furthermore, should the requirements change, as they often do, then the same consultants may redefine and resell the same systems, with yet more support and maintenance contracts. In some countries, this technology to government supply chain is a perpetual activity which accounts for an enormous amount of business in monetary terms and, importantly from a political perspective, maintains significant numbers of public sector employees. Depending upon one's point of view, it may be posited that such a situation is an important factor with respect to job creation and the perpetuation of commerce. Alternatively, one might adopt the view that it represents a huge waste of resources that might be better deployed for the common good. In any event, such a situation is an embedded reality within our contemporary, political world.

Within all of this activity there is another, very important factor which often has serious implications for the efficiency and effectiveness of government agencies. This is the assumption that, somehow, the provision of technology absolves personal responsibility and eliminates the need for personal initiative. We see this again and again as government agencies become increasingly ineffective in parallel with the introduction of massively expensive technology projects. A good example of this is in law enforcement where the available technology is, in fact, very impressive compared with what was available just a decade or so ago, and yet crime levels seem to be soaring. Every day in the media we read some horror story about serious mistakes being made by police forces which one could not imagine being made 20 or 30 years ago when common sense, personal responsibility and a sense of purpose and pride in the role played a much more important part. The same seems to be the case within public sector education, where classrooms are overflowing with computer technology and yet standards in both teaching and student achievement have fallen alarmingly. Public hospital and health systems, particularly in the UK, are an absolute disgrace with respect to their inefficiency and the standard of care being realised for patients. Again, the media are full of stories of unqualified 'doctors' being recruited to key, and very lucrative positions, patients dying unnecessarily due to an alarming lack of basic care, other patients dying of infections contracted in the hospitals themselves due to a lack of basic cleanliness and care. Ambulances often fail to arrive in anything like a timely manner, resulting in more unnecessary deaths. And yet, the information technology within the health system is all pervasive and has represented a massive investment which no doubt would have been better spent on medical equipment or training for personnel. One could continue with an almost endless list of examples of almost inexplicable inefficiency which, in general, has the effect of deskilling the associated workforce while reducing the quality of life for society as a whole. In almost every case, the cause is rank bad management, supported by the ridiculous assumption that, somehow, the provision of technology will solve all such ills. Consequently, more technology is brought in and, not surprisingly, the situation worsens. The technology then becomes a convenient scapegoat as everyone blames the computer systems, rather than the lack of intelligent policy which resulted in their procurement. Another faintly ridiculous aspect of all this is the reliance that operational personnel place in the technology, often to the point of stupidity as they stick rigidly to whatever the technological process suggests, regardless of the reality of a given situation which might require a completely different approach. In such a manner, we are deskilling an entire generation.

We stress this aspect of the effect of technology upon roles and responsibilities as a warning against the folly of making similar assumptions with respect to biometric technology. The technology, used intelligently, may provide some worthwhile benefits and assist our endeavours in many areas. If used unintelligently, it will simply add a layer of confusion and lead to the further erosion of skills and common sense within the operational areas where deployed. We must not, for example assume that the introduction of biometric technology to border control procedures removes the need for skilled and experienced immigration officers who are able to apply common sense and reason, based upon experience, to a given situation. Similarly, in areas of law enforcement and criminology, law enforcement officers should not rely upon the technology, but simply appreciate it as another tool within a comprehensive and varied toolbox, underpinned by good quality training, operational experience and more than a modicum of common sense.

Naturally, all of the above applies equally to the private sector, although one would have hoped that in this area, a little more control over spending and realised benefits might be exercised. However, seeing how some of the larger organisations and utilities have implemented technology does make one wonder about this. Administrative efficiency certainly seems to have eroded almost to a point of complete collapse in many such organisations, the result being a severely impacted service, and the degradation of operational value to customers. The key message of this section is therefore that the provision of technology is not a replacement for managerial responsibility, either in the public or private sector. Furthermore, the technology should not become a self-serving entity that soaks up additional resource which might have been better deployed elsewhere. The same principle holds true with respect to biometric and identity management technology.

Law Enforcement

It was natural perhaps for law enforcement agencies to embrace biometric technology. After all, they had been using fingerprints for over a 100 years in order to identify criminals and, in more recent times, had developed automated fingerprint identification systems (AFIS) with which to match fingerprints against large databases using sophisticated pattern matching and other techniques, albeit in an off-line manner. The ability to match a live fingerprint against such a database, even if not quite in real time, represented a useful step forwards for law enforcement agencies. In addition, other biometrics, such as facial recognition for example, might prove extremely useful when combined with associated surveillance technology. Even so, it took a while for law enforcement agencies to truly grasp the potential of biometric technology within their sphere of operations. Having done so, they have now embraced the technology to such a degree that they may be in danger of placing too much reliance upon what is, after all, a fallible technology.

An example of the extent of this activity is the way in which, in the USA in particular, law enforcement has effectively hijacked immigration and border control processes for their own purposes. In this instance, the innocent are effectively being criminalized by having their fingerprints taken, matched against criminal records and then stored in what is, after all, a criminal database. In effect, millions of innocent citizens are being turned into criminals. Their crime being to have entered the USA mostly for purposes which will benefit the country, such as business or tourism. The pretext upon which this hugely significant social development has been introduced is the fight against terrorism. Several years after its implementation, no significant terrorists have been apprehended via this channel, to the author's knowledge as of the time of writing. Of course not – they would not be naive enough to volunteer their fingerprints in this way. Indeed, since the introduction of this idea, terrorism and serious crime have tended to increase in various areas around the world. However, from a political perspective, the concept provides politicians with a vehicle with which to claim that they are taking steps to protect their respective countries. Citizens will no doubt have varied perspectives as to the efficacy of such schemes, as well as the value of surrendering any vestige of privacy and dignity in return for such political rhetoric. Nevertheless, such powerful political ideas tend to take root and many countries are now following a similar path, albeit with slight variations. One might well ponder where this is all leading and what it means for future generations.

This intrusion of law enforcement into processes which are not criminal, but simply a part of everyday human activity, actually represents a very significant social change. Such huge changes have consequences and we shall no doubt see these reflected in future societal models. The creation of an 'us and them' relationship between state and citizen may or may not be sustainable over the longer term, especially when coupled to other national or societal ills such as economic recessions, a reduction of the quality of important functions such as education and healthcare and the general sense of well-being. These are dangerous waters to be sailing in. Especially so when the personal information gathered is passed to almost anyone who wants it or is willing to pay for it, thus creating an ever stronger control over individuals from both a political and commercial perspective. It may well transpire that, longer term, this stance from law enforcement of criminalising the innocent, actually does more to disenfranchise normally law abiding citizens and thus create more crime, than any good it could possibly have done in reducing terrorism. There is a particular danger here among impressionable youngsters, both male and female who, with a little inducement from those with a vested interest, will willingly adopt the stance of living up to expectations. After all, if they are treated like criminals from the outset, they may as well behave like criminals. However illogical this may seem, we must remember that, increasingly, the human race is producing many millions of youngsters who have no opportunity of a proper education, little or no ethical parental guidance and who are swamped with frivolous and suggestive communications, mostly of the wrong kind. The gap between the haves and the have-nots is increasing in many societies who consider themselves civilised and, furthermore, in many cases the have-nots are increasingly those who once considered themselves reasonably well placed. This is an interesting, but potentially worrying situation. The idea that such societal ills may be remediated by ever-increasing control over citizens by government may appear interesting to some from a theoretical perspective. However, if such controls are seen as failing to improve society while simultaneously robbing citizens of their dignity and right to privacy, the effect will be one of reducing the quality of life for everyone, and potentially setting the scene for a more radical change, as has happened throughout history. In this context, the manipulation of law enforcement for political purposes is a development which we should consider very seriously. From a technology perspective, we should equally consider what exactly it is that we are putting in place and why. We might also consider how such a capability might be used in less stable times, and by whom. In the previous chapter, we suggested the creation of a Biometrics Constitution. Such an entity is perhaps long overdue. After all, we can do much better than this.

Terrorism and Serious Crime

In 2007, the author prepared an extensive paper entitled 'Studies Into Serious Crime and Terrorism' for an international conference on the same theme which was to take place in Istanbul. Ultimately, the conference was cancelled, but the paper was adopted and published in the 2007 digest of the Galatasaray University (Galatasaray Universitesi Hukuk Fakultesi Dergisi) and may no doubt still be accessed from that source. The paper sought to place terrorism in perspective, focus upon the root ills of contemporary society and propose a practical way forwards which may easily be realised by an international consortium. A pertinent paragraph from the paper is herein reproduced.

When a child is born, it is not born a terrorist. Neither is it born a Muslim, Jew, Hindu, Buddhist or Christian. It is neither a democrat or republican, nor a socialist or conservative. It knows neither hatred or envy. At birth, it is simply a pure, unspoiled miracle of nature, beloved of its mother and ready to set out upon its pathway in life. Any ideas of violence, hatred and dishonesty are accumulated along the way, according to a combination of life experiences and direct family and peer influence. It is a strong child who can develop independently of such influence.

Therein lies an important truth. Terrorists are not terrorists because of a lack of personal identification and surveillance technology. Organised criminals do not follow their particular path in life because of a lack of the same. What we are witnessing in this respect is a symptom of other, deep rooted societal ills. Consequently, the problem will never be solved by any amount of technology. Furthermore, as we have already seen within the border control scenario, the imposition of such technology upon society as a whole achieves little in the way of addressing such issues or even apprehending those involved. This is hardly surprising if we think about it logically. Firstly, the assumption that a terrorist or serious criminal has to cross a border in order to perpetrate his or her chosen crime is faintly ridiculous. A study of terrorist attacks over, say, the past 30 years or so reveals that this is hardly ever the case. Secondly and equally ridiculous is the notion that the imposition of such controls is going to change the attitude of those who decide to follow such a path, especially as for those in appropriate positions, such a path is a particularly lucrative one. One must conclude therefore that the deployment of technology in this manner, without a deeper understanding of the associated societal issues, is largely a political exercise. The problem is, in following this political doctrine we are likely, if we are not very careful, to throw the baby out with the bathwater so to speak, by adding increasing layers of operational complexity while disenfranchising those who might otherwise be allies in the real fight against crime. Of course, we do need a proper law enforcement framework and such a framework should use technology as and where appropriate to support intelligent policies. We should beware however of embracing technology with an evangelist's fervour simply to support political agendas. Such an approach often leads to unfortunate complications.

In order to address such societal ills, as discussed, we must address them at the root source. We must understand what combination of conditions pushes individuals down such paths and seek to eliminate them. A critically important factor in this respect is education. With proper education comes understanding and capability. With understanding and capability, societies may shape their destiny in such a manner that hardly allows for the combination of conditions previously described. Of course, there will always be exceptions which need to be handled appropriately. However, in an intelligently conceived society, such exceptions will be few and far between. A key to handling them is a justice system which is seen to be fair and reflective of the natural justice which every human being understands. Such a judicial system will include a penal system which focuses on rehabilitation and industry at the individual level, ensuring that those involved will exit the system with a better set of understanding and capability than that harboured upon entry. Within our intelligent society, education and justice systems will be administered by capable agencies, staffed by properly trained individuals who understand factors such as responsibility and respect. You would think that, in the twenty-first century, those simple building blocks would, by now, have been in place in most civilised societies. The reality is, sadly, rather different. In the absence of such building blocks, the societal ills simply fester and regenerate, waiting for any excuse or opportunity to flourish.

A good example with which to illustrate this point is Britain. A once proud country whose administrative systems were often the envy of the world, where order prevailed and citizens had a sense of belonging and duty. A country who gave so much to the world in terms of science, technology and administrative process. Where education was taken seriously and students had a healthy respect for teachers. Where the law enforcement agencies were seen as friends of society. Indeed, the British 'Bobby', as was, was an integral and important element of all local communities and was affectionately respected accordingly. Where hospitals were administered with military precision coupled with sympathetic understanding and technical excellence. A small country whose young men in their hundreds of thousands gave even more to the world during the Second World War by laying down their lives for a democracy and way of life which they believed was worth preserving, while their women folk worked all hours in munitions factories and elsewhere to support this effort. Where ordinary citizens took in their stride, horrendous bombings during the blitz that made hundreds of thousands homeless across the country, and continued with a resolute calmness and composure which has never been witnessed since in any community. This spirit and sense of belonging was partly a factor of an education system which taught respect and offered a grounding in common sense and the primary subjects which served the individual well in whatever path they chose. Furthermore, this took place within a social environment where justice was seen to be on the side of the law-abiding individual and administrative affairs were conducted on behalf of the community with some level of integrity.

Compare that reality with the chaos and overt corruption with which modern Britain is now administered. The education system is in tatters and has been dumbed down to such an extent that many teenagers are leaving school in a state of semi-literacy and qualifications, such as they are, have become almost meaningless in terms of reflecting individual capabilities. A complete absence of discipline and respect characterises the majority of public sector schools, whose teachers seem to be little concerned with the welfare of those in their charge. No wonder that, for those who can afford it, private schools seem the only viable way of providing a meaningful education. The public health system is similarly in tatters and has become effectively useless for many, even though they have paid for it all of their working lives. Law enforcement has weakened to the point where local agencies effectively give up and, in some city areas, refuse to even patrol. The British Bobby, as once known and loved, has effectively disappeared from most communities. Curiously, in each of these examples, the individuals within these administrations have become very highly paid, as have the politicians at both a local and central level, distancing themselves ever further from grassroots society. Curious also, that all this is taking place within what has become known as the 'surveillance society' where there are more CCTV cameras per capita than anywhere else in the world. Where personal information has been passed on and sold to anyone who wants it, and where the worst perpetrators of this, against every tenet of their own data protection and privacy acts, are government agencies themselves. Where a recent study identified that there are more active links between commercial organisations and government ministers in Britain, than almost anywhere else in the world, a factor which usually reflects serious corruption in a proportional manner. Where elected members of parliament have been systematically defrauding the already over-generous expense system in their hoards, and see nothing wrong in this. Is it any wonder that, in spite of all the technological surveillance, serious and violent crime has risen in Britain to alarming and unprecedented proportions? Furthermore, the judicial system seems to be biased much more towards the benefit of criminals than victims, ensuring that this heinous level of serious social crime continues unabated. Do we really believe in our wildest dreams that any amount of technology is going to address these issues as they currently stand? Of course not. So long as we lack the courage and integrity to address them at root source, so long shall they proliferate. We have used Britain as an example, but no doubt the same could be said of many countries, to one degree or another. It is curious, is it not, that such societal decay runs in parallel with what we like to call the technology age? It need not be like this of course. But we must learn to place technology in a proper perspective. Technology has its place in the fight against crime, if used intelligently and to support robust and just operational processes. If manipulated in relative isolation, simply as an instrument of politics, then it has no hope whatsoever of addressing the societal ills so beloved of politicians for rhetorical purposes. If we are to create a better world for our descendants, we must acknowledge these realities and have the courage to inspire and initiate change. There are undoubtedly some good things we can do with biometrics and identity management technologies, but we should not confuse these with the politics for which they are often hijacked. It is time to reconsider such matters.

11

Scope Creep

One of the most prevalent and often destabilising effects within large-scale systems, particularly, but not limited to those within the public sector, is scope creep. This occurs when a system conceived for a specific purpose is pressed into service for other purposes, for which it was not properly designed. The result is often reflected in both operational performance, stability and, in many cases, relative security. This affects not only the technical infrastructure but, importantly, the data held within these systems. The source of scope creep is often political in one way or another. With respect to systems within the public sector, this often arises because one government agency wishes to access data held by another. Furthermore, this often occurs across international boundaries, further confusing the picture with respect to the effective management of data. In addition to technical considerations, there is an attendant issue with respect to the fact that citizens or systems users believe that the system is operating as intended whereas, in reality, something quite different is happening. Often, individuals have absolutely no idea what is really happening to their personal information.

As data is passed between systems and accessed by different parties, it is of course easily corrupted, modified or appended to. Indeed, this is precisely the aim of some systems which seek to collect and correlate data from a number of sources. In doing so, an assumption is made as to the accuracy of the original data. If this is inaccurate, then such inaccuracies will be promulgated throughout the various links and parallel systems. Once such scope creep and attendant third party links have occurred, there is no effective control over who has access to the data, for what reason and with what access authority. It may well be that one agency chooses to modify or update data according to its own requirements, in isolation of the original source data, leading to various versions of the truth being maintained. When important decisions are made in relation to the data, then which version of the truth will prevail? Scope creep with respect to any system is an undesirable thing, but when it involves personal information and aspects of identity management, then it is a particularly risky affair.

This brings us back to clarity of purpose and good systems design. If the operational requirement has been properly defined and documented, there is no reason why the system should not be designed precisely to meet this requirement in a robust and secure manner. Such a design will include all necessary links and interfaces and, once deployed, should be left alone to function as intended. Furthermore, the operational processes associated with such a design would also have been thoroughly developed and tested, negating any necessity to change. However, if such a system is subsequently modified in order to cater for new political agendas, then both the operational integrity and associated processes are immediately compromised. Of course, such scope creep can and sometimes does occur before the original system is even deployed, resulting in a continuous cycle of changes to the specification as the system is being developed, making it very difficult to pin down precise functionality and operational process. Such a situation explains how large-scale systems in the public sector often seriously overrun both their delivery schedule and associated budgets. Such scenarios should not really exist in the twenty-first century, and would not exist if projects were properly managed from the outset according to logical conventions.

Let it again be stressed that such situations are particularly serious when dealing with systems that process personal information. When biometrics are added to the mix, we additionally introduce all manner of assumptions around the associated data, as discussed earlier within this volume. Scope creep, for whatever reason, is to be avoided if we are to create and maintain robust, ethical systems.

Societal Development

There is another aspect of the politics around technology and its implementation, which might best be described as a broader impact upon societal development. This may become either positive or negative depending upon the technology in question and the perceived benefits that it brings, assuming of course that such benefits are properly understood. When the technologies in question are aligned predominantly with governmental control over citizens, then such developments may be considered very important as they form part of the relationship between citizen and state. Politicians would do well to understand this mechanism and its potential. Of course, political administrations may decide to simply ride roughshod over any such considerations and implement whatever level of control they can exert with the help of technology. Such a strategy doubtless appeals strongly to many administrations. However, if citizens are increasingly alienated as a result, then societies can start breaking down and this will have an adverse effect upon serious crime and underground activities. Not only does all history show this to be true, but a quick glance around the world as it is today reveals some interesting examples and degrees of this truth. In extreme examples, the situation can become unstable and lead to dramatic, if not catastrophic change. Strong words perhaps, but government agencies should nonetheless think very carefully about the use of certain technologies, how such usage is perceived, and how it will develop in future years and for future generations. Given that, in civilised countries at least, the fundamental idea of democratic government is to represent the views of citizens and manage national affairs on their behalf, the notion of increasing control under an 'us' and 'them' arrangement may not sit too comfortably with some sectors of society. To discuss, or even contemplate such matters will be seen as politically incorrect by many in government. However, we must not hide from such discussion, as to do so would be to constrain our understanding in some very important areas.

Biometric and identity management technologies are potentially very powerful, especially when aligned with other contemporary developments in information technology. They provide a level of surveillance and control which has hitherto been unavailable to global society. Such levels of power may be used more or less sympathetically according to the administration wielding them. Unfortunately, we have not got off to a good start in this respect, as technology is increasingly being used to control and exploit individuals without their permission or, indeed, without them having any say in the matter at all. This reality reflects a fundamental disrespect for the individual which is, frankly, alarming. If such trends continue, what does the future hold for our descendants? And what happens when the information which allows for such control falls into the hands of administrations that subsequently come in conflict? It seems that no one is prepared to stop and ask such questions. Perhaps it is time that we did so. Make no mistake, these technologies have already had a dramatic impact upon global society, and their implementation has caused previously respected legal instruments to be ignored and bypassed by both the public and private sectors. This, especially within administrations who describe themselves as democracies, represents a significant change to the very fabric of society. Whether such change is positive or negative may depend upon one's point of view. However, change is change and we should be sensible of its implications before rushing too quickly down any particular technological avenue. The pace of change in recent decades has been unprecedented and we have perhaps acquired the habit of accepting and implementing every strand of new technology as it surfaces, without really considering the broader implications. Such new technologies are, in turn, developed purely from a commercial perspective and fuel some of the world's largest industries. While that is understandable and indeed a necessary part of technological evolution, we should learn to consider the implementation of such technologies much more deeply and not just to blindly accept the propositions from technology suppliers. In particular, we should consider the longer term societal implications and ensure that we are implementing technology in an ethical and sustainable manner. This is particularly pertinent with respect to biometric technology, for reasons already discussed within these pages.

Such discussion should not be viewed as alarming, but simply as one of the many strands that any intelligent administration will consider as part of its ongoing technological and administrative strategy. Of course, societies are constantly in a state of flux and change may in itself be considered a constant. However, we surely need to ensure that, as far as is possible, such change is positive and generally enhances the quality of life for the majority. If change were to start going in the other direction, aided and abetted by technology, then that would equally surely be a bad thing. In order to understand where change is going and what the overall effects might be, we must be able to openly discuss all such possibilities and use such discussion to inform our strategy. An ill-informed or non-informed strategy will be a strategy out of control, and that, one might posit, is not the sort of societal development we are seeking.

Review Questions

1. How important is technology from a political perspective, and why?
2. Discuss the technology supply chain from a political perspective.
3. Discuss the use and efficacy of technology as used for law enforcement purposes.
4. Define scope creep and discuss the implications thereof.
5. Discuss the politics of technology in society.

The Future

12

Abstract In this chapter, we acknowledge the desirability of understanding trends and predicting the future with respect to information technology and its usage, whilst highlighting some existing areas which are particularly interesting in this respect. We predict a wider usage of identity management from an intelligence perspective, using personal transactional information to inform a broader business intelligence, both from an internal organisation perspective and from the broader commercial and marketing perspective. Such intelligence gathering is supported by tools providing functionality such as centralised log management and correlation across disparate information sources, often close to real time. Biometric-related information, such as likeness scores for example, might provide for some interesting systems-related intelligence and we discuss such matters accordingly.

We consider both the likely progress and associated issues with respect to virtualisation, including challenges around configuration. Such discussion leads logically to the concept of cloud computing, with which we may experience many challenges, including those around information security and identity management. In this context, we predict a proliferation of cloud identity management services and federated identity models, and posit that the proliferation of cloud technology may lead us into completely new ways of thinking around identity management. Biometrics may have a part to play, although there are some attendant challenges which will need to be carefully considered.

We predict that an even greater proliferation of online services and the use of mobile technology will ensue, bringing additional challenges and a new wave of sophisticated cybercrime. We also introduce the TOLL (Total On Line Licensed) model and question factors such as control, ownership, responsibility and data security. We suggest that, hand in hand with TOLL, the concept of professional services will expand and become a major consumed component of many organisations in both the private and public sectors. We additionally consider systems design and the migration towards web services, components and associated architectures as an operational systems model, as well as technology usage from the broader perspective, including ongoing challenges such as complexity, security, ownership, trust and identity theft. The pace of technological change is both exciting and not a little worrying in some respects. This chapter introduces some food for thought in this context and hopefully inspires further discussion.

J. Ashbourn, *Guide to Biometrics for Large-Scale Systems: Technological, Operational, and User-Related Factors*, DOI 10.1007/978-0-85729-467-8_12,
© Springer-Verlag London Limited 2011

Introduction

In casting one's gaze to the future, the picture may easily be obscured by the mist of incorrect assumptions or portended vision of the unexpected. We cannot predict with absolute accuracy what the future has in store for us. However, we can make informed predictions based upon past and current trends and can also foretell, at least to some degree, the challenges that await us. Indeed, looking to the future is a necessary part of managing today's activities both for the public and private sectors. Just as the past can inform what we do in the present, so too may intelligent or inspired visions of the future. Time itself is an interesting medium. In this section, we shall discuss various aspects of the future, as related to technology in general and biometrics and identity management in particular.

Trends

There exist many parallel trends reflecting various human endeavours at any one point in time, including, of course, the development and usage of technology. Within the context of this particular work, there are some interesting trends which we might usefully acknowledge and understand, whether we are a technology developer, systems integrator, commercial organisation or government agency. Some of these trends are discussed below.

Intelligence and Identity Management

The term 'identity management' was first used by the author more than 20 years ago when foreseeing that, what we used to call access control, would develop into a more sophisticated set of functions covering a broader spectrum of activities and encompassing a new range of technologies. Nevertheless, the popular view of identity management remains centred around access control and the administration of access control, whether in relation to internal systems or external access to commercial or governmental systems. In either case, we seek to provide access to services and systems functionality to known individuals based upon their particular access privileges. We tend to achieve this via the use of directories which, rather like the concept of a printed telephone directory, provide lists of known individuals, aligned with a set of credentials which provide access to a defined set of services. Within such a framework we may also define groups into which we may subsume both individuals and services of a like nature, facilitating a straightforward administration of the whole. Within a small organisation or a limited service, the management of access in this manner is relatively straightforward. As organisations grow in size or services become more widely available, the administration of such a mechanism becomes proportionally more challenging. Furthermore, security becomes more of an issue, necessitating different approaches such as two factor authentication or the use of certificates and keys. Nevertheless, the fundamental principle of seeking to grant access to functions, services and information, only to those who may legitimately use them, remains.

But things are changing. Whereas an integral component of identity management has been to provide an audit trail, this function has primarily been used in a retrospective manner in order to investigate breaches of access or other events of interest to the implementing agency. A recent trend has been to develop this concept of an audit trail into a broader intelligence gathering mechanism which may be used in a variety of ways in order to support a more general business intelligence function. The idea being that, within our information age, information of any kind is a valuable commodity and, information appertaining to the actions of an individual, is of particular interest, albeit to different entities for different purposes. Within an organisation, such intelligence may be used to track the activities of an individual and understand how they are working and functioning in relation to their position, including the times at which they usually undertake certain functions. This is no doubt of value from a human resource management perspective and may also be valuable from an information security perspective, especially, for example, if a sudden change to a given routine is noticed. Within a commercial context, understanding a customer's online activities and preferences is considered extremely valuable from a marketing perspective. Furthermore, such information has an inherent value in itself and may be sold on to third parties (albeit intruding upon the privacy of the individual, in contradiction of many data protection acts). Government agencies have also realised the commercial potential of the information they hold about individuals, however collected, and routinely provide such information to the private sector as well as exchanging it with other agencies. Of course, it is not just organisational access or web-based activities which may be harvested in this way. Any situation whereby the user has a token associated with their identity may be monitored, including the use of credit cards, ATM machines and even corporate loyalty cards.

Given this reality, however questionable some of the more commercial aspects of it may be, it is perhaps inevitable that, within the organisational sphere, there will be a growing trend of merging identity management with business intelligence. Such a trend is supported by sophisticated analytical tools such as centralised log management, as well as the inherent functionality within identity management specific tools. It is thus a simple matter to correlate such information and provide an increasingly complete view of associated activities. This is, of course, very useful from a security perspective as, what may have previously been considered as disparate events, may be correlated together in context. Such capabilities may also be useful from a systems management perspective, especially in relation to version control, patch management and similar activities. Consequently, there are many potentially useful aspects around a more intelligent usage of identity management information, providing of course that the tools being used are correctly configured and hold accurate information. This last point is particularly important as the configuration of many such tools is by no means a simple business. If configured poorly or incorrectly, then the information provided as a result may not be relied upon.

A further, and very interesting factor, is the prospect of automation within such tools, providing them with the capability of essentially real time, or close to real time, activity monitoring and the automated generation of alerts and reports, accordingly. However, we must acknowledge that such systems are not in themselves intelligent. The intelligence must come from their configuration by members of the implementing project team who really understand the organisation and its various systems. It is for this reason that such systems can rarely, if ever, be installed and commissioned successfully by third party systems integrators. To create an intelligent configuration, including all the necessary links and feeds from other systems, requires an in-depth understanding of both the organisational technical architecture and the attendant business processes, including of course, in this context, identity management. When we add biometrics into the mix, there are some interesting factors to consider. Should we, for example, in addition to recording instances of binary match and fail transactions, also record the transactional score which, as you will remember, reflects the degree of likeness between the reference biometric and the live sample? Doing so might provide us with an interesting insight into transactional performance, including equivalence of performance across operational nodes. If we do so, then there will be a further degree of integration involved. In addition, what assumptions will we be making as to the results of any biometric identity verification transaction from a business intelligence perspective? There are some interesting concepts with which to grapple in this context. Similarly, with respect to online systems if a biometric is involved, there is the question of non-repudiation and, again, the assumptions made with respect to a biometric. There is no doubt that we shall see an increasing coordination of identity management and business intelligence, using information from access transactions, in association with other information, to inform our view of operational activity. There is similarly no doubt that we shall encounter challenges with respect to the provision of such functionality and that we shall have to tread carefully, especially with regard to assumptions made due to the correlation of disparate data. Such challenges may of course be overcome, although we should not assume that making such transitions will be easy. The success of any such enterprise will no doubt be proportional to the attention to detail and the amount of time that we are able to bestow upon it.

Virtualisation and the Cloud

One of the more significant developments in recent times has been the contemporary model of virtualisation whereby applications and data may reside upon a virtual computing machine which may, in turn, reside upon any available hardware platform within the virtualised architecture. The theory of course is that the available technical infrastructure within a given organisation may be more efficiently exploited by matching processing power with the computational requirement on a dynamic basis. Thus, an application may not be tied to one physical computer, but may be moved around within the infrastructure according to load. In addition, several applications may be run within their own virtual machine upon one host server, providing a degree of operational isolation, providing that sufficient resources are available. The concept is not so far removed from the original model of networked computing and the sharing of processor cycles, but there are important differences from a dynamic perspective. Some of these will revolve around versioning and configuration and some, naturally, around identity management within such an environment. The user's credentials must be available to every potential instance of the application and must be pertinent to the precise configuration. This should, in theory, be managed transparently by the virtual machine management layer. However, things are often not as straightforward as they might at first appear and we might encounter some interesting scenarios in this context, including around the logging of transactional information. Virtualisation may actually be a poor choice of approach in many operational instances. Nevertheless, it will be marketed strongly and many organisations will follow the trend without necessarily understanding the implications. In particular, when the virtualisation is provided as a third party service using third party hardware, over which the client organisation has absolutely no control. This complicates many functions, including the tailoring of business intelligence and regulatory compliance. It also complicates effective identity management and, if biometrics are utilised, the related architectural configuration and associated management of the biometric functionality.

Such ideas are further extrapolated into what has become known as the cloud. Cloud services seek to supply not only the infrastructure but, increasingly, applications, all hosted by a third party. Furthermore, identity management as a cloud service is increasingly being proposed, however the relative sophistication of such proposals currently varies quite considerably. In many cases, it is predominantly a matter of providing some sort of single sign on capability, with perhaps some limited user provisioning. In others, there is talk of federated identities and externally hosted directories. Organisations embracing the cloud concept should consider such matters in some depth. In simple terms, one might wonder how an existing organisational identity management model, complete with its various policies and provisioning capabilities, is to be integrated into a third party hosted cloud infrastructure. And at what cost? It is curious that, under the pretext of saving costs, cloud services introduce many new costs which will be over and above that previously met by clients. In the context of identity management, especially for any sizeable organisation, there will undoubtedly be costs of both migration and, quite possibly, additional ongoing costs due to the provision of externally hosted identity management services which were previously included as a part of everyday IT management. A likely scenario is that, with cloud infrastructure providers unable or unwilling to provide sophisticated identity management services, existing companies specialising in directories and identity management will offer an intermediate service which, while compatible with the cloud service provider's architecture, provide a finer level of configuration and control from the cloud client's perspective. Indeed, such services are already in the pipeline and, by the time this book is in print, will no doubt be well established. Of course, from the client's perspective, this equates to additional ongoing cost, coupled to a loss of absolute control over this vitally important factor. However, it may be that our way of thinking about identity management will be changed irrevocably by the advent of cloud computing. It may be that we lean towards the idea of federated identities and seek to place tighter control upon other aspects of information security. Such a model is interesting to contemplate. No doubt those who are keen on identity theft and malicious activities in general also find the idea of interest. This is inevitable as, when we introduce any new concept within the field of information technology, there will be a parallel activity among fraudsters and others who will seek to introduce equally revolutionary exploits. We must try to anticipate their efforts as we design our new infrastructures and this is especially the case with respect to identity management.

The idea of biometrics utilised within cloud based identity management raises some interesting questions. Where, for example is the biometric check undertaken? If we plan to undertake this locally, then the opportunity arises to spoof the binary result as it enters the

12

cloud. If we undertake the check within the cloud, then registration becomes an interesting issue, as does maintenance of the reference database and its alignment with personal data which may come from a different source. In addition, what happens in the case of biometric capture device hardware refresh? How is calibration achieved and, as mentioned several times within this work, how will equivalence of realised performance be maintained? There are ways around all of these issues and a capable third party supplier should be able to design an architecture and methodology which combines reasonable performance with transactional security. However, implementation will need to be handled with care, especially if a federated identity model is envisaged. The cloud is no doubt here to stay as it offers technology suppliers some unique advantages with respect to their business model. Furthermore, for many users, migrating to the cloud will effectively represent a one-way street as extricating themselves from it will prove extremely difficult once they have gone down this road. This, of course, is the whole idea from the technology supplier's perspective. With respect to the reliable use of biometric technologies in the cloud, there is still some work to do.

Online Services

Another huge change that we have seen in recent times is the provision of online services. Initially, this was implemented as bulletin boards and simple email facilities but, with the advent of the World Wide Web, the opportunity to offer both information services and commerce over this channel has been quickly exploited. Nowadays, there is very little in the way of everyday transactions that you cannot undertake via the Internet. Finance, banking, shopping, healthcare, government, travel, education, employment, entertainment and a host of other functions, may all be accessed via the Internet using a simple web browser. This brings a great deal in terms of convenience, but also opens some doors onto vulnerabilities from a security perspective, including around identity management. Simple real-time hacks to break into organisational servers and steal information have given way to sophisticated methods of extracting information by stealth, often by planting Trojans onto targeted machines in order to monitor transactions and siphon off important information. The scale of such scams with respect to stolen credit card numbers caused the payment card industry to issue its own security specification in the form of the Payment Card Industry Data Security Standard, with which merchants are obliged to comply. While this will not eliminate all such fraud, it will at least ensure that the infrastructure of compliant merchants is configured to a reasonable standard from a security perspective. However, payment card fraud is simply one of many strands of malicious activity which can affect online transactions.

A common denominator for most online services is that they require a degree of identity management in order to have some degree of confidence that the person accessing the service is who they believe them to be. Typically, this is orchestrated via the familiar user name and password model. Of course, if these credentials are compromised and subsequently used by an impostor, then the service provider has no way of knowing this, as they do not know who is actually on the other end of the line, so to speak. In instances of fraudulent online credit card transactions, the fraudster must also have the full details of the card, including the security number printed on the back. This would usually imply that the card is present at the time of the transaction and has possibly been stolen. Fraudsters can of course act quickly and if they have the user's online credentials, which they may have acquired via a monitoring agent or even a web browsers history if the browser has not been configured securely, then acquisition of the credit card, or its full details, will see them using it quickly in a variety of situations. Again, this is only one form of online scam. There are many others, including breaking in to personal banking transactions and all manner of impostor activities. However, obtaining the personal details and user credentials of the targeted victim is key to many such fraudulent activities. A small step further and we are in the realms of identity theft, which can have very serious consequences indeed for the victim.

We risk labouring the point about online fraud to emphasise the all-pervasive presence of the Internet in society and the challenges that this brings. We might similarly emphasise the situation with information theft, bogus web sites and many other such ills which have been created by this technological development. The interesting point here is that this perceived explosion in online services, however revolutionary it may have seemed, is likely to be just the beginning. Government agencies and commercial organisations alike are gearing themselves up for a world where the provision of many services will only be possible via the web. Even broadcast media is moving more and more in this direction. When this point is reached, the attractiveness of the web for organised criminals will be similarly enhanced. Denial of service attacks in particular will no doubt become more sophisticated and will be implemented upon a broader scale. Consider also the implications for cloud computing and professional services hosted by third parties. If the cloud goes down, everything goes down with it, including your business if you have placed a full reliance upon this mode of operation. This simple fact will not have escaped the organised crime fraternity. Forget any assurances provided by technology suppliers, because if such a catastrophe were to occur, such matters will be the least of everyone's problems.

Such considerations bring to mind many matters, including secure infrastructures, resilience, disaster recovery processes and, our old friend, identity management. For it is compromises in identity management, at all levels, which often provide the intelligence needed for the fraudsters to strike. Consequently, as the world moves increasingly towards the provision of online services, often via networks and mobile devices which already leave something to be desired from a security perspective, the concept of identity will become increasingly important. As technology suppliers, service suppliers and device manufacturers ponder such matters, the concept of biometric identity verification will no doubt occur to many of them and we shall equally no doubt see some interesting implementations of the technology in this context. Such developments will introduce various technological challenges, as already discussed, together with challenges around operational processes and the assumptions made about the efficacy of biometric identity verification transactions. Nevertheless, there may be some valuable advances made, perhaps in the way that biometric technology might be integrated with other identity management technologies in order to provide mechanisms which offer a higher confidence than those available today. The proliferation of online services may actually drive a new wave of thinking around identity management, and such thinking will necessarily encompass the concept of biometrics, even if not implemented as currently envisaged.

Mobile Technology

Mobile technology has been racing ahead with all manner of new functionality and form factors with the mobile phone in particular adopting a capability well beyond that of telephone conversations. Such developments may be more significant than many suppose, especially as much of the marketing is targeted towards the younger generation who have grown up within the mobile information age and, perhaps, have some different expectations of the associated technology than those which their forebears may have entertained. A quick look at both the hardware and software offerings in the mobile phone sector will quickly verify this marketing approach. However, there is a parallel marketing drive towards business users and an effective merging of functionality. Social networking, games and online entertainment functionality thus merges with the ability to synchronise the mobile device with specific computers and networks, providing an effective extension to the office for mobile workers. In addition to mobile phones, there remain a plethora of laptop, notebook and netbook mobile computers which share similar functionality. From a mobile phone network perspective there are of course bandwidth constraints which may place limits on file download sizes and interactive capabilities, although localised wireless networks can offer more in this respect and, in any event, the network technology will tend to develop in order to provide the functionality that users, or perhaps marketing executives, desire.

We thus have a situation wherein mobile phone users may place telephone calls, send and receive text messages, send and receive email messages, access and browse the Internet, play games, watch movies, listen to the radio, run applications, synchronise with a remote computer and access files, take photographs, collaborate on social networking sites, receive direct marketing messages from service providers, verify their precise location via GPS and access maps, and a host of other functionality. Similarly, from the hardware perspective, such devices have become quite sophisticated, with high resolution touch screens, integral QWERTY style keyboards, high resolution imaging devices and other features. More conventional computing devices such as notebook and tablet computers are starting to replicate some of these features with integral imaging devices, touch screen and variations of wireless connectivity. It is hard to ignore such developments, or the pace with which they are taking place. Clearly, mobile technology is going to become increasingly important within the broader information technology sphere. Consider also the parallel developments around virtualisation and cloud computing. Already we have virtual machines on mobile phones, enabling one hardware device to provide effectively several mobile phones which may be used for different purposes or on different networks. We also have a move towards operating systems in the cloud, as currently expressed via the Google Chrome operating system, as well as a wide range of business and leisure applications hosted in the cloud. Such developments lead us increasingly towards the possibility, if not probability, of dumb devices, whether laptop or notebook computers or mobile phones, who utilise their functionality in terms of both operating system and applications, solely upon a subscribed online basis. Let us call this the TOLL (Total On Line Licensed) model.

Under the TOLL model, all the important infrastructural and operational functionality is provided by third parties. This will of course include security and the management of identity. There are all sorts of things which might be achieved with encrypted communications and locked down device configurations, but who will be in control of such things? And how easily may they be compromised? The TOLL model certainly raises some interesting questions. No doubt, as devices, operating systems, middleware and software continue to be developed, the concept of biometrics will surface from time to time. There are many ways in which biometrics might be implemented on mobile devices. Touch sensitive screens might be used, for example to capture fingerprints, or small capacitive fingerprint sensors may be integrated into the hardware. It may even be possible to run a signal through a Plexiglas display cover and pick up an interference pattern, as was suggested well over a decade ago. Integral imaging devices may be used with facial recognition systems, although the matching algorithms may need to improve somewhat, but there is little doubt that such improvements will be made. They might also be used for iris recognition, where the matching algorithms are already of a high standard. Voice verification may be employed upon mobile phone devices. There are all manner of possibilities in this context, even if the biometric is used as a second factor for authentication purposes, or maybe used simply to release a certificate from a mobile device. Currently, for the Blackberry device, it is possible to use a wireless smart card reader. It would be a small step to integrate biometrics into such a model and there are various chip on card technologies which may undertake the biometric match right on the card itself. With a little creative thinking, service providers may easily integrate biometric technology with the mobile model. With respect to the TOLL model, the requirement for secure identity verification becomes even more pertinent. When considering such matters, we should think in terms of a total architecture rather than an end point device. When the total architecture has been robustly conceived, we may overlay an equally robust operational process. Such a process must necessarily include a secure registration model which may be transportable across different types of organisation. It must also include a support and maintenance model which is geared towards managing biometric configuration and sustainable operation. These are challenges, no doubt, but they are not insurmountable challenges. It will be interesting to witness future developments in this area.

Service Industries

The provision of services has mushroomed as a business model, with telecommunications providers becoming Internet Service Providers, mobile network providers and more, all at substantially higher costs than people were used to paying for related services. Similarly, the entertainment service providers have created very lucrative business models around what used to be provided at little or no cost. In the information technology arena, technology suppliers have realised that they can make as much, if not more, from supplying professional services, than they do from the core technology. They have managed to manipulate the market in such a manner that clients pay extra for items like support and maintenance, when this used to be supplied for nothing as part and parcel of the product. Even manuals are no longer supplied, forcing clients to pay extra for any related information. One might view such developments as something between progress and organised crime, depending upon one's perspective. Nevertheless, for better or for worse, we have very much become a service-based society. This model will doubtless continue and expand into many different areas in the coming years. A case in point is the provision of cloud computing, including hosted infrastructures and hosted applications.

The cloud computing model is set to expand almost exponentially within the next few years as potential clients believe all the hype without understanding the implications. From the relatively simple model of hosted infrastructure, wherein a client organisation may simply rent processing power for a finite time period, we shall see the creation of more complex models whereby almost everything except your organisation specific data is provided by the service provider, as described via the TOLL model in the previous section. Whether it is wise to place your core operational functionality in the hands of a third party, who you do not even know, is a matter for conjecture. However, commercial organisations and government agencies alike have a habit of following like sheep where technology is concerned and, once a few key players have trodden this path, others will quickly follow, however illogical the journey might seem. As the concept becomes increasingly adopted, it will occur to many that factors such as data security, disaster recovery and identity management are typically not robustly defined within such models. This will pave the way for a whole brace of add-on services to be developed and provided, at additional cost, in order to complement the host service. Such add-on services will themselves mutate into a multitude of variations, each with their own buzzwords and fancy phrases to be discussed at IT conferences everywhere. The whole will develop into a giant, global jambalaya into which clients will pour in their organisation specific data and hope that it somehow survives unscathed. Individual users will likewise provide their personal information, possibly into federated identity management schemes, to be stirred in with the mix. One slight problem with this model is that the hotplate which keeps the jambalaya simmering is not just one hotplate, but hundreds, or even thousands of them, distributed across the world in locations that only the service provider knows. Indeed, even the service provider may not know where they are, as it is likely that service providers will increasingly use third parties to supply and manage the physical infrastructure.

The question is, how will this model develop in the future. The TOLL concept may seem attractive to some organisations and government agencies in terms of removing any concern of infrastructure, software and all that goes with it, including security. This may prove to be a short-sighted approach. However, having got this far, the service providers will be looking for the next logical step which, in many cases, may be actually taking over the core business. Thus, we would have the concept of virtual organisations, whereby the business organisation is nothing more than a few individuals coordinating a collection of services provided by third parties. This model would even seem to fit some government agencies quite well, as they could wash their hands of the necessity to actually manage their own administrations. The problems herein are manifold. Prominent among them are the absence of ownership, responsibility and accountability. When things go wrong, and of course they will, who is going to take responsibility and see that they are put right? The top-level organisation? They will not be able to as they do not have any control over the operation. The service provider? Of course not, they are simply providing a service to the client organisation. There would be some serious issues to attend to in this context alone. Furthermore, there would be innumerable issues from a technological responsibility perspective, not to mention those from an operational transaction perspective. And identity management? We must think very carefully about where such models are leading. The transition from real industries to service industries changes many of the concepts of support and, ironically service, with which we have been familiar in recent decades. We have already witnessed this in what is curiously called 'customer support' as practiced by many large organisations in the financial, retail and other sectors. This is what happens when monopolies are allowed to develop. The same could happen to organisations themselves as monopolies develop with respect to the provision of IT-related services. Again, we have already witnessed this in the real costs of support and maintenance with respect to conventional models. No doubt some would posit that this may simply reflect the twenty-first century societal evolution. Nevertheless, we should consider such matters very carefully. With respect to biometrics and identity management, much may depend upon the scale. Within a small- or medium-sized operation, a discreet, self-managed system may continue to work well. Upon a larger scale, perhaps for multinationals, one can foresee a move towards federated identity and perhaps multi-factor authentication. For systems in the public domain, such a model may also appear attractive to government agencies. In order to facilitate such a model, it may be that we use the available technologies in different ways to those implemented today. The service industry element of this may bring some quite radical changes, indeed, it may even change the way in which we think about the concept of identity with respect to everyday transactions altogether. Make no mistake, services industries are changing, and will continue to change our world.

Systems Design

It is interesting to note how the concept of systems design has developed in recent times. From an application perspective, in the past, we have tended towards holistic, properly compiled code which contained most of the required functionality and ran efficiently upon the platforms for which it was designed. More recently, the advent of interpreted code environments such as Java and Microsoft's dot Net have tended to proliferate. In the case of Java, this has provided a degree of portability across platforms, albeit at a slight cost in performance. Within the dot Net environment, certain basic functionality is taken care of within the run-time environment, allowing developers to concentrate more on core functionality, although only for Microsoft platforms. The ubiquity of the Internet has driven a multi-layered architecture wherein web front ends connect to middleware, which in turn connects to back-end databases and core applications. Within such an architecture, many basic functions are provided by web services: blocks of reusable code which may be called by the application or, indeed, multiple applications as required. We are thus moving increasingly into a modular development and implementation environment whereby applications tend not be holistic, but rather comprise of a series of functional components, some of which may be reused or perhaps bought in from third parties. Many refer to this model as a Service Oriented Architecture wherein such modular services are often available via a service bus. On the Internet, the service bus may effectively be the Internet itself, as functional components may be called from other third party locations. In such a manner, related services may be grouped and offered via a single web portal, even if not provided by the same supplier. We are no doubt destined to see more of this, particularly as mobile devices become more widely used to deliver services in close to real time. Abstracting often used functionality into logical blocks, whether as web services or something else, makes sense in this context as specialist knowledge for a given function may be encapsulated and reused by others.

In the future, applications may be quickly conceived, built, tested and deployed by relying increasingly upon this service-based model. Such an approach will be particularly pertinent to those offering cloud computing services, whereby generic applications may be easily customised towards specific requirements via the adoption of functional modules arranged in a particular manner. The ease of construction and delivery will be considered to outweigh any issues around support and maintenance of the functional modules. This already happens to a degree, but we are likely to see a somewhat deeper and more seamless integration in this respect. Identity management becomes interesting within such a model. Within a discreet, closed environment, we would traditionally have used a directory service, hosted upon the discreet network, together with the appropriate administrative workflow. This is fine for a discreet environment where all users are known to the system. In the cloud however, things might become more interesting as the concept of federated identity will increasingly be considered, together with an identity as a service approach. If one may simply append identity management to a broader application on a 'plug-in' basis, and then allow users to interact with this as a service, then some interesting possibilities present themselves. Such services will no doubt quickly be available from technology suppliers who specialise in these areas. Integrating biometric functionality into such a model will be a little more complex, depending upon the approach taken. If individuals are in control of their own biometric, perhaps via a token such as a smart card for example, then this might be verified locally upon the initiation of a given transaction. The workflow from that point onwards might not use the biometric itself but some other form of token or certificate. A primary factor in this context will be the registration process and the confidence that may be held around such an identity. If a fraudulent identity is created at source, then this will of course proliferate throughout all subsequent activity. A development of this thinking may be that of anonymous identity verification, whereby the system does not actually need to know the identity of the individual in explicit terms, but merely that they are entitled to the service and have been authenticated to a degree concomitant with the perceived risk from a transactional perspective. In pertinent cases, a unique identifier may be used throughout the end-to-end transactional workflow in order to associate with an identity, should it ever be necessary to do so, thus alleviating the need to capture and store personal information for every transaction. There are many potential variations on a theme which may be explored. The primary factor here is to understand large-scale systems architectures and applications, especially when provided partly or largely by third parties, and the data flow throughout these systems. Biometrics and identity management functionality may then be overlaid upon this architecture in a manner which is practically realisable, ethical and sustainable. In some cases, this may require a complete rethink of how we view identity management and, certainly, the use of biometrics. We should not shrink from this challenge as it may represent the inspiration we need to take a significant step forwards with respect to practical identity management for the future.

Technology Usage

The use of technology may be broadly subdivided into two categories. Firstly, the use of contemporary technology, which is readily available, albeit sometimes with a cost of entry for early adopters. Secondly, the use of pioneering technology, which may not yet be main-stream but which has perhaps a special relevance to a given organisation. With respect to the use of available technologies, before such technologies may be used to good effect, they must be properly understood and placed in context. In most cases, this will necessitate an organisational function in order to monitor related developments and be able to relate them to the operational requirement. This is often not as straightforward as it might sound, as often such a function will be at the mercy of supplier-provided information which is often rather ambiguous as to the actual availability and status of a given technology. In this respect, it is typical that supplier organisations will somewhat overstate the capabilities or development status of a new product or technology, partly in order to be able to gauge response from potential users. Even when a product is launched, it may not function or perform in quite the manner that pre-release information has led people to believe. It is for this reason that many organisations wait for the second version of a product or technology before investing in it. Here lies a dichotomy. In order to realise business or operational advantage in a competitive manner, one must employ the best technology available within a given business sector. On the other hand, the risk of being an early adopter, particularly of radical new technology, may be very real. A balance must be struck between the two approaches which align with the operational situation of the organisation. In many cases, such a situation may not arise at all. For example, if the operation is functioning quite happily and effectively on technology which is 10 years old and may be easily supported, then there may be no need to change anything or to seek new approaches. This is actually an important factor that many organisations do not seem to understand, as they have been lured or coerced into a constant upgrade cycle which, while suiting the technology suppliers, actually places them in a perpetual state of inefficiency and uncertainty. In other cases, it may be important from a marketing perspective to exploit new technologies and function-ality appropriate to that market. However, in such a case, one should be highly selective and not just blindly accept every new development that comes along. Bear in mind that the adoption of any new technology has both a cost and a risk.

The other area of pioneering technology is particularly interesting. It is difficult to predict which emerging technologies are going to have such an impact that they signifi-cantly change the way we go about things. These are sometimes referred to as disruptive technologies because of their overall effect. Often, they come about almost by accident when something quite different is being researched and, suddenly, the broader relevance of one particular strand is appreciated and developed accordingly. Sometimes this happens within the same laboratory, sometimes it is someone else who spots the potential and develops it, perhaps for an entirely different market. Modern history is peppered with many such incidents. Sometimes, the reverse seems to happen when a technology area which everyone agrees has tremendous promise, simply fails to mature and deliver on that promise. From an organisational perspective, being aware of such background research and understanding its potential might be regarded as a valuable asset. Even if it is not appropriate to become involved in trials or community research projects, such an intelligence may well usefully inform future strategy. These days it is quite easy to discover such information, especially via officially backed community research programmes, or simply by keeping up-to-date with organisations engaged in relevant research.

Currently, there are various interesting pockets of research which may well impact upon the operation of large-scale systems. One such area is that of super efficient or 'green' networks whereby the power usage of computing would reduce my orders of magnitude. If such a goal is realised then, coupled with large-scale compact data storage, the whole computing infrastructure could suddenly become significantly larger, or otherwise accommodate a good deal more processing capability. This, in turn, might facilitate an increased capability for dynamic links and the cross referencing of information in order to provide enhanced services. Significantly increased communications bandwidth is another area which could bring changes in how we provide or receive information, with the possibility of video almost everywhere including, where applicable, high resolution video. Of course, with all this additional information, the prospect of information overload becomes very real and potentially confusing with respect to the relationship between client and service provider, in both the private and public sectors. For these reasons, the ability to conduct intelligent searches, detect patterns within data and perhaps tag metadata will no doubt become an area of priority within some sectors. The perennial research area of artificial intelligence may find some new and worthwhile strands to pursue in this respect.

Against this exciting research and development backdrop, we might usefully consider the position with respect to biometrics and identity management. It is expected that progress will be made with regard to biometric matching algorithms and, consequently, the performance of biometric systems in general. One area which might be less obvious is perhaps concerned with the capture of the live biometric and whether different materials or other technologies might facilitate a step change in this context. We have already referred, in this work, to the concept of equivalence of realised performance across operational nodes and this may also be an area where real progress could be made, especially where multi-modal biometrics are employed. Perhaps there will be totally new biometrics emerging for specific applications. The links between human factors and machine intelligence might also throw up some interesting ideas. Then there are the established areas of identity credentials, directory systems and so on, which might benefit from some radical rethinking. In any event, we should be sensible of related research and development and remain open minded as to the possibilities offered by such developments. We may be on the verge of some very significant changes within the broader area of IT and how we use it.

Challenges

There exist many challenges with respect to the implementation of technology in general and these are often proportional to the overall scale and scope of the systems concerned. With respect to the use of biometrics and identity management within large-scale systems, such challenges may lie partly within the specialist technology area of biometrics and partly within the more general technology area, while additional challenges will exist around the integration and interoperability between the two. It would be inappropriate to attempt to list all of these challenges within this work as such a list would quickly become unhelpful within the context of many systems and applications. Instead, a few key areas will be highlighted in order to emphasise the point that, with any large-scale undertaking within the sphere of information technology, it is not so much the technology itself which presents challenges, but the way in which it is implemented coupled to the operational processes associated with such an implementation. Such matters need, ideally, to be very carefully considered before the system is designed. Only then may we achieve a systems design which is closely aligned with clarity of purpose and, consequently, likely to be sustainable and reliable.

Complexity

One of the enemies of any system is complexity. When a system becomes over complex, any functional processing or workflow necessarily becomes complex and adds further complexity to the whole, thus generating something akin to a positive feedback model. Adding layers of infrastructure, such as that inherent in virtualisation and cloud computing, adds additional complexity as the same processing and workflow now has to navigate throughout these additional layers. Furthermore, if these layers are administered by third parties, then there are likely to be additional interface layers to negotiate. In recent years, we have perhaps had a tendency to over-complicate things by constantly adding layers of technical complexity in order to provide a more sophisticated functionality. The problem with this approach is that, when things need to be reconfigured, for whatever reason, the difficulty in doing so is correspondingly enhanced. Furthermore, testing becomes more difficult and problematic as there will be a myriad of dependencies, some of which you may not even be aware of. Another issue is the maintenance of an understanding of the whole, which may prove extremely difficult when multiple layers are involved. Not fully understanding the architecture upon which your system is running has, of course, implications of its own.

As the operational architecture becomes more complex, the operational processes similarly follow suit as they have to accommodate and anticipate such an architecture. When things go wrong, as they will, the fallback processes become additionally complex as they must cater for a myriad of possible eventualities. In order to do this successfully, they must understand all of these possibilities. Yet complexity is also the enemy of understanding. It follows therefore that simplicity is what we should be aiming for. Simplicity comes from a combination of clarity of purpose and good systems design. Within such a model the systems architecture should be sufficient to support the operation, but no more. Its messaging should be as direct as possible, its processing undertaken at the optimal point and there should be no unnecessary links and feeds to other systems. Administrative functionality should exist simply to support the primary operation and should be streamlined accordingly. These are all basic tenets which should accompany all good systems design. However, the road to good systems design seems sometimes to become obscured by technology marketing aspirations.

Security

Following on from complexity is the subject of security. It goes without saying that the more complex a system becomes, the more difficult it becomes to maintain security. Even defining security may prove troublesome in some instances. Security of what? Where? And under what conditions? Security should be aligned with risk, but how is risk perceived and defined in relation to a complex multi-layered system? A good starting point is to understand, really understand, all the transactional data flows which exist within the broader system, together with the architecture that they traverse. This will allow for the relative security of the data to be evaluated at each point and ensure that suitable security measures are in place, from the point of origin to the stored transaction, if indeed storage is necessary. When a system is constructed from various components supplied by various vendors and cobbled together by a lead systems integrator, understanding security in this way may become difficult. It is nonetheless important as, without such an understanding, vulnerabilities will undoubtedly exist. A necessary component of security is of course access control, in order to ensure that only those authorised may access or manipulate the data for which they are authorised. The administration of the access control must in itself be secure and this may be facilitated by good systems design and robust processes including a proper segregation of duties. There are various tools which may be employed in this context; however, some of them introduce complexities of their own which may not be necessary within the operational scope of many applications. One must be wary of utilising top heavy tools simply because they are described as industry leading or have impressive sounding functionality. In some cases, the introduction of these heavyweight tools causes a good deal of disruption, soaks up resources and may actually introduce vulnerabilities that were not previously present. This is not necessarily a criticism of the tools themselves or their suppliers, but rather an acknowledgement that buying in a brace of tools with the assumption that this is going to solve all organisational issues is a tactic which rarely works and often backfires. For all aspects of our large-scale system, including security, the starting point must be absolute clarity of purpose, translated into technical architecture and operational process, both of which should be minimalist and elegant. In such a manner, it will be possible to maintain a close understanding, and therefore control over the system in its entirety. Having arrived at such an elegant solution, one might usefully employ the logging functionality inherent in operating systems, middleware and applications, in order to understand and monitor what is actually happening throughout the system. Once again, one may purchase sophisticated tools with which to manage this function, but such tools will be useless if the detailed understanding of the overall systems architecture and functional flow is not in place. If the understanding is in place, then such tools may provide a little additional event correlation, if indeed such correlation is needed. The security challenge will naturally increase if third party networks are utilised, as the organisation will simply not be aware of what is happening on this network. Service providers will of course issue all manner of assurances, but such assurances will be of little import if your data is seriously compromised. Organisations should think very carefully about the wisdom of hosting operational data on third party networks, not just from a security perspective, but also from a business continuity perspective should anything go wrong. Any assurances from service providers will quickly evaporate into the atmosphere in the event of such an occurrence. This is not a matter of deliberate deception on their part, it is simply that no one can absolutely guarantee security of operation under such architectures. We would be foolish to imagine otherwise. The challenge therefore is to understand your core operation and related operational processes and overlay these upon a systems architecture and design which offers the least exposure to risk. There are no short cuts in this respect and no such design may be purchased out of a box. We must strive to maintain both an ongoing clarity of purpose and a detailed understanding of both the technical architecture and operational process. This is particularly pertinent with respect to biometrics and identity management.

Ownership

As we move further towards distributed networks and service-based architectures, the concept of ownership becomes increasingly interesting. We may contemplate this strictly in relation to data flows and the responsibility for the security of the data at various points, or we may consider the situation around the use of the data at various points and the possibility of manipulating, appending to or otherwise processing such data. We must additionally be sensible of the fact that, very often, this data will be replicated and may reside in several places simultaneously, thus raising the possibility of synchronisation errors. Under such an eventuality, one might speculate as to the responsibility, depending upon the in-place operational process, the individuals concerned, whether administrative or operational, and a host of other factors. Ideally, the implementing organisation should be fully responsible for the total end-to-end transaction and associated storage and archiving of the transaction, including all associated data, especially when including personal information. However, when such data is routinely shared in such a hotchpotch manner as is the case in both government, industry and commerce, it may be difficult to trace the precise point of any compromise or leaks associated with the data. Extrapolating operational functionality into the virtualised cloud will exacerbate this problem, as data will reside in a multitude of instances upon physical infrastructure of which the host organisation has no comprehension. Ownership of the data and its security under such conditions may become extremely complicated, and may be subject to the varying jurisdiction of multiple countries. If personal data has been entrusted to the host organisation by individuals, how will the host organisation manage and protect this data upon infrastructures which are totally outside of their control? They cannot. Furthermore, any assurances to the contrary will be worthless. With respect to identity management and the use of biometrics, this raises some interesting and slightly worrying issues. There may be ways in which we can implement some robust management processes in this context. However, the situation will require a good deal of thought coupled to an intelligent use of networks. Currently, such an in depth consideration seems to be elusive, as does the concept of ownership and responsibility. Perhaps we need a complete revision of associated legislation, coupled with a user's charter to govern the permissible use of personal information by government agencies and the commercial world.

12

Verification and Trust

It is a curious thing that once an identity has been established and given a reference of some kind, we tend to assume that it is legitimate. From that point onwards the identity proliferates throughout systems, almost as though it had a life of its own. Its actual legitimacy will depend upon the rigour of process undertaken at the point of establishment. The criminal world understands this point, rather better it seems than do government agencies, hence the relative ease with which it is possible to obtain a fraudulent passport, and hence identity, simply via the provision of a few breeder documents and statements which are easily falsified. Once the fraudulent identity has been created it will perpetuate unless, by chance, it is discovered to be a fraud. Goodness knows how many fraudulent identities have thus been created by government agencies and will perpetuate for as long as their owners wish them to. Such a fraudulent identity may or may not assume a new name. It may be an existing name, but with a fraudulently conceived status of qualification or entitlement, there exist many variations upon the theme. In any event, once successfully created, it will become accepted and trusted accordingly. With regard to identity management, appending a biometric to such a fraudulently created identity simply adds weight to its perceived authenticity. The criminal world must have thought it was their birthday when government agencies started to rush out biometric enhanced identity documents and invited people to participate in various early adopter schemes. The opportunity to quickly establish a number of fraudulent identities was no doubt not lost on them. The practice continues with sloppy registration processes, often based more upon operational expediency than intelligence or security. The point is stressed because, once an official fraudulent identity is created, it may be subsequently used for a number of fraudulent purposes with little or no risk of ever being discovered.

This brings into question the level of trust which we place in a perceived identity, without really understanding how that identity has been established. The national identity example is used, but the same holds true of identities created for commercial or social purposes. For example, it is common for individuals who use social networking sites to do so under one or more aliases, never revealing their true identity. In such a manner, social interchanges and transactions may be undertaken in privacy with little redress in real terms. If something goes wrong, the identity is simply dropped and the user fades into the background. Thus, nearly every individual in the world has at least two identities. Their true identity and their officially perceived digital identity. Hopefully, in the majority of cases, the two are in alignment, at least to some degree. However, this cannot be assumed. The digital identity of the individual is now in the hands of so many third parties that, while the fundamentals may be aligned, the detail may become increasingly detached according to what information has been appended, and just how accurate this information is. Consequently, mistakes may easily be made with respect to either the denial of an entitled service or the granting of a service or benefit to which the individual is not entitled. There are two fundamental elements involved: the basic identity of the individual and the transactional history and associated built profile. The two should really be considered separately from an identity management perspective, but rarely are. From a technology perspective, it makes little difference what technologies we apply in order to facilitate access control or transaction verification. If the base identity is in error, then this error will simply be perpetuated throughout the systems involved. The better or stronger the supporting technology, the greater the misplaced trust we shall have in the identity. Of course, we must have secure mechanisms in place which do not allow for the identity to be tampered with from a transactional perspective. However, we should understand what perceived identity really means. When biometrics are involved, this can work in both directions. The fraudsters can take advantage of registering an identity of their choice using a biometric, in the understanding that the biometric will always be matched and the identity accepted. On the other hand, law enforcement agencies may believe that they have matched a biometric and identified an individual when, in fact, the identity they have matched against is incorrect. It all comes down to the assumptions made about biometric technology and the confidence held in the information aligned with an identity. The key is the biometric registration process. Once a legitimate identity has been verified and created, we must take great care of it. Currently, this is not the case as it is shared and replicated through so many systems and bound too closely with a transactional history that may or may not be correct. This whole situation needs thinking through very carefully.

Identity Theft

Given the above section, it is little wonder that identity theft has become so prevalent. Due to the sloppiness around both government and commercial processes, it is relatively easy to gather a good deal of information appertaining to a targeted individual. Appending a single relevant reference can often be enough to effectively steal the identity and use it fraudulently. In such cases, it is often extremely difficult for the true holder of the identity to repudiate the fraudulent usage and re-establish their good credentials. The more pervasive the collecting and storing of this personal information, the higher the risk. Is it not curious then that governments have effectively abandoned data protection and privacy legislation and are allowing the collection of personal information for no legitimate purpose and quite in contrary to the tenets of such legislation, by both commercial and government agencies? To the extent that it is no longer possible for citizens to obtain basic services such as insurance or the provision of utilities without divulging a great deal of personal information which has absolutely nothing to do with the transaction at hand. Similarly, when travelling or, increasingly, simply holding a telephone conversation with their bank. This has all been established under the pretext of security, and yet has nothing to do with security in a real sense. It is simply information harvesting on the basis that the more information held about an individual, the more control may be exerted over that individual. Extrapolate this thinking into the cloud and you have a recipe for greatly enhanced identity theft. The more identity theft that occurs, the less confidence may be had in the concept of identity as currently understood. The less confidence, the more information harvesting and the more identity theft, leading to further eroded confidence. It is a vicious circle which has serious societal implications. If we are to improve upon this situation, we must re-consider the whole concept of identity and re-establish a strong legislation around data protection and privacy. The current free-for-all situation is serving no one well. The challenge therefore is to have the intelligence to realise this, and the will to develop a better, fairer system. There are many ways in which this may be achieved.

12

Review Questions

1. Explain and discuss current technology trends and the impact they exert from a societal perspective.
2. Discuss the potential issues around identity management within a cloud computing architecture.
3. Discuss biometrics and identity management with respect to future developments in mobile technology.
4. Discuss the future with respect to service industries and the implications for organisations in both the private and public sectors.
5. Define and discuss likely challenges with respect to future technological developments and their practical implementation.

Epilogue

13

This book is primarily about biometrics and yet we have travelled through a broad landscape of systems and related issues. This is necessary as biometrics and identity management do not exist in isolation, but are a component part of larger systems, whether computer based or not. They should therefore be considered in context. And yet, in the early days this was not the case as a disproportionate focus was centred upon the biometric capture device and the associated matching algorithms. Biometrics, initially, were considered predominantly as a mechanism for automated physical access control, as a replacement for the cards and tokens then widely in use. No wonder it took a long time for the technology to gain a wider acceptance, but note the link between this wider acceptance and a defined purpose, in this instance heavily influenced by law enforcement and border control. The situation represents an interesting example of the need to have the requirement clearly defined before applying the technology to it. Even so, the manner in which biometrics was applied to this perceived requirement left something to be desired. The technology, hyped beyond its natural capacity, tended to be bolted on as an afterthought and, consequently, many lessons were learned the hard way. The plethora of overnight biometric experts has slightly given way to a more reasoned appreciation of the technology within major systems integrators, although the transition is incomplete and one still hears an awful lot of nonsense being propagated by ill-informed entities posing as specialists. A brief trawl through the Internet will expose a good deal of such nonsense and unsubstantiated claims around the technology and its capabilities, surprisingly, sometimes from organisations that are otherwise considered to be well established. It is pertinent therefore to take a step backward and reconsider the use of such technologies within the broader operational context.

As mentioned elsewhere in this work, the starting point should be an absolute clarity of purpose as to the broader operation and its associated policies. Once such a clarity is established, a robust systems design may be developed with which to support it, in parallel with an equally robust set of operational processes. The technical architecture may be designed according to best practices and with proper diligence with respect to security, scalability, sustainability and of course with due regard to data protection and privacy legislation. Consequently, there is no paint by numbers approach to the integration of biometrics and identity management. It must be designed at source if it is to be effective. Certainly, technology suppliers may supply guidance as to communications protocols and general configuration with respect to their particular devices, but this is a detail. The fundamental

J. Ashbourn, *Guide to Biometrics for Large-Scale Systems: Technological, Operational,*   **189**
and User-Related Factors, DOI 10.1007/978-0-85729-467-8_13,
© Springer-Verlag London Limited 2011

13

precepts need to be properly understood and integrated into the original design. Such a methodology will be particularly important with respect to virtual infrastructures and cloud computing. Naturally, there will be a long line of technology suppliers offering a bolt-on solution, typically portrayed as identity management as a service or something similar. A parallel line will contain vendors offering to host a federated identity service. They will all claim reduced costs, better management and better security. In some cases there may be some justification to such claims but, mostly, what they will really be offering will be an additional layer of complexity coupled to a loss of organisational control, at an increased operational cost. If this is what organisations want, then there will be plenty of options from which to choose. However, there may be better ways of going about things.

Given the current reality, it may be a good time to initiate a new wave of research into biometrics and identity management, with the focus not purely on the front end devices, but upon end-to-end transactions within a systems context, taking account of recent trends towards virtual environments. Within such research, new architectures may be proposed which place biometrics under the control of the individuals to which they pertain and which do not compromise privacy. One might foresee various ways in which this could be accomplished, perhaps using tokens which remain under the control of the user. Such a token might contain one or more unique identifiers, used for different purposes, which might only be released via the biometric, which, by the way, could also be matched upon the token. There are many potential variations on such a theme. A parallel line of research might completely rethink the registration process and how this might be securely undertaken. Indeed, the whole concept of identity and how it is used within society might be re-evaluated with new ideas and proposals developed from the ground up. And, of course, biometric matching algorithms may continue to be developed. There is much that could be achieved with some intelligent research in this context, but we need to change the academic emphasis. To date, the programmes which do exist tend to focus on how biometrics work and what the current applications are. This is not enough. We need to dig much deeper into the concept of identity, biometric verification and both contemporary and future technological architectures. Such research could be multidisciplined, encompassing elements of social science, psychology, mathematics, physics and computer science. Consequently, several departments within an academic institute might collaborate, or several academic institutes might collaborate upon a national or international basis. In this respect, a variation upon the Verus Mundus theme might be appropriate. Verus Mundus is a programme created for the benefit of schools and young students with a view of widening awareness and building skills with respect to the Earth sciences. A similar framework might usefully be established with which to research identity management in the twenty-first century.

We have also spoken of politics within this book as politics are interwoven with corporate activities upon a variety of scales and, consequently, cannot be ignored. Hence, we have three roads of technology, politics and application to consider. Furthermore, these three roads weave their way through a landscape of society and social issues which similarly cannot be ignored. At present, we are at a particular point along these converging roads and we have arrived at this point as a result of various historic views, activities, political aspirations and technological development, aided by a catalyst of commerce. Our roads have now broken out onto a plateau from which they might continue in any number of directions. This plateau, upon which many other developments are taking place, provides us with the opportunity to completely rethink biometrics and identity management. Indeed, we must do this as the current situation has failed, in some respects, to deliver the claims made for both the technologies involved and the effect of their implementation. We are at a point in time where we could usefully develop a second generation approach to the use of biometrics and the concept of identity management in the broader sense. There will of course be opposition to any such development, from those who have a vested interest in maintaining the status quo. However, if we are to realise an ethical, operable and sustainable approach to future identity management, then we need to develop this second generation. There are several elements which might usefully come together in this context. We have already mentioned the importance of developing new architectural models and further developing the base technology. In addition, we need to develop something akin to the Biometric Constitution as already suggested elsewhere in this book, and we need to establish a non-political, non-commercial, independent centre of expertise with which to orchestrate these activities. The author has already outlined such a model in his Credo Congregatio idea and this may be further developed for this purpose.

There are many good and useful things for which we can utilise biometric technology in order to bring benefits to both the individual and the service provider, provided we do so in an ethical manner, which preserves privacy and supports data security. This is not difficult to do if we approach it in the right manner, as previously discussed. However, there is also a dark side to many contemporary developments in computer science and this book would be failing in its duty if it ignored these potentially darker factors, not all of which are directly concerned with identity management. Among these, the concept of cloud computing has, in particular, many dark sides. Entrusting your operation to an infrastructure in which you have absolutely no idea of its physical location or by whom it is administered, really does not make very much sense. And yet, thousands of organisations will undoubtedly go down this route, many of them giving up perfectly good infrastructures currently under their control for this conceptual model which will be totally out of their control. Using such an infrastructure will necessarily involve identity management which will entail personal identity credentials and associated personal information also being extrapolated to this unknown network, which might straddle several geographic areas and international boundaries. If this cloud infrastructure collapses, or even suffers a serious degradation, what is the impact for all those organisations using this infrastructure? If part of the physical infrastructure is hosted in a country thought to be friendly but which subsequently becomes less so, and such changes can happen overnight, what happens to the overall service? And what better target could possibly exist for political activists and terrorists than an infrastructure upon which major organisations and various government agencies rely? Of course, the service providers will come up with all sorts of assurances around how they can quickly redeploy facilities via virtualisation techniques and how they can quickly restore capacity in an emergency and all manner of other guarantees, all of which, in times of trouble, become utterly worthless. We are placing ourselves in a situation whereby the prospect of a serious data catastrophe becomes very real. Moreover, upon a less catastrophic scale it is possible, or even likely, that a data breach in the cloud will go unnoticed by the client organisation, at least until well after the event, by which time tracks will have been effectively covered.

From a personal information and identity perspective, the fact that an individual's personal information resides, no doubt with minor variations, in a multitude of places with currently no effective data protection or privacy in place renders this information of increasingly questionable value. Adding a biometric to it simply enhances the assumptions made as to its authenticity. Relatively large-scale identity theft becomes a real possibility under architectural models currently proposed. Furthermore, transient identity theft, whereby the identity is stolen for one brief transaction and then another identity stolen for the next, will be a particularly difficult crime to pin down if we allow this free-for-all of personal information to continue. There is also the question of valid identities being appended with information which completely changes their complexion and the manner in which they are perceived, for good or ill, effectively creating identities which are at the same time, authentic and meaningless. There are many other issues around contemporary information technology and its usage which we could articulate, although that would be somewhat outside the scope of this book. It would suffice to say that we need to bring such concerns out into the open and ensure that they are properly discussed and understood.

We often boast about the pace of technological development; however, the concept of technological change being pushed through simply because it is possible, while it may suit technology suppliers very well, is not necessarily always in the best interest of society as a whole. The kaleidoscope of confusion created by this runaway pace of development has already had a serious impact upon global society, in a manner which is not as yet universally understood, and we need to start thinking a little more carefully about our usage of technology, particularly in the computer science field. We need to have a better perspective upon exactly what it is that we are enabling, and how such developments might be used in both a positive and negative manner. This is as pertinent to biometrics and identity management as with any other factor within the broader sphere of information technology. More so in some ways, as the link between a biometric and the individual is a particularly personal one. We can use this technology in ways which are positive and which provide benefits to the individual, but we need to think this through very carefully, hence the suggestion of a second generation biometrics and identity management approach.

We have covered a lot of ground in this book and have discussed various pertinent factors. Now is the time to collate all of our experience to date, take a long hard look at the broader scenario and work together to bring about this second generation approach. An approach which, finally, can make good use of the available technologies in a manner which is sympathetic to both societal and operational aspirations, while providing clarity of purpose and a clear path forwards. We can do this. We just need the will to start.

Where do we go from here? If you have enjoyed reading this book and agree, in principle, with the need to change and further develop our approach towards biometrics and identity management, then you may wish to contact the author who will be pleased to collate any such responses and work towards establishing a centre of excellence in this context. This might represent a useful first step upon the plateau. From here we may develop sustainable models which bring a new understanding to the concept of biometrics and identity management.

Index

A

Absorption, 19
Access control cards, 25
Access controls, 18, 19, 21, 24–26, 32, 33, 45–47, 55, 59, 61, 98, 107, 120, 122, 123, 130, 131, 172, 186, 188, 191
Access rights, 54, 121
Access to information, 120–122
Acoustic properties, 19
Active monitoring, 100
Administrative access, 66
Administrative rights, 44, 53
Administrative strategy, 168
Administrator access, 26, 60
Administrator privileges, 123
Administrator rights, 60
Age, 7–11, 30, 91, 125, 132, 135–137, 149, 165, 173, 178
Ageing, 9, 136
Age related change, 91
Age related factor, 136
Aldus Huxley, 149
Algorithm, 17, 19, 20, 34, 47, 54, 57–60, 100, 141, 159, 179, 184, 191, 192
Alphonse Bertillon, 8–9
Ambient noise, 19
Analysis, 7, 20, 22, 29, 30, 58, 64, 105, 137
Analytical tools, 173
Anatomical features, 3, 8, 23
Anatomical measurements, 4–11
Anatomic measurement, 7
Ancient civilisations, 4–5
Ancient Egyptians, 2, 4, 5, 8
Anger, 146
Animals, 2–4, 6, 12, 30, 40, 146, 148
Anonymous biometric, 35, 44
Anonymous biometric systems, 35, 44
Anonymous identity verification, 182

Anthropometry, 7, 8, 10
APEX, 100–105
Application servers, 122
Application software, 66
Archaeology, 6
Artificial brains, 4
Assumptions, 17–18, 44, 63, 64, 70, 85, 114, 115, 117, 121, 149, 153, 160, 161, 163, 166, 167, 172, 174, 177, 186, 189, 194
Astronomy, 7
Atavism, 6
Attended transaction, 53
Attitude, 12, 76, 88, 89, 125, 134, 136, 137, 148, 150, 163
Audit logging, 46, 63–64
Audit trail, 45, 54, 57, 64, 100, 103, 109, 120, 173
Autism, 90, 140
Automated fingerprint identification systems (AFIS), 20, 33, 41, 57, 58, 161
Average error rate, 77, 135

B

BANTAM, 36, 37, 59
BANTAM Program Manager, 37
Behavioural, 7, 15, 20, 23, 92, 93, 133, 135, 136
Behavioural biometric, 20
Behavioural changes, 136
Behavioural expression, 92
Behavioural traits, 7, 15, 23
Behaviour traits, 148
Benefit entitlement, 21
Benefit fraud, 28, 43
Benefit provision, 19
Bertillonage, 8
Biological brain, 4
Biological reactions, 145

J. Ashbourn, *Guide to Biometrics for Large-Scale Systems: Technological, Operational, and User-Related Factors*, DOI 10.1007/978-0-85729-467-8, © Springer-Verlag London Limited 2011